SHAKESPEARE
IN THE
CINEMA

THE **SUNY** SERIES

CULTURAL STUDIES IN CINEMA/VIDEO

WHEELER WINSTON DIXON | EDITOR

SHAKESPEARE IN THE CINEMA

Ocular Proof

STEPHEN M. BUHLER

STATE UNIVERSITY OF NEW YORK PRESS

Published by
State University of New York Press, Albany

© 2002 State University of New York

For information, address State University of New York Press,
90 State Street, Suite 700, Albany, NY 12207

Production by Marilyn P. Semerad
Marketing by Fran Keneston

Library of Congress Cataloging-in-Publication Data

Buhler, Stephen M., 1954–
    Shakespeare in the cinema : ocular proof / Stephen M. Buhler.
        p. cm. — (The SUNY series, cultural studies in cinema/video)
    Includes bibliographical references (p.) and index.
    ISBN 0-7914-5139-9 (alk. paper) — ISBN 0-7914-5140-2 (pbk. : alk. paper)
        1. Shakespeare, William, 1564–1616—Film and video adaptations. 2. English
drama—Film and video adaptations. 3. Motion pictures—History and criticism. I. Title.
II. Series.

PR3093 .B84 2001
791.43′6—dc21

                                                                        2001020008

10 9 8 7 6 5 4 3 2 1

CONTENTS

————— ◇ —————

ILLUSTRATIONS

◇

ACKNOWLEDGMENTS

◇

Performance is a collaborative exercise; so too is scholarship. I wish to express my gratitude for the assistance I have received from so many collaborators (and co-conspirators) in bringing *Shakespeare in the Cinema: Ocular Proof* to press.

The staff and management at a number of libraries granted me access to film prints and unpublished shooting scripts for many of the versions and adaptations discussed here. Most helpful were the Film and Television Archive at the University of California, Los Angeles; the Motion Picture, Broadcasting and Recorded Sound Division at the Library of Congress; and the Folger Shakespeare Library. More than my own thanks go to Kenneth Rothwell not only for his distinguished, trail-blazing work on cinematic Shakespeare, but also for organizing a three-day festival, "A Century of Shakespeare on Screen," for the 1996 World Shakespeare Congress in Los Angeles, which uncovered and screened several rarities. Jerry Ohlinger's Movie Material Store in New York and the Nostalgia Factory in Boston were instrumental in locating the publicity stills that serve as illustrations for the book. References to Shakespeare's works are taken from *The Riverside Shakespeare*, second edition, ed. G. Blakemore Evans (Boston: Houghton Mifflin, 1997).

Portions of the following chapters have been published previously: some of the descriptions of versions of *Othello* in chapter two and elsewhere have been reworked from "Ocular Proof: *Othello* Films on Video," *Shakespeare* Magazine 3.3 (Fall 1999): 17–19; the beginning of chapter four was adapted from "'By the Mass, our hearts are in the trim': Catholicism and British Identity in Olivier's *Henry V*," *Cahiers Elisabéthains* 47 (April 1995): 55–70; the discussion of Kenneth Branagh's

A Midwinter's Tale and *Hamlet* in chapter six is based on "Double Takes: Branagh Gets to *Hamlet*," *Post Script* 17.1 (Fall 1997): 43–52; part of chapter seven's commentary on the Ian McKellen/Richard Loncraine *Richard III* is taken from "Camp *Richard III* and the Burdens of (Stage/Film) History," *Shakespeare, Film, Fin de Siècle*, ed. Mark Thornton Burnett and Ramona Wray (London: Macmillan, 2000), pp. 40–57. I am grateful to the editors and publishers for permission to use material that appeared on their pages.

The University of Nebraska-Lincoln has generously supported this study with grants from its Research Council, with release-time from the Department of English, and with an intellectual environment that encouraged such inquiries. Colleagues in English, in Film Studies, and in the Medieval and Renaissance Studies Program have provided valuable suggestions about specific plays and films and about general approaches and connections, most notably Wheeler Dixon, Gwendolyn Foster, Robert Haller, Stephen Hilliard, Peter Lefferts, Carole Levin, Shirley Carr Mason, Ruth Nissé, Paul Olson, Nick Spencer, Pamela Starr, and Alan Yates. Research assistants contributed greatly to this book's development, especially Sarah Croft, Nichole DeWall, and Steven Werkmeister. I gratefully acknowledge the contributions of my students at Saint Anthony High School in Long Beach, California; at the University of California, Los Angeles; and at the University of Nebraska-Lincoln. If a sense of discovery expresses itself here, it reflects many shared hours of exploration and discussion in the classroom.

My interest in performance issues and their connections with pedagogy was sharpened as a high school instructor and as a teaching assistant for Albert Hutter and John Clark at UCLA. My appreciation for such concerns intensified during a 1992–94 humanities institute funded by the National Endowment for the Humanities and hosted by the Folger Institute: "Shakespeare and the Languages of Performance" brought scholar-teachers together to engage with ways of bringing the excitement of stage and screen production more fully to bear in Shakespearean instruction. My academic life has been immeasurably enriched by time spent with program director Lois Potter, with then-Executive Director of the Folger Institute Lena Cowen Orlin, and with the institute's participants and presenters: Sally Banes, Harry Berger, Carol Brobeck, Ann Christensen, Ralph Alan Cohen, Ann Jennalie Cook, Mary Corrigan, Kurt Daw, Michael Goldman, Eva Hooker, Geraldine Jacobs, David Kranz, Kathleen Lynch, Thomas MacCary, Jean-Marie Maguin, Deborah Montuori, Kate Pogue, Milla Riggio, David Sauer, Michael Shea, Susan Snyder, Audrey Stanley, Evelyn Tribble, Garry Walton, and Jane Williamson.

The community of scholars interested in film adaptations of Shakespeare is a congenial one and I am happy to have benefitted from conversations, pointed commentary, and occasional controversies with fellow members of it. Along with many others already named above, I am indebted most to such colleagues as Debbie Barrett-Graves, Susan Bennett, Thomas Berger, David Bevington, Mark Thornton Burnett, Samuel Crowl, Peter Donaldson, Michael Friedman, Diana Henderson, Peter Holland, Bernice Kliman, Douglas Lanier, David Linton, Megan Lloyd, Philip McGuire, Sharon O'Dair, Jean Peterson, Renee Pigeon, Donald Rude, Roberta Rude, Lisa Starks, Robert Willson, Susan Wing, and Ramona Wray. I know there are others that I have neglected to thank and I hope they will accept my apologies along with my gratitude.

At the State University of New York Press, I am indebted to the patient efforts of James Peltz and Marilyn Semerad, along with the expert copyediting of their vendor Lisa Metzger. Thanks to series editor Wheeler Dixon for being haunted by my proposal and to the readers of the manuscript, whose comments and criticisms did all they could to make this a better book.

Without the support, encouragement, and indulgence of my wife Carla and daughter Tess, my intellectual adventures might still be possible, but would be far less meaningful and enjoyable. They have my deepest—and ongoing—thanks.

CHAPTER ONE

◇

Introduction: The Shakespeare Test

That's what I like about Shakespeare; it's the pictures.

—Al Pacino, *Looking for Richard*

The making of Shakespeare films dates nearly from the start of commercial presentations of the cinematic medium. In the earliest screen adaptations from Shakespeare, there were palpable tensions at work, not only between aesthetic and financial objectives, but also between developing notions of what film is and does. One filmic impulse is to document, but with Shakespeare there are any number of subjects worth documenting: the playtext, a particular theatrical realization of that playtext, or the historical conditions reflected or represented in either playtext or stage version. Another filmic impulse is, of course, to tell a story: here, too, Shakespeare's playtexts offer an embarassment of rich possibilities. Further complicating matters are the uneasy, inescapable relations that the genres of nonfictional and fictional film bear with one another. The problem of distinguishing between modes of representation and ways of manipulating materials (Plantinga 9–12) is as old as narrative filmmaking itself, and Shakespeare very quickly became part of the developing dilemma.

It was in the 1890s that Georges Méliès pioneered the practice of storytelling through the exciting new medium; he also pioneered the practice of borrowing from familiar materials, such as the Faust legend in *The Cabinet of Mephistopheles* (1897) or Charles Perrault's account of *Cinderella* (1899). Méliès would later borrow from Shakespeare—an abridged *Hamlet* and a film, starring himself, about the composition of *Julius Caesar*, both in 1907—but his were not the first Shakespeare films. Back in 1899, film's documentary capacities had already been exploited to record performances from Herbert Beerbohm Tree's London production of *King John*; this likely comprises the very first Shakespeare film. Long believed completely lost, Tree's *King John* survives in at least one sequence—part of the title character's death scene (McKernan 1–2). Yet another filmic impulse, carried over from theatrical institutions, is to deliver a product embodied by a recognizable star performer. In what survives of the film of *King John*, Tree is as much the draw and the focus on screen as he was on stage.

These impulses combine and compete not only in this first Shakespeare film but in many, if not most, of its successors. This book investigates what the Shakespearean project reveals about individual films and about film in general. Presenting a cinematic version of one of Shakespeare's playtexts invariably foregrounds questions of film's identity as a cultural production. The play's the thing both to bring pressure upon the technical and affective "natures" of the medium and also to highlight its relations to theater and the entertainment marketplace. Shakespeare's own status as cultural icon underscores film's relation to strata of culture and to self-identified centers of culture such as museums and academia. His otherness as a figure from the past and his long-standing appeal to non-English speaking audiences enhance film's ability to serve in both transgressive and institutional capacities within national boundaries and beyond.

Most studies of Shakespearean film have understandably concentrated on what the medium of cinema reveals or obscures about Shakespeare: productions are evaluated in terms of fidelity to the text, compromises between Elizabethan stagecraft and changing filmic convention, actors' performances and directors' achievements in "realizing" the playtext. Here, I will regularly address such issues but will be more concerned with how filmmakers have approached their task of adapting Shakespeare for the screen and what results as film and as interpretation from their strategic choices. The challenges implicit in the task of realizing Shakespeare in the cinema have inspired—or provoked—many different strategies of identification, negotiation, and transformation. Even so, there are identifiable, shared patterns at work among several films. I suggest that focusing on shared patterns of adaptation can allow Shakespeare to illuminate the medium for filmgoers, just as his works have helped define the medium for filmmakers. The similarities stem from a nearly universal point of departure: an encounter with a classic text, especially one produced by a cultural figure as imposing as Shakespeare, places no small stress upon screenwriters, directors, designers, actors, and production companies more generally. The attempt to mediate between that text and either a specialized or a mass audience forces filmmakers to confront the nature of film, its relation to viewers, and its relation to cultural norms of art, gender, power, and profit.

My subtitle, *Ocular Proof,* is taken from Shakespeare's *Othello,* a tragedy about desire and trust, envy and suspicion, identity and otherness. The phrase signals the kind of testing—another meaning of "proof"—to which film is subjected when linked with a Shakespearean text. The next chapter will examine three films that are inspired by this play to explore cinema's status as a representational medium: the 1922 German version directed by Dimitri Buchowetzki, the 1955 Soviet version directed by Sergei Yutkevich, and the 1995 retelling by Oliver Parker.

The third chapter explores documentary approaches to making Shakespeare films. When film is defined by its power to document events, it may maintain a subordinate role not only to the playtext but to the stage. Strategies of deference and, occasionally, resistance will be considered in connection with some of the earliest films: the chapter includes, along with the 1899 *King John,* a 1913 *Hamlet* with Johnston Forbes-Robertson; a 1936 Metro-Goldwyn-Mayer short, *Master Will Shakespeare,* which in the guise of documentary offers a fanciful biographical sketch of the playwright; Stuart Burge's 1965 film of the National Theatre *Othello* featuring Laurence Olivier; the 1969 film of Tony Richardson's *Hamlet* featuring Nicol Williamson; and finally, *Looking for Richard,* Al Pacino's film documentary of a never-realized version of *Richard III.*

The fourth chapter considers what happens when film is primarily defined by its commercial aspects, especially by audience appeal as established by popular performers who are cast in Shakespearean roles. This is illustrated by the 1929 United Artists *The Taming of the Shrew* with Mary Pickford and Douglas Fairbanks; the 1935 *A Midsummer Night's Dream* directed by Max Reinhardt and William Dieterle, featuring several Warner Brothers contract players; the 1936 MGM *Romeo and Juliet* featuring Norma Shearer, Leslie Howard, and John Barrymore; and two films directed by Franco Zeffirelli, the 1966 *The Taming of the Shrew*, which starred Elizabeth Taylor and Richard Burton, and the 1990 *Hamlet* featuring Mel Gibson and Glenn Close.

The fifth chapter focuses on cinematic versions of Shakespearean plays that assert themselves as films as distinct from theater: that is, they exploit—and often advertise—the medium's illusionistic powers or its radical plasticity. Such films can overtly address such issues, with Olivier's 1944 *Henry V* a prime example as it restages both Elizabethan-style performance and nineteenth-century "historical" settings before building to 1940s-era naturalism in the battle scenes. Other examples of self-consciously filmic approaches are: silent versions of the plays produced by the Vitagraph Company in the United States from 1908 to 1911; the 1954 *Giuletta e Romeo* directed by Renato Castellani; the 1962–66 *Othello* directed by Liz White (not shown until 1980); the 1969 *A Midsummer Night's Dream* directed by Peter Hall; *Roman Polanski's Film of The Tragedy of "Macbeth"* from 1971; and Baz Luhrmann's *William Shakespeare's "Romeo+Juliet."*

Several strategies of cinematic adaptation build upon the revisions of Shakespeare that dominated pre-1900 theatrical practice, especially in the tradition of companies led by actor-managers. The sixth chapter will consider the rivalries and interdependencies at work in the careers of the three actor-directors who crafted some of the most influential Shakespeare films: Laurence Olivier, Orson Welles, and Kenneth Branagh. A primary concern will be the cinematic medium's connections with past and contemporary directorial practices; further emphasis will be placed on the kinds of exchanges—both borrowings and rebuttals—that occur between and among these filmmakers. Initial examples will be taken from Olivier's 1948 *Hamlet* and 1955 *Richard III*, with some reference to his earlier *Henry V*. Welles's 1948 *Macbeth* was overshadowed by Olivier's *Hamlet*; his 1952 *Othello* enters into dialogue with his rival's success and the 1966 *Chimes at Midnight* enters into debate with his contemporary's view of the Henriad and of Shakespeare generally. Branagh's 1989 *Henry V* and 1996 *Hamlet* clearly engage with the filmic and the financial precedents set by Olivier, but also react to Welles's innovative approaches and cautionary example. These issues are explored in Branagh's "rehearsal" for a cinematic *Hamlet*, his 1995 film *A Midwinter's Tale* (see Figure 1).

The seventh chapter considers Shakespeare and transgression, the social dynamic that both challenges and shapes cultural norms. Shakespearean playtexts present a number of opportunities for transgressive

FIGURE 1. Kenneth Branagh advises Michael Maloney on one of Hamlet's soliloquies during the filming of 1995's *A Midwinter's Tale* (*In the Bleak Midwinter*). Photo courtesy of Jerry Ohlinger's Movie Material.

gestures, both within filmic conventions (the ubiquitous asides and soliloquies) and sociopolitical conventions (cross-dressing, a range of sexualities and gender roles, class-based coding alternately reinscribed and critiqued). These opportunities pertain whether or not the film-makers situate themselves "with" or "against" the Shakespearean play-text; the cultural significance of Shakespeare as author and authority allows for considerable conformity as well as transgression. Examples involving gender issues include what may be the second Shakespeare film ever made, a 1900 vignette featuring the legendary stage actress Sarah Bernhardt as Hamlet; the 1920 German *Hamlet: The Drama of Vengeance* in which the young prince turns out actually to have been a woman; Paul Czinner's 1936 *As You Like It*; and Kenneth Branagh's 1993 *Much Ado About Nothing*. Sociopolitical approaches to film and to Shakespeare recur in Joseph L. Mankiewicz's 1953 *Julius Caesar* and 1971's *Peter Brook's Film of William Shakespeare's "King Lear."* Both Franco Zeffirelli's 1968 *Romeo and Juliet* and the 1995 *Richard III* adapted by Ian McKellen and Richard Loncraine touch on the interrelation between political and sexual identity. While McKellen and Loncraine effectively engage with the camp aesthetic, yet more assertively transgressive adaptations of Shakespeare can be found in Derek Jarman's 1980 *The Tempest*, Peter Greenaway's 1991 *Prospero's Books*, and Trevor Nunn's 1996 *Twelfth Night*.

The eighth chapter examines the linguistic and cultural translations that shape non-Anglophonic films intended as versions of Shakespearean playtexts. The strongly political significances of many of these films regularly coincide with their engagements with issues of linguistic authority and cultural influence—both welcome and unwelcome. Italian filmmakers, inspired by the settings for many of the plays, were early pioneers in adaptation. Films made in Germany both point toward and look back at the enormities of the Nazi regime. Engagements with the burdens of Stalinism are evident in such Russian films as the 1955 version of *Twelfth Night* and Grigori Kozintsev's later adaptations of *Hamlet* and *King Lear*. Japanese explorations are provided by Akira Kurosawa in his 1957 *Kumonosu-djo* (*The Castle of the Spider's Web*), a rerendering of *Macbeth* (shown in the United States in 1961 as *Throne of Blood*), in his 1960 *The Bad Sleep Well* (based on *Hamlet*), and ultimately in *Ran* (*Chaos*), his 1985 revisioning of *King Lear*. Examples from France include the early *Shylock*, adapted from *The Merchant of Venice* in 1913; *Les amants de Verone*, a 1949 revisiting of

Romeo and Juliet; *Ophélia*, Claude Chabrol's 1962 seriocomic dissection of adaptation and translation; and, from 1987, Jean-Luc Godard's deconstructed *King Lear*.

My conclusion concentrates on three Shakespeare-inspired films marking 1999 as the centennial of Shakespeare in the cinema. Michael Hoffman's production of *A Midsummer Night's Dream* continues the star-delivery approach, going so far as to transform Bottom into a romantic lead, the better to accommodate one of the film's biggest box-office draws. That decision, however, is but one of many indicating the filmmaker's uneasiness with the Shakespearean playtext and with the precedents in Shakespeare films he feels he must follow; Hoffman may be envious of the freedom often enjoyed in versions of Shakespeare in languages other than English. No such linguistic resentment appears in the giddy pastiche *Shakespeare in Love*, which wittily appropriates every Shakespearean tag that it can while paying tribute to the history of Shakespearean performance on stage and on screen. Finally, Julie Taymor's *Titus* reconnects with recent innovations in stagecraft and rediscovers a long-neglected play.

In all of these films, we can see the conjunction or collision of different motives, aims, means, and ends. Filmmaking is a commercial enterprise, not unlike the playacting of Shakespeare's day. But, as Pierre Bourdieu has observed about other forms of "symbolic capital" (74–76) , Shakespearean plays have been invested with so much cultural significance that they seem to stand beyond economics altogether. As a result, they have come to stand for culture itself, in its elitist and egalitarian aspects; they have represented culture both as social construction and as a bridge between nations, peoples, and times. No wonder, then, that film's own uncertain and unsettling relationship with culture becomes a major part of the story when Shakespeare is adapted for the cinema. It turns out, after all, that the play's one thing among many, many others that provide the bases for Shakespearean film.

Three more preliminary comments.

First, several well-known and influential screen productions that connect with Shakespeare have been relegated to cameo status. Because of the emphasis on film itself, this book will address versions primarily intended for video release only when they have recognizably influenced a later, different film production. Similar strictures apply to cinematic versions of plays written as stage derivations from Shakespeare: witty travesties like *Rosencrantz and Guildenstern Are Dead* and expansive musicals such as *Kiss Me Kate* and *West Side Story* will receive only brief mentions. This is, in part, an attempt to impose some limits on a vast area of study; it is also, more importantly, a recognition of how such works vastly increase the interactions among performance codes appropriate to different media. There are more than enough negotiations at work between and among the "film codes" (Guntner and Drexler 31–32)—the cinematic conventions associated with specific genres—employed in Shakespearean adaptations.

Second, several of the productions that are discussed here have not always been accepted as "canonical" versions of Shakespeare (Holderness 63–64). At times, adherence to models of specifically literary criticism has hindered the study of Shakespearean film (Collick 6–8). Resulting analyses have privileged the work of acknowledged auteurs, while often eliding the difference between them and canonized authors. Other dynamics—especially commercial ones—in filmmaking could be either ignored or dismissed, as differences between "high" and "low" Shakespeare were exaggerated (Levine 1991, 169–72). That critical moment seems to have passed. There has recently been an explosion of studies interested in situating Shakespearean performance more surely in contemporary contexts: see, for example, the collections edited by Bulman, by Boose and Burt, and by Burnett and Wray; see also individual studies by Howlett and Willson, with many others.

Consequently (and finally), this study endeavors to place all Shakespeare films amidst the cultural practices, economic pressures, career trajectories, and audience expectations that shaped their production and reception. For that reason, I will make reference to directors' other films, to actors' other roles, to screenwriters' other works, and to the markets that studios targeted—even when these are not specifically Shakespearean. Too often, Shakespeare films have been considered in isolation from other cinematic works and from each other: silent film versions of the plays, for example, have been aggressively marginalized, even by some of their most devoted students. Twentieth-century (and later) filmic texts participate in a range of discursive networks as broad as those that framed Early Modern texts, such as Shakespeare's plays. Film, Shakespeare, and their interactions can best be understood when, as Leah Marcus has recommended for literary studies, "a wider historical and cultural matrix" is seen "as constitutive, an integral part" of their networks (23). There is much to be learned, especially, from examining how the worlds of film connect with the scenes of Shakespearean stagecraft, in which boundaries are happily, disturbingly, and deliberately blurred and redefined. Shakespeare's lines constantly oscillate between commerce and art, audience and player, high and low, comedy and tragedy, male and female, power and resistance, play and life. So, in their multifarious way, do the movies.

CHAPTER TWO

◇

Ocular Proof:
Three Versions of Othello

> OTHELLO: Be sure of it. Give me the ocular proof,
> Or by the worth of mine eternal soul
> Thou hadst been better have been born a dog
> Than answer my waked wrath. . . .
> IAGO: You would be satisfied?
> OTHELLO: Would? nay, and I will.
> IAGO: And may; but how? How satisfied, my lord?
> Would you, the supervisor, grossly gape on?
>
> —Shakespeare, *Othello*

It may have been inevitable that *Othello* be one of the most frequently filmed of Shakespeare's works. For Western audiences especially, the play is inherently spectacular in its explorations of race: Shakespeare imagines the passionate conjunction of black with white and stages it in ways guaranteed to captivate and disturb not only his earliest audiences (Maus 574–78), but many to follow. The story can be very simply outlined. Othello, a Moorish general who now serves Venice, marries Desdemona, daughter to one of the city-state's leading citizens. Through the machinations of Iago, a disaffected officer, Othello is convinced that his new bride has been unfaithful and murders her. One of Iago's most effective tactics is to persuade Othello that his very blackness—as well as his older years, his lack of "gentility," and his status as foreigner—makes him an unnatural mate for the white, young, genteel Venetian. Shakespeare adapted the story from a novella by Giraldi Cinthio that indeed stresses the unsuitability of the match; one of the remarkable changes wrought in the play is the problematization of that idea (McPherson 56–68). The sight of the fair Desdemona with her new, dark lord can both inspire and challenge a number of visceral, but culturally conditioned responses to race.

Other forms of cultural conditioning—those deeply affecting our notions of dramatic representation—have shaped later audiences' response to the play. The ascendancy of illusionistic approaches first on the stage and later in film and video, with their emphasis on the impressions of realism or (paradoxically) naturalism, has profoundly complicated the process of mounting a production of *Othello*, whether for stage or screen. If Othello himself is figured as a black African, illusionistic productions must endeavor to make the racial embodiment believable. To avoid facing such challenges, several critics (and not a few directors, including Jonathan Miller) have denied that race is a major factor in the play. One rather evasive way to justify such a claim is by proposing that Othello is classified, after all, as a Moor, a term that could describe any number of peoples from the Mediterranean and beyond. The North African Othello was popular on eighteenth- and nineteenth-century stages, in part reflecting Samuel Taylor Coleridge's assertion that "to conceive this beautiful Venetian girl falling in love with a veritable negro" was in itself "monstrous" (qtd. by Newman 143). A white performer impersonating a "blackamoor"—the term appears in Queen Elizabeth's edict expelling African slaves from England (McDonald 296)—could, at times, be deemed too much. The nineteenth century also witnessed, however, the first black performer to adopt the role: Ira Aldridge enacted Othello to consistent acclaim throughout Europe (Hill 17–27). The list of his successors includes other pioneers such as Morgan Smith and, in the early twentieth century, Edward Sterling Wright; it bears no greater name than that of Paul Robeson, who portrayed Othello on a London stage in 1930 and, after unconscionable delays, appeared in the role on Broadway in 1943.

Robeson's legendary runs elicited both admiration and, from some observers, revulsion. Some critics and commentators in London combined both reactions (Vaughan 188–90); observers of the trial runs at Harvard and Princeton in 1942 and of the very successful New York production in 1943–44 were generally positive. A larger audience was also involved, though, and the notices from people who would not have permitted themselves the opportunity to attend were, not surprisingly, negative. Errol Hill notes that after *Life* magazine ran a photo feature article about the New York *Othello* with Robeson, its editors received letters of outrage, one of which decried "the horrible, indelible, undeniable and terrifying fact that there are white men with so little respect for themselves that they would cause to be printed the picture of a Negro man with his arm around a white woman in a love scene" (129). The intensity of such a reaction helps to explain how slowly U.S. theater practice changed in the wake of Robeson's triumph. It would take decades—along with the tireless efforts of civic rights activists on a variety of fronts—before actors such as Moses Gunn, William Marshall, and James Earl Jones would be accepted as Othello. Now, in the early dawning of the twenty-first century, it is difficult for audiences to accept a non-black performer in the role either on stage or on screen.

The naturalistic approach that has dominated commercial theater and film contributed to this striking reversal. Once black performers had confirmed Othello's kinship with them, it became more difficult for white performers first to elide questions of race (although the "North African" interpretation was regularly revived) and ultimately to address them. On stage, the attempt to impersonate blackness culminated in Laurence Olivier's performance for the National Theatre in 1964. In recalling his characterization, Olivier insists that he "had to be black . . . had to feel black down to [his] soul" and so underwent a three-hour makeup job for each performance, appearing on stage with what he considered the appropriate wig and with burnished, dark-brown skin (Olivier 1986, 153). He aimed at "verisimilitude"—and, remarkably, at least one critic praised him for it (Spoto 330)—also by assuming a Caribbean-inflected voice that owed its basso profundo qualities in part to recollections of Robeson. Only Olivier could get away with it and perhaps only at that time and place: certainly no other white actor has since attempted such an impersonation. If the goal in realizing the play is a naturalistic study of Othello's blackness in relation to white society, then it would be advantageous to cast in the role black performers who have far more extensive experience in, to paraphrase Olivier, being and feeling black.

But performative strategies that go beyond naturalism have also insisted on Othello's blackness. Even the film version of *Othello* featuring Olivier is self-consciously theatrical in its effects—and such theatricality works against filmic naturalism. I will examine that film in greater detail when considering the documentary approach to cinematic Shakespeare (see chapter three; see also Buhler 1999, 18). Here, I want instead to focus attention on the interrelation between modes of presentation and the issue of blackness in three film versions of the tragedy of the Moor of Venice. Two of them, films directed by Buchowetzki and by Yutkevich, are decidedly non-naturalistic in approach; the third, directed by Oliver Parker, inconsistently but intriguingly breaks away from naturalistic conventions. A central component to non-naturalistic filmmaking is its acknowledgment of artifice. As Colin MacCabe astutely observes (64), "realist" filmmaking in all its forms hastens to conceal that art by means of an imposed continuity and coherence; so, for that matter, does the kind of traditional film theory advanced by André Bazin. Disruptions in presentational mode and abrupt shifts in both cinematic and acting technique can break the realist illusion and thereby allow space for envisioning specifically how social realities are constructed. Such cinematic practices suit the complexities of *Othello* very well.

Dimitri Buchowetzki's film *Othello* was made in Germany in 1922 and combines the period detail that retains considerable appeal in today's "heritage" filmmaking with unabashedly expressionistic acting styles. The title role is played by Emil Jannings, already an established performer—having honed his craft with the Deutsches Theater and its influential director, Max Reinhardt—but still anticipating his appearances in F. W. Murnau's *The Last Laugh* (*Der letze Mann,* 1924) and Josef von Sternberg's *The Blue Angel* (1930). (See chapter four for Reinhardt's collaboration with William Dieterle for the Warner Brothers 1935 *A Midsummer Night's Dream.*) Iago is Werner Krauss, another product of the Deutsches Theater. Krauss's ability to convey sinister benignity in the title role for Robert Wiene's *The Cabinet of Dr. Caligari* (1919) would suggest an aptitude for playing the outwardly "honest" ensign. Krauss, though, grates rather than ingratiates; his filmic Iago is the embodiment of the neglected soldier, whose brethren made up a sizeable component of the film's original audience in defeated and disillusioned postwar Germany. Kenneth Rothwell astutely notes how this Iago is "curiously evocative of Adolf Hitler" for later viewers (Rothwell and Melzer, 211) and this visual association with that embittered veteran of the Great War intensifies our sense of the racial and racist bases of Iago's campaign against Othello. An awareness of Krauss's later work in collaboration with the Nazi regime, often portraying duplicitous Jews (as in the 1940 film *Jud Süss*), does nothing to lessen our unease. Krauss's appearance as Mordecai, the Shylock figure in the 1925 film *The Jew of Mestri* (the U. S. title for *Der Kaufmann von Venedig*—that is, *The Merchant of Venice*), foreshadows this aspect of his career.

The film, however, sends mixed messages on the issue of race. While the makeup for Jannings's Othello marks him as unmistakably black, his words—at least those that appear on title cards for U. S. release—suggest a different racial identity. When called to account by the Venetian Senate for his marriage with Desdemona, this Othello asserts that there is no difference in their bloods, since he is "son of an Egyptian prince and a Spanish princess." The emphasis on blood can refer nearly as easily to noble status as to race, however. In one crucial scene, Krauss's Iago evinces sharp distaste at physical contact with Othello: before he can bring himself to show the handkerchief that will intensify the Moor's suspicions, he uses it to wipe the hand that has smoothed Othello's brow.

The business with the handkerchief is emblematic of the freedom with which Buchowetzki, as scenarist as well as director, treats his source materials; he incorporates and rearranges elements directly from Cinthio along with Shakespeare's revisions. As the film opens, Iago has not yet learned of his rival Cassio's appointment to the office Iago desired, that of Othello's lieutenant. We see his deep—and public—disappointment as Othello makes what is clearly a difficult decision in front of the Duke (here named, more accurately than in Shakespeare, the Doge) and the assembled senators and choice citizenry. Following the lead of Reinhardt's stage practice, Buchowetzki provides a larger on-screen audience for the dramatic events at key moments throughout. Crowds of concerned Venetians discuss how Cyprus may be defended from the Turk if Othello is under arrest for his secret marriage; they cheer when Desdemona happily proclaims Othello her new lord and husband. On Cyprus, crowds cheer the announcement of the failure of the Turkish assault and the nuptials of Desdemona and Othello at their reunion. Later, the populace hears rumors of an impending attack from a reorganized Turkish fleet; these lead to anxiety over the shift in command from Othello to Cassio. Nearing the film's conclusion, the citizens are in turmoil upon learning of Othello's arrest; Cassio, the faithful lieutenant, must personally face the crowd with more dreadful news than they had expected, that of the general's death. Barbara Hodgdon has detected a kind of proto-Axis triumphalism in the film's conclusion, but such a view implies a Mark Antony–like demagoguery not to be found here. Hodgdon further argues that the public scenes contribute to the director's dual marginalization and objectification of Desdemona (228–29). In his choices, however, Buchowetzki preempts any impulse to make the tragedy purely personal and thereby reduce, for many viewers, its political and cultural significances—including the dismissive discourse toward women in which Iago participates and that he employs so destructively. Buchowetzki utilizes both massive sets (the doge's palace, Venetian canals, Cypriot public squares) and assembled multitudes to reinforce the larger social contexts and consequences of Iago's villainy and Othello's fall.

The director rearranges and sometimes creates events to increase sympathy for Othello. In this version, Brabantio is surprised by his daughter's marriage to the Moor not because he didn't see it coming but because he explicitly forbade it. Jannings's initial interpretation of Othello is imperiously calm, making good use of an imposing physical presence. This general need not bare his head to anyone; he keeps his hood on even when speaking with the Doge. Jannings is nevertheless able to convey emotional nuances such as doubt over not promoting Iago and tender solicitude in his concern over Desdemona. He apologizes to her when she is startled at his entrance to the church where they will be wed; as Desdemona, Ica van Lenkeffy responds by gazing lovingly at him. He removes the hood—she is already the "general's general" of Iago's later description—and they kiss, passionately. This image of black and white in loving accord is immediately followed by an intercut scene where Iago goads Roderigo, who had haplessly courted Desdemona, to alert her father that she is now in the "gross clasps of the Moor." The filmic audience is doubly challenged: once by the "spectacle" of the interracial kiss and again by the enactment of one all-too-common response to that spectacle by a buffoonish pawn. After their marriage, Othello presents Desdemona with the fateful handkerchief and tells her then (far earlier than in Shakespeare) of its significance. She accepts it, there in the church, as they embrace once more. Later, once they have arrived safely in Cyprus, the married lovers are playful, indulging in a game of hide-and-seek.

In a silent film, without the full psychological impact of Iago's language, Othello's descent from this loving trust into murderous suspicion might best be engineered in other ways. Krauss's Iago is more a stage-manager than a rhetorician, but the character's malevolent brilliance survives. He overhears Desdemona tell his wife, Emilia, about the handkerchief and begins his campaign to wrest it from her. While persuading Emilia (played by Lya de Putti), Iago apparently employs some of the jewels that Roderigo intended for him to give to Desdemona. As it turns out, the gifts were unnecessary: he sees the handkerchief while Emilia is busy unpacking clothes after the voyage from Venice and simply takes it from her; she protests, if to no avail, and also becomes a far less problematic character. He brings about Cassio's disgrace in a drunken brawl, as in Shakespeare, but in the film he plants the seed of suspicion in Othello even before that scheme comes into play. This Iago deepens the suspicion by asking Emilia to keep from Othello any information about Cassio's visits to Desdemona (which, as in Shakespeare, Iago also advises) in order to win her support for Cassio's reinstatement. Iago, of course, lets slip what he has asked his wife to conceal.

The newly engendered division between Othello and Desdemona is expressed visually, in a motif that will be reprised throughout the history of Shakespeare film. Disgusted with what he believes to be obstinate lies from Emilia, Othello runs to another chamber, where he finds Desdemona at needlework. They are separated by a stone wall, with a window punctuated by thin columns. Othello is framed by the columns furthest away from Desdemona, and as she freely admits Cassio's visit—and pleads his case—Jannings's Moor reaches through the window only to withdraw his hand and embrace one of the stone bars. Similar images would be explored and exploited by directors of Shakespearean film such as Olivier, Welles, Yutkevich, and especially Castellani. Despite the visual sign of his doubt, this Othello has not yet completely succumbed to jealousy; he will hold on desperately to some trust in Desdemona. Roderigo unwittingly stands in for Cassio, serenading Emilia at Desdemona's window (an ingenious inversion of Don John's plot in *Much Ado About Nothing*); not even after Othello nearly chokes the syllable "Cass—" out of Iago to identify the singer is he convinced of her infidelity. When Iago confronts him with the handkerchief he claims to have "found" at Cassio's, Jannings's Othello goes into paroxysms of jealous rage. Ultimately, he tries to undermine the persuasiveness of Iago's evidence by shredding the handkerchief with his teeth, calling for still stronger "Proof! Proof!"

A summons from Venice for Othello to return to the city and leave Cassio in charge at Cyprus gives Iago the opportunity for ocular proof. Upon hearing the news, Othello had wavered; on hearing Desdemona speak on Cassio's behalf, he had struck her once and been restrained from doing her further injury and shame. Iago tells Cassio (played by Theodor Loos—another former member of Reinhardt's ensemble) about the summons but suppresses information about Othello's response. Instead Iago urges him to visit Desdemona once more, asking her to help Othello accept the orders. This done, Iago drags Othello to witness Cassio leaving Desdemona's chamber: "You asked for proofs, my lord." The growing violence of Jannings's Othello seems ready to explode here and now; Krauss's Iago seems, for once, uncertain of what will follow. Othello tells Iago that in return for Cassio's death he will receive the long-desired lieutenancy. He is unable to give an answer to Iago's next question, "What of her?"

Jannings's performance has been much criticized for its extravagance in these later scenes. Rothwell makes an irresistible pun in accusing the actor of literal "scenery chewing" in the handkerchief scene (Rothwell and Melzer 211); Robert Hamilton Ball out-Iagos Iago when he describes the darkly made-up Jannings in the role as "almost animal, gorilla-like in face and passion without dignity or tragic intensity" (279). There is, I would counter, considerable dignity not only in Jannings's depiction of Othello before Iago's machinations, but in his expression of a long-cherished faith in Desdemona that persists as this Iago smothers it. There is also tragic intensity, but of the expressionist, not the naturalistic, variety: the painful despair Jannings would body forth as both the doorman in *The Last Laugh* and Professor Rath in *The Blue Angel* is palpably here in the 1922 *Othello*. After learning from an unmoving, parade-ground straight Iago that Cassio (as Iago believes) is dead, Othello weeps uncontrollably. His final meeting with Desdemona begins tenderly, but quickly accelerates into wrathful violence, observed by Emilia. She destroys his explanation of the deed with a simple account of how her "husband stole that handkerchief of me." Jannings's Othello pushes her away in disgust and then quickly realizes what, if true, Emilia's words would mean. Shakespeare's Desdemona survives strangling just long enough to attempt to throw suspicion away from her husband, her murderer; Othello is moved to admit the deed. Here, Othello's own persistent but insufficient belief in his wife moves him to credit Emilia's version of events. He moves back, horrified, from Desdemona's body.

In Buchowetzki's version, Othello completely avenges himself on Iago, dispatching the now-craven villain with one thrust of his dagger. (Othello is given the lines assigned to Lodovico in the play describing Iago as a "Spartan dog.") He is reconciled with the wounded Cassio, who will replace him in Cyprus, and returns to Desdemona's bed for a last kiss and to pay for her death with his own. Outside, the citizens of Cyprus are in turmoil: "Othello is arrested, O woe!" reads the title card. Cassio is shaken by the sight of the slain Othello and Desdemona but still accepts the responsibilities of his new office. He tells the crowd that Othello is dead and prays for God's "mercy on his poor soul." As Cassio bows his head, the screen slowly fades to black.

The film's release in the United States provides yet another melancholy coda. Ben Blumenthal, one of the film's producers, specialized in the exchange of German and American films across the Atlantic. He was much encouraged by the reception of *Othello* upon its New York release in 1923: reviewers were enthusiastic and audiences exceptional for an independent production (Ball 284). Several factors, though, worked against more general distribution—with exhibitors' reluctance outside the metropolitan centers of the northern United States perhaps the most insurmountable obstacle. The film's subsequent neglect (also due to its independent status) made it, however, a prime candidate for transfer to video format. It is now one of the most widely available examples of Shakespeare on silent film, so the images of Othello with Desdemona once withheld from motion picture screens can readily appear—if in faded glory and with abrupt, obviously spliced cuts—on television monitors.

Three decades after Buchowetzki's adaptation, another Russian-born director tackled *Othello*. The context for production, though, was not Germany in the aftermath of World War I, but the Soviet Union in the early days of the post-Stalinist era. In fact, 1955 witnessed the production of two Soviet Shakespeare films, a sumptuous *Twelfth Night* (see chapter eight) along with Sergei Yutkevich's equally opulent *Othello*. Both films boast vivid color, lavish sets and costumes, striking locations, and stirring music; in the case of *Othello*, the filmscore was provided by Aram Khatchaturian, one of the Soviet Union's best-known composers (his "Sabre Dance" remains an orchestral staple in pops-style concerts). For the first seven minutes and more of the film, music is all we hear. Before the credits appear, Yutkevich adds a scene to the play that takes us into the mind of Desdemona; after the credits, we see Othello and Desdemona solemnizing their vows in an ornate church. No word is audible, not even the priest's prayers. No sound other than the musical score is heard until Yutkevich cuts abruptly to Roderigo pounding on a door and crying out, "What ho, Brabantio! Signior Brabantio, ho!" (1.1.79) at Iago's instigation. Yutkevich had been present at the creation of Soviet film in the silent era, a stalwart of the avant-garde who had survived the Communist Party's push of all arts toward socialist realism. His opening sequence is, in part, a celebration of the relative cultural thaw of its time, a review of film history, and a send-up of the deliberately "inspirational" epics (often depicting Stalin himself) the Central Committee of the Party insisted upon.

The return to silent film practice is not, however, a strategy of avoidance: Yutkevich is not afraid of Shakespeare's language. The original film employs Boris Pasternak's Russian translation and the version released in the West offers capable readings of Shakespeare's lines, although the dubbing is often—and unintentionally—asynchronous. Language is a prime subject of the story here, even before it is heard. From the very first scene, Yutkevich explores—as Shakespeare does—the effect language can have on vision. The opening shot reveals Othello with his back to us, facing Desdemona (played by Irina Skobtseva) and her father Brabantio, who are listening intently to the Moor's accounts of his exploits. Othello uses a large, intricately decorated armillary sphere both to trace his travels and to invite his auditors into his permeable world. After he leaves, Desdemona goes to the chamber window, with light reflecting off the water of a canal and shining on the exterior wall of Brabantio's house. It seems she wants to keep Othello in view as long as possible. After a lingering look, she turns and walks back toward the sphere. She turns it slightly and for a moment her eyes follow its surface's movements. As her gaze glides away from the sphere, Yutkevich pulls into extreme closeup on Skobtseva's face. The screen then dissolves to show how Desdemona imagines Othello: a storybook hero who goes through daring campaigns, endures life as a captive, and returns to command more glorious than before. The fanciful nature of her imaginings is reinforced by whimsical effects; her idealization of Othello is established by constant low-angle shots. Even his eyes have authority: while still a galley slave, Othello keeps his overseer from whipping him by the sheer force of his gaze.

The 1922 *Othello* had highlighted expressivity in its efforts to replace Shakespeare's language with action, gesture, and Iago's literal plotting. Yutkevich's version incorporates language and its effects, which are not as controllable as either Othello or Iago believe. Before the Venetian senate, Othello reproduces the initial impact his rhetoric had on Desdemona. Once again turning a globe, he casts a powerful spell upon most of his listeners: two young servants in the council room are shown utterly rapt at Othello's account. "This is the only witchcraft I have used," he asserts (1.3.168) and it is potent magic indeed. But Brabantio remains unmoved and Desdemona herself has gone beyond the outlines of the Moor's story: she wants it to be not just a romance, in its earlier sense of an adventure narrative, but a romantic comedy. From this point on, Skobtseva's Desdemona will try to be one of Shakespeare's comic heroines.

Her and Othello's departure from the senate is filmed with all the trappings of an exultantly happy end. The doting couple makes a stately descent down sunlit steps to the water's edge; Khatchaturian supplies a triumphal march as accompaniment. Yutkevich, though, adds another hint of the dangers to which Othello and Desdemona are oblivious: here, she drops the handkerchief on the steps; Iago picks it up and returns it, humbly. All seems—and only seems—more than well. When Desdemona lands at Cyprus, she is dressed in doublet and hose, as though she were Viola in *Twelfth Night* or Rosalind in *As You Like It* adopting male garb. Upon his arrival, Othello runs up six flights of steps to reach her, embrace her, and kiss her in front of cheering throngs. Through all the pains and humiliations that follow, Desdemona holds onto her belief in the eventual return of the happy endings she has experienced.

Yutkevich shows Desdemona's imaginings as well as her attempts to realize them. This access to subjectivity is paralleled in the presentation of Iago. Andrei Popov's portrayal concentrates on the character's agreeable bluntness: as in Shakespeare's play, it does not occur to his observers that such a plain-spoken individual could have anything to hide. Theatrical audiences know otherwise, thanks to a series of coruscating soliloquies that reveal Iago's malign depths. In this film version, the revealing speeches—even the asides—are delivered in voice-over, as internal monologues, reinforcing a sense of depth. Having first shamed Cassio and then sent him to Desdemona for aid, Iago contemplates his unfolding scheme as he gazes into an ancient well. "And what's he then that says I play the villain [?]," (2.3.303) Iago muses. Looking at his reflection in the water, he sees himself as others do—a man apt in giving his friends free, honest, and reasonable counsel. He will go on to persuade Othello to accept not only this image of Iago, but the images Iago offers of Cassio, Desdemona, and the Moor. The scene ends with Iago shattering his reflection with two sweeps of his hand and the voice-over concludes: "So will I turn her virtue into pitch, / And out of her own goodness make the net / That will enmesh them all" (2.3.327–29).

In the long exchange from 3.3 in which Iago destroys Othello's image of Desdemona, Othello is physically enmeshed. Walking along the Cyprian coast, the characters first pass some fishing boats, then several nets hung up to dry on shore. As Iago utters his ironic warning, "O beware, my lord, of jealousy" (3.3.167), Othello finds it harder and harder to pass through the snares. When Othello himself accepts Iago's version of things—that Desdemona, in loving him, embodies "nature erring from itself" (3.3.229)—he faces the camera in medium shot, stopped short by a fine-mesh net. Iago soon takes his leave and Othello must work through his doubts alone, in soliloquy. Sergei Bondarchuk's interpretation of the character is expansive, grandly expressive: in marked contrast to Iago's interior thoughts, Othello's soliloquies are given aloud. In this speech, he begins by expressing his conviction that Iago is a man "of exceeding honesty" and keen knowledge "Of human dealings." This is followed by a howl of grief, as the full significance of honest Iago's words now hits home. He looks into the same well Iago had visited, seeing himself just as Iago desires: because he is "black, / And have not those soft parts of conversation that chamberers have," because he is "declined / Into the vale of years" (3.3.265–68), he cannot keep Desdemona's love. He imitates Iago's gesture, breaking the image in the water with his hand, dramatizing the snares of the naturalistic approach. Racial categories are often "naturalized" visually, most efficiently by illusionistic approaches that conceal their artfulness. Othello himself has already used language to this end, as instructed by his adopted culture and his cultural tutor and supposed ally, Iago.

Another visual echo marks Iago's delivery of the "ocular proof" Othello believes he wants. The Moor has taken emotional refuge on board his ship, after Iago shares an invented memory of Cassio talking in his sleep. In his cabin, Bondarchuk's Othello delivers the fragmented speech haunted by the word *confess* in a towering passion reminiscent of Jannings's performance in the role. He tries to climb back on deck but falls backward down the steps in a fit. After Iago finds and revives him, they look out of a window as they plot Othello's revenge. Cassio has appeared on the dock and Iago goes to speak with him, urging Othello to overhear the conversation that follows. We see Othello at the window, light reflecting from the water as it did upon Desdemona's window. Iago's frame of reference has completely supplanted hers. When Bianca appears with Desdemona's handkerchief, the frame provides its own interpretation. Cassio's emotional distance from Bianca has already been established in the filming of the scene in which he gives her the handkerchief, not realizing it is Desdemona's. Like the stone window dividing Othello from Desdemona in Buchowetzki's version, a wrought-iron gate keeps Cassio and Bianca from true intimacy: they banter and she receives the important token through its bars. Cassio's cavalier attitude toward Bianca feeds Othello's rage, since he believes it both applies to his own wife and confirms her fallenness.

Even now, Desdemona's counterplot of romantic comedy persists and has its charms for Othello. He has seen his handkerchief bandied about by Cassio and a courtesan; in response, he has expertly practiced sword handling while avowing he "will have [Cassio] nine years a killing" (4.1.169). In Shakespeare's play, Othello himself immediately changes tone: "A fine woman, a fair woman, a sweet woman!" He is not being ironic, here. Iago immediately senses a loss of resolve and urges, "Nay, you must forget that." In Yutkevich's film, Desdemona's voice reminds Othello of the other vision, the other narrative, the other world she represents. We hear her singing and then see her on a small boat, attended by Emilia, in full song; her singing has previously been heard during part of Iago's grand temptation of the general. Othello falls back on a bed; with her voice still on the soundtrack, he praises her as "an admirable musician." Believing her to be corrupted, he nonetheless insists that Iago acknowledge "the pity of it." Popov's Iago leans his head over Othello's from the other direction, promoting his inverted vision of things. When Iago counters that Desdemona should be strangled in bed, "even the bed she hath contaminated," Bondarchuk's Othello alternates between laughter and tears in approving. At that moment, Desdemona's voice vanishes from the soundtrack. Her song will not be heard by Othello any more.

She sings once more, though, giving voice to "The Willow Song" that foreshadows her death. It is heard in Russian, as are all the film's songs, and Skobtseva's delivery may add to a possible obscurity for English-speaking audiences. Her manner, though subdued, is confident. She remains the comic heroine almost to the end, aided by reaction shots of Emilia, who even betrays a certain boredom with the song. In the conventions of comic romance, servants are allowed to hold at arms' length the idealism of their betters; a similar dynamic is at work in Shakespeare's play, where Emilia and Desdemona argue about what men and women may rightly or wrongly "do." Othello's appearance on the scene changes the story and also the style of performance. We return to the expressionist mode, literally with a vengeance. When Othello informs Desdemona she is about to die, she utters a brief prayer: "Then Lord have mercy on me" (5.2.57). He answers with "Amen" and the organ music that accompanied the wedding scene returns. Othello stretches his hands to her and, as he approaches, we finally see through his eyes. The camera adopts his point of view as it tracks toward Desdemona, his arms framing her. Almost immediately, we shift to her perspective: Othello stalks closer, glowering, bathed in red light. The melodramatic effects intensify for the actual murder, as the camera quickly pans right to a candle extinguished by a gust of wind that wordlessly echoes a line at the beginning of the scene: "Put out the light, and then put out the light" (5.2.7)—part of Othello's preparations for his wife's murder. As organ music resounds once more, we see branches waving in the wind.

Further confirming this Othello's incapacity "to dissemble" or to sustain interiority, his hair turns white as a consequence of the murder. Jannings's Othello had greyed noticeably under the strain of Iago's campaign, but the guilt of Bondarchuk's Othello is made visible like the mark of Cain. Yutkevich's revival of the practices of silent expressionism seen in Buchowetzki's film has more personal sources as well; he had adapted expressionist styles for his own theater and film work in the 1920s. His collaborators at the time included not only Sergei Eisenstein but also Grigori Kozintsev, who would produce two masterpieces of Shakespearean film in the 1960s (see chapter eight). As Peter Donaldson has observed (1990, 95–97 and 112–13), Yutkevich clearly learned from Welles's 1952 film version of the play. Welles, too, explores the powers of reflection and vision in Shakespeare's playtext and he also places special emphasis on Othello's moment of recognition (see chapter six). Here Yutkevich shines light directly upon Othello's eyes, with Bondarchuk's face in extreme closeup—a tragic and more stylized version of the early shot of Desdemona. There are additional echoes of Welles's version in the concluding shots of Othello and Desdemona lying in state, and of the captive Iago, but Yutkevich's daring juxtapositioning of styles sets him well apart from his illustrious predecessor.

Yutkevich earned Best Direction honors at the Cannes Festival in 1956; the judges were impressed by his mastery of individual styles and his skillfully abrupt shifts from one to the other. In this, Yutkevich is authentically Shakespearean: the plays are filled with what some readers have considered unseemly mixtures of high and low, of tragic and comic. Given Yutkevich's often aggressive cuts, his dramatic changes in camera angle and point of view, and his foregrounding of genre conventions in film, lapses in the timing of the dubbed dialogue scarcely detract from the experience. Neither does the survival of the original Russian for the songs. Yutkevich refuses to naturalize his source materials, his medium, or its conventions—a refusal that contrasts sharply with Bondarchuk's later career as actor-director (Cohen 318–20) in film adaptations of Mikhail Sholokhov's *Fate of a Man* (1959) and Leo Tolstoy's *War and Peace* (1965–67). What does detract from the experience of Yutkevich's *Othello* is its most readily available video version, which has been copied from a well-worn, black-and-white print of a film originally filled with remarkable uses of color. Yutkevich uses vibrant color throughout, especially in bright, sun-drenched exterior shots and in marking the splendor of Venetian pomp. Such effects have been severely muted—when they survive at all—in the transfers first to black-and-white film and then, from that source, to video format. Intriguingly, given the weight of Soviet history, the most significant colors are red and white. When he arrives on Cyprus, Othello wears a brilliant red cloak. After dismissing the troops and proclaiming a holiday in honor of both the peace and his marriage, he leads Desdemona to a high platform. As they watch the sunset, he wraps his cloak around her and they become one figure on the battlements. At the end of the film, Othello carries the lifeless body of Desdemona onto the same platform. After stabbing himself—"And smote him thus!" (5.2.352)—he returns to Desdemona and uses the white cloak that he wears as a shroud for them both. Their final kiss is hidden from view. That spectacle is denied us.

Oliver Parker's 1995 version of *Othello* revels in the spectacular. For the most part a naturalistic presentation, conforming with the conventions of mass-market film production, it nevertheless includes elements that resist those conventions. The emphasis on naturalism has in itself one salutary consequence: for the first time in a general-release film, the role is portrayed by an African-American actor, Laurence Fishburne. At the same time, though, naturalistic conventions privilege spectacle. The first on-screen kiss between Fishburne's Othello and Irene Jacob's Desdemona is presented as truly something to behold: not only does Roderigo spy on the newly married couple there in church, but Othello himself keeps watch, unwilling to close his eyes as their lips meet. When the couple is reunited on Cyprus (and this Othello rides up the city's steps, on a powerful charger), not only is their passionate kiss open to public view, but so too are the reactions of the observers. Parker focuses on the onlookers, who are far more subdued—perhaps even critical—than those seen in Yutkevich's film. Not even Cassio (played here by Nathaniel Parker) seems entirely at ease with the display, though he smiles: he and Emilia both avert their eyes. A less ambiguous instance of unease is recorded by Herbert Coursen in a study of this film's use as a classroom aid. He reports how a white, female observer "covered her eyes as Othello and Desdemona kissed" (126).

We, as spectators, are allowed glimpses of the marriage's consummation as well. After Othello proclaims the holiday on Cyprus, the newlyweds repair to their new chambers. In explaining why Fishburne was chosen for the role, Parker has described the actor as "all danger and sexuality" (Starks 64); this interpolated love scene emphasizes both qualities almost to the exclusion of any other. Fishburne's Othello carries Desdemona into the room, and they share in blowing out the lamps as they pass. Parker apparently means to foreshadow the final scene's "Put out the light" and the tone is not significantly brightened by lines borrowed from a different context: "The purchase made, the fruits are to ensue; / That profit's yet to come 'tween me and you" (2.3.9–10). In the play, Othello says this to Desdemona in the presence of Cassio and several attendants. The lines not only express physical desire, but also help to mark the trust placed in Cassio during the celebrations. Here, it is instead a very private exchange marking our access to Othello's and Desdemona's intimacy and especially to Othello's body. Fishburne undresses as "exotic," Moorish-sounding music is heard on the soundtrack, possibly part of the festivities outside; the camera pans up from his bare feet along his still trousered legs and focuses, in moderate closeup, on Othello's hands removing his belt. As Lisa Starks notes (71–72), the film exploits Fishburne's association with recent roles, especially as Ike Turner in *What's Love Got to Do With It* (1993), in ways that fetishize Othello as the black aggressor of racist—and popular—stereotype. At first, Desdemona seems fearful, as she retreats from him, almost hiding behind the bed. Soon, though, she finishes undressing and their lovemaking follows: to establish its tenderness, the raucous drums fade from the soundtrack and lush strings accompany a solo flute. We see flower petals on the bed, which may be another indication of conventional romanticism or a sign of Desdemona's virginity prior to marriage. Finally, the screen offers an emblematic image of their hands, black and white, knitted together.

Othello, here, speaks mostly with his body: Fishburne is given only a small portion of the character's lines in the play (and, unlike many of his co-stars who had more extensive experience with Shakespeare, he didn't negotiate for restoration of cut lines). He doesn't speak with his own voice, opting instead for a vaguely "North African" accent. Even as he summarizes the story that won Desdemona's love, the physical scars from battle and brand from slavery speak most eloquently here. His conviction that Cassio and Desdemona have betrayed him is also expressed visually. The Othello of Buchowetzki's film had dreamed of their embraces, awakening in anquish only to be comforted by Iago with the handkerchief. After Fishburne's Othello has fallen victim to Iago's plot and his own doubts, Parker lets the audience witness still worse imaginings about Desdemona and Cassio: Othello dreams of being, even more outrageously, the "supervisor" of Iago's gibes, discovering them in bed together. Even after he wakes, he cannot shake the images: he imagines Cassio's and Desdemona's hands linked as a white-on-white "correction" of the earlier scene. Recalling Brabantio's parting shot—"She has deceived her father and may thee" (1.3.299)—he leaves the marriage bed and the still-sleeping Desdemona. Their separation is further confirmed, with images, in the scene depicting Othello's physical fit of jealousy. In an armory, filled with weapons and massive links of chain, Iago repeats Cassio's alleged confession. Othello again imagines the pair making love and grabs the chains in an attempt to stay upright as the fit comes on. Instead of the speech about confessions and "Noses, ears, and lips" (4.1.41–2), we see Othello's imagining of these body parts (and tongues, too) in a scene of sexual passion. The chains suggest that Parker intends we see Othello enslaved not only by his jealousy but by the racist categories Iago has led him to internalize. The diminishing of Othello's voice tends to align the film with other stereotypes, nevertheless.

Iago has the most commanding voice in the film, here provided by recent film's most popular Shakespearean actor and director, Kenneth Branagh. His own Shakespeare films will be examined more closely in chapters six and seven, but two of their characteristics, one interpretive and one technical, apply most pertinently here. First, Branagh's Shakespeare films assert an undeniable likeability in many of the plays' leading roles, including not coincidentally those he performs. From young King Henry in *Henry V* (1989) and Benedick in *Much Ado About Nothing* (1993) to his subsequent portrayal of Hamlet, Branagh eagerly asks audiences to root for these characters. They are the heroes, after all; they are also the most accessible characters on screen. Branagh may be one of the canniest practitioners of what Mas'ud Zavarzadeh terms "the cultural politics of intimacy" (115–16). So it is fascinating to see the same mannerisms Branagh uses as Benedick applied to the role of the villainous Iago: the same breezy delivery of lines, the same curious combination of almost-forced joviality with genuine discoveries of often-overlooked laughs. (The success in making explicit the comedy of several scenes is also due to Michael Maloney's performance as Roderigo.) The glib congeniality not only makes Iago's persuasiveness believable—when this man gets serious, it must really be so—but also unsettles our understanding of his roles in other films: just how sincere are Branagh's Henry, his Benedick, and his Hamlet?

Second, Branagh as director refuses to let Branagh the actor look directly into the camera; barely one of his characters' great soliloquies is addressed to us. Branagh's gaze is almost always averted—the only exceptions are a reaction shot in *Much Ado*, some of Hamlet's responses to the Ghost, and one of Berowne's speeches in *Love's Labours Lost* (and even then primarily because it serves as a lead-in for a musical number). Parker, though, insists that Iago face the film's audience. Wheeler Dixon's analyses help greatly in appreciating the impact of Iago's soliloquies here. Dixon persuasively argues (63–76) that overtly returned cinematic gazes and addresses can serve to alert audiences that the screen always "looks back," that most films (especially mass-market ones) impose a dynamic of surveillance in exchange for the guilty safety of a voyeuristic relation to spectacular images. The overtly returned gaze can disrupt this exchange as it disrupts the tacit naturalization of materials and of subject matter that also dominates commercial film. The carnivalesque potential in this disruption explains why the returned gaze is usually reserved for comedy, as in Branagh's shocked response to what his character has overheard in *Much Ado*. Parker daringly applies the returned gaze to tragedy. This is not so much that we can get to the "truth" of Iago, which would result from the naturalistic effect of soliloquy, but that we can face our presence in front of the screen, which responds to the performative effect of soliloquy. As a result, we are confronted by our involvement with—and either our complicity or implication in—what occurs as entertainment and as aesthetic experience.

When Branagh's Iago first addresses us, he is poised over a set of overdetermined symbols: a chessboard upon which the black and white pieces stand in for Othello, Desdemona, Cassio. The returned gaze helps to underscore not only the obviousness of the symbolism but the arbitrariness of the racial games Iago will play. In the second of the film's soliloquies, where Iago promises us that he will transform Desdemona's "virtue into pitch," Branagh removes a charred, still-smoldering log from a fire to smear sooty ashes over his own hand: the gesture toward the burnt-cork used in white impersonations of blackness also adds to a sense of the constructedness of racial identifications. His Iago then stretches his hand forward to blot the screen, indicating that Iago's version of blackness and its significations will now dominate. That Iago appears impervious to the still-hot embers may also suggest that he is a kind of White Devil (an Early

Modern expression common enough to be used as a Jacobean play's title), at home in hell's flames; at the end of Shakespeare's play, when Othello realizes what Iago has done, he looks for the cloven feet that folklore says devils should have (5.2.283). But Branagh likely feels the pain: he may be covering the lens in order to cut short the take and hide his discomfort. Together, these effects undermine the naturalization of categories—such as the meanings assigned to white and black—and of performance.

As I have indicated above, Parker's film does not consistently resist naturalization. In fact, the interpretation of Iago goes so far as to "explain" his vendetta against the Moor as the result of unacknowledged homoerotic desire. At the end of the film, the Venetian envoy Lodovico not only demands that Iago "Look on the tragic loading of this bed: / This is thy work" (5.2.359–60) but also drags the wounded Iago to the bed upon which the bodies of Othello and Desdemona lie. Branagh's Iago then crawls upon the bed, apparently still trying to separate the lovers—or, at least, to impose himself upon them. Even here, the overt "look back" complicates matters: Iago climbs part way on top of the couple and then lies back, turning his gaze toward us. The white man's story has prevailed, we are shown, and not only by this disruptive image. In this version, Othello is provided a weapon—so he may both atone for his crime and escape capture—by Cassio, who subsequently dissembles: "This did I fear, but thought he had no weapon" (5.2.356). It is also Cassio who opens the window of the fatal chamber, letting in sunlight. One recalls Parker's decision to have Othello draw his sword when confronted by Brabantio and the officers he has recruited to arrest the Moor. Many stagings emphasize Othello's cool command here as he urges all to "Keep up your bright swords" and "Hold your hands" (1.2.59, 81b); the character adds that "Were it my cue to fight, I should have known it / Without a prompter" (83–84). Fishburne's Othello wields a formidable blade, backed up by Iago and Cassio, who also point weapons at their general's adversaries. Perhaps in phallic competition with Othello, Iago has drawn his dagger as well as rapier. While the image participates in the film's presentation of Othello as "dangerous" (see Figure 2), it also shows Othello as endangered. Our hero should watch his back, as the saying aptly goes, since both Iago and Cassio combine—if not conspire—to ensure Othello's death.

It is worth noting that, for months after the film's relatively brief circulation in most markets, Parker's *Othello* attracted African-American audiences. Some of the lasting interest must have been due to Fishburne's charismatic presence. This was the focus of a cover story feature on the

FIGURE 2. Laurence Fishburne, "dangerous" and endangered in Oliver Parker's *Othello* (1995). Photo courtesy of Jerry Ohlinger's Movie Material.

film in the African-American periodical *Jet* ("Laurence Fishburne Stars"). The article quotes Fishburne's account of the character as a "warrior, a poetic soul . . . someone who's never been in love before [and is] naive in the ways of love"; it also praises director Parker's stated intention to concentrate on Othello rather than Iago. The value that the publication placed on the film is made evident by another story in the same issue, one that reports the death of the magazine's pioneering and inspirational executive editor, Robert E. Johnson. Despite this development, *Othello* nevertheless remained the cover story—and the article's praise of how Fishburne had "powerfully mastered the tragic character" ("Laurence Fishburne Stars" 35) attracted sizeable audiences. Some of the film's appeal to African-Americans must also have been its insistence on presenting a problematic spectacle—the interracial embrace—framed by explorations of the constructed quality of so many of its enduring problems. As an African-American man commented after seeing this Othello kiss Desdemona, "That's all he has to do. He doesn't have to say anything" (Coursen 126). The comment can be heard as both admiring and rueful, as a response to Parker's version and also to the play and its history on film. That lesson, which can be derived from the content of the play, also responds to the conjunction of an overall naturalistic approach and nonillusionistic techniques as they are filtered through the cultural conditioning and resistance so central to a viewer's experience.

CHAPTER THREE

— ◇ —

Documentary Shakespeare

OTHELLO: When you shall these unlucky deeds relate,
Speak of me as I am; nothing extenuate,
Nor set down aught in malice.

—Shakespeare, *Othello*

In his study *Rhetoric and Representation in Nonfiction Film*, Carl R. Plantinga reviews the enduring problems and pitfalls of defining what a "nonfiction" film is and of further categorizing a film as a "documentary." Drawing upon and reacting to the work of theorists such as Edward Branigan, Noël Carroll, and Bill Nichols, Plantinga suggests a definition that acknowledges both the intentions of a film's makers and the expectations of its audiences: nonfiction films "assert a belief that given objects, entities, states of affairs, events, or situations actually occur(red) or exist(ed) in the actual world as portrayed" (18) but their power of assertion depends on an audience's ability to "gauge that a film has been indexed" as nonfiction or documentary in intent (19). The history of Shakespeare on film has regularly been shaped, though, by different kinds of assertions and different claims of intent. Shakespeare documentaries that concentrate on the stage usually claim both that what audiences are seeing did happen "as portrayed" and that their experience as filmgoers prevents them from fully appreciating what occured in the "actual world" of the theater. One pseudo-documentary (relying on fanciful "re-enact-ments"), *Master Will Shakespeare* (1936), offers the counterclaim that the cinematic experience can provide a truer account—or, at least, a fuller realization—of the playtexts that serve as bases for stage performances. The persuasiveness of this assertion depends on a deliberate blurring of the boundaries between fictional and nonfictional film. Finally, the most recent exercise in Shakespeare documentary, Al Pacino's *Looking for Richard* (1996), makes its assertions neither about a stage performance or a film realization of a play but about the processes of discovery a playtext may require and inspire. Not only does the answer to "what occurs or occured in Shakespeare?" change; so too does the definition of *what.*

When publicity stills and the surviving scene from Herbert Beer-bohm Tree's 1899 production of *King John* are seen today, over a century later, the entire filmic project can strike viewers as more a set of souvenirs than a purposive document. Luke McKernan has argued that this *King John* "was a poor record of both the production of the play, but then it was intended as neither . . . [it was meant] to provide what amounted to an advertisement for Tree's production, or better still a news report" (1–2). Something of a coherent narrative might have been communicated, nev-ertheless. In the absence of the three (or more?) missing sequences, it is dif-ficult to conjecture what impact a sequential screening may have had on Tree's ideal audience—"those perfectly familiar with the play [who] could recall the lines appropriate to the action" (Ball 304). Given that some later silent versions, most notably the 1913 *Hamlet* with Johnston Forbes-Robertson, address exactly such an audience, the apparent choice of scenes in *King John* could have provided a compressed account of the perfidy and fall of its deeply problematic protagonist. As such, it could also serve as a documentary of the overall interpretation and performance.

The first scene, as reflected in publicity stills (Kachur 55–62), con-firms King John as consummate politician: he is cannily able to persuade Hubert to assassinate the king's young nephew, a rival claimant to the throne, without directly requesting the deed or promising any reward. The next scene shows Arthur's mother, Constance, in desperate grief at Arthur's capture. The climactic scene shows the king himself brought down by the corrupt political milieu he has shown himself incapable of rising above. Struck by a fever at the battle of St. Edmundsbury, John is taken to Swinstead Abbey, where is he poisoned by one of the monks pos-sibly in revenge for his past defiance of papal authority. Ironically, the king had decided to yield to Rome in hopes of preventing the battle.

As it exists now, the film shows Tree as King John already seated as he begins the speech describing the pains of both the fever and the poison: "Ay, marry, now my soul hath elbow-room" (5.7.28). Dora Senior, playing the king's son, Henry, steps toward him and takes Tree's hand, apparently at the prince's question, "How fares your Majesty?" (5.7.35). Tree turns away from her, reflecting the bitterness of John's lines, which rail against his son and followers because they do not "bid the winter come / To thrust his icy fingers in my maw, / Nor let my kingdom's rivers take their course / Through my burn'd bosom" (36–39) and cool his raging fever; Tree clutches at his chest as he silently mouths the lines. Senior kneels and takes Tree's hand again for Henry's expression of sorrow and empathy, "O that there were some virtue in my tears, / That might relieve you" (43–44). Tree pulls his hand away, clawing at it with his other hand, as he expresses the king's inability to accept the gesture or even to feel the tears without guilt-ridden agony: "The salt in them is hot. / Within me is a hell [Tree clutches his chest once more], and there the poison / Is as a fiend confin'd to tyrannize / On unreprievable condemned blood" (45–48). John's callousness toward Arthur, his brother's son, has led only to estrangement from his own son. The major fragment ends here. Another fragment shows Tree rising from the chair, apparently in preparation for the king's death. This scene continued—or another vignette followed—with the crowning of the prince as Henry III (who would reign for well over fifty years), offering hope for stability after the chaotic events precipitated by his father's political schemings.

All in all, this would provide a compelling shorthand account, if only for audience members deeply familiar with this lesser-known play. For most viewers, however, the sight of performers like Tree and Julia Neilson (in the role of Constance) and the sheer scale of the experience provided ample excitement. William Kennedy-Laurie Dickson, the director, filmed these scenes for the British Mutoscope and Biograph Company in 68mm, presaging such widescreen Shakespearean spectacles as Stuart Burge's 1965 *Othello* and Branagh's *Hamlet*. (Dickson, building on the work of Eadweard Muybridge, developed the kinetoscope in Thomas Edison's workshop. Leaving Edison, he cofounded American Mutoscope and Biograph in 1896; soon after, he returned to England to found that company's British counterpart, which pioneered newsreel-style documentaries.) On smaller screens, the empty spaces separating Tree from the actors on either side of him merely suggest a resistance to adapting stage blocking to the needs of a motion picture camera; on a larger screen, the original audiences might have seen the spaces as highlighting the king's isolation. As first presented, then, the 1899 *King John* offers an abridged cinematic analogue to the experience of seeing Tree in this stage production. In fact, the film premiered in British, American, and European theaters on the same night that the play reopened at Her Majesty's Theatre, September 30. Another reproduction of a stage experience was a highlight of the 1900 Paris Exposition, which included the developing phenomenon of sound film. The duel scene from Sarah Bernhardt's production of *Hamlet*, with the Divine Sarah herself in the title role, was screened to the accompaniment of a wax cylinder recording of the dialogue and sound effects. (For more on this film and its contribution to "Transgressive" Shakespeare, see chapter seven.)

At the same time, such films usually suggest that there is no real substitute for having been present at these performances. They are presented as memorials, already removed from the vitality of the theater. In 1913, at the age of sixty, Johnston Forbes-Robertson started bidding farewell to the English stage with reprises of some of his most celebrated roles. The series of commemorative performances, which ran from late March to early June at Drury Lane, began and ended with *Hamlet*. Forbes-Robertson had revolutionized the role sixteen years earlier, in a production hailed by no less exacting a critic than George Bernard Shaw (who had advised the actor on the play generally). The Gaumont Company persuaded Forbes-Robertson to preserve the 1913 production on film. At the time people recognized that the "new mechanical device" that is the motion picture camera, as described by the reviewer for the *Pall Mall Gazette*, "lends some degree of permanency to the essentially personal ephemeral art of the actor" (qtd. by Ball 192). In this way, the medium of film could preserve for generations to come some aspects of an electrifying and profoundly influential interpretation of the role. The original idea, though, was to allow a wider audience to witness, if at a cinemagraphic remove, the culmination of a distinguished player's long experience with the role. The "new mechanical device" is subordinated to the medium and institution of the stage.

The 1913 *Hamlet* does, at times, fit the stereotype of staginess all too well. In fact, the relative narrowness of the conventional camera's frame—no widescreen visuals this time—often prompts the director, E. Hay Plumb, to squeeze into it all the elements that might spread across the width of a proscenium arch stage. The resulting effect of claustrophobia is not linked to any interpretive theme. In part this is because Forbes-Robertson's Hamlet could indeed "be bounded in a nutshell, and count [himself] a king of infinite space" (2.2.254–55), so free and force-ful is his intellect. The exchange with Rosencrantz and Guildenstern that includes this self-assessment, from act 2, scene 2, appears in this version, although Hamlet's erstwhile fellow students are transformed to "ambas-sadors" according to a title card. Forbes-Robertson's Hamlet is breezily comfortable in parrying with the informers sent from his uncle, step-father, and king. This prince inhabits a very different world from Elsinore and can be contemptuous of its demands; as an actor, Forbes-Robertson is never condescending, but sometimes does betray an indifference toward the camera. At one point, he moves out of frame in mid-speech, while the cinematographer tries valiantly to swivel the fixed camera around to bring him back into view. He unapologetically delivers long speeches, with only a few gestures to suggest where we are in a given passage, unlike Tree's approach. Even so, Hamlet's words are so much more familiar than King John's that lipreading Forbes-Robertson's delivery of the lines conveys an uncanny impression of "hearing" his performance.

Some efforts were made to capitalize upon film's flexibility and potential expansiveness: exterior shots, including a rocky shoreline and an idyllic garden, convey what Shakespeare's verbal scene-painting cannot in this medium; double exposure effects of the sort pioneered by Méliès lend a spectral insubstantiality to the Ghost (who walks through Horatio and the two guards, Marcellus and Barnardo); closeups are used to advantage in drawing our attention to the poisoned sword and cup Claudius and Laertes have prepared for Hamlet. Most impressive of all, for many view-ers, is the happy conjunction of Forbes-Robertson's restrained perfor-mance style and the scrutiny of the camera at moderately close range. Shaw had particularly praised the actor for capturing a central truth about the character: Hamlet's "intellect is the organ of his passion" (Shaw 3: 203). The synthesis of logic, intensity, grace, and control that seemed so striking on stage lends itself readily to the naturalized screen.

The degree of realism that a naturalistic approach to film makes possible becomes the theme of a curious documentary short entitled *Mas-ter Will Shakespeare*, produced by Metro-Goldwyn-Mayer in conjunction with their 1936 release of *Romeo and Juliet*. The film, dubbed a "Minia-ture" (rather than a vulgar "Short") in the opening credits, combines shots of twentieth-century Stratford-upon-Avon and London with fanciful re-enactments of important public and private moments in Shakespeare's life. *Master Will Shakespeare* also intersperses visuals from the exterior of the Folger Shakespeare Library—a frieze that serves as background for the credits—and, most likely, from the interior as well: in asserting that Shakespeare felt a special fondness for *Romeo and Juliet*, the film offers a reverential closeup of the 1597 quarto edition of the play. Through dramatic re-enactments, young Will can be seen tramping through the English countryside en route to London, holding patrons' horses outside the Blackfriars Theatre, and getting his first break when hired as a prompter by James Burbage. Through the conflation of newsreel footage, travelogue-style commentary, and such authoritative images as the Folger Library and its prized holdings, the film indexes itself as documentary and thereby presents its contents as "explicit claims about reality" where Shakespeare is and was concerned.

The screenwriter, Richard Goldstone, has more in mind than bringing to life any number of truths, half-truths, conjectures, and lies about the playwright; in trying to draw attention to the MGM *Romeo and Juliet*, he also wants to impress upon the audience Shakespeare's suitability for the screen and for them. In the voice-over narration, Shakespeare is compared with "Stage-Struck Sally" and "Footlight-Fascinated John" who dream of taking Broadway or Hollywood by storm. The legend about Shakespeare tending horses provides a parallel to would-be performers and writers winding up waiting tables. When the film proposes that Shakespeare improvises superior dialogue while prompting an actor who has forgotten his lines, it also insists that positive audience reaction ensured that young Will would be commissioned to rewrite entire scenes and ultimately to compose new plays.

Director Jacques Tourneur (who would later create such horror/cult classics as *Cat People* and *I Walked With a Zombie*) shows this process in action, giving us a chance to see what has been lost to the ages: a manuscript draft, complete with corrections and an unmistakably authorizing signature, of a Shakespearean original. We also see the playwright in action, coaching his fellow performers, always "demanding realism" in their acting. In short, Shakespeare is cast in a prophetic role, preparing the way for the technology, techniques, and dominant presentational modes of Hollywood cinema. To bring this point home, the narration further informs us that Shakespeare was hindered by primitive performance conditions, in which the dramatic illusion was constantly shattered by the practice of casting boys in women's roles and by the absence of scenery. We are asked to wonder what Shakespeare, from his vantage point "high in the seventh heaven," must think of his work being presented on the screen. Because of his love of beauty—which in his day could be represented "only in his words," not physically on the stage—he must approve, we are told, of the lavish sets and the casting. As a sample of the scenery, the Capulets' gardens are shown; to persuade audiences of the aptness of the casting, clips follow from the film, featuring Leslie Howard as Romeo and Norma Shearer as Juliet. Howard's suitability for Romeo has been visually established by the actor portraying Shakespeare, who resembles Howard most when an older, sadder Will recites from Romeo's final speech. A further link with Howard's performance is made when we hear, along with these words, music from Tchaikowsky's ballet, as used in the feature film. The question of Shearer's age is more problematically answered by closeups of the actress as Juliet and by the narrator's recitation of lines from Enobarbus's speech in praise of Cleopatra: "Age cannot wither her, nor custom stale / Her infinite variety" (*Antony and Cleopatra* 2.2.234–35)!

William Guynn has analyzed the "oscillation of modes of expression" that occurs in the documentary film: its "nonfiction-effect" is produced by the competition between authoritative commentary and intermittently autonomous image-discourses (157). A pseudo-documentary (akin to propaganda films), *Master Will Shakespeare* hopes to instill that effect in its viewers, like thousands of "historical" shorts and corporately produced "educational" films, with the further goal of affecting consumer behavior. This film fails in large measure because voice and image here have so clearly ceded both authority and autonomy to a master-text involving the major film production of *Romeo and Juliet*. (Remarkably, MGM revived *Master Will Shakespeare* in conjunction with its 1953 *Julius Caesar*.) Even without the complication of overt marketing within a film (wittily parodied by the use of Shakespeare-inspired advertising slogans in Baz Luhrmann's *Romeo+Juliet*), any genuinely documentary approach to Shakespearean filmmaking needs to allow for competition between the visual and commentary discourses. One way of eliding the problem is to incorporate re-enactments as part of a narrative film, as in Olivier's *Henry V*. Another way is to make the major film itself a document, to return to the strategies seen in the 1899 *King John* and the 1913 *Hamlet*. Two film versions of Shakespeare's plays in the 1960s—Stuart Burge's film of the National Theatre *Othello* with Laurence Olivier and Tony Richardson's film of his raucous Roundhouse *Hamlet* with Nicol Williamson—take strikingly different approaches toward those documentary strategies. Al Pacino's 1996 *Looking for Richard* engages more fully with the "nonfiction-effect," in part by documenting a production of *Richard III* that exists only within the making of the documentary.

Burge's 1965 *Othello* has been roundly criticized for its "staginess," which is similar to finding fault with water for being wet. One of the film's producers, Anthony Havelock-Allan, announced its intentions upon its release: "to recreate completely the atmosphere, effect and immediacy of the theatre performance, using the basis of film technique . . . the whole object was to capture the absolute magic of the theatre on this occasion" (qtd. by Manvell 117). The specific occasion, of course, was Olivier's performance. In order to "share the experience" with "millions of people throughout the world, who would not have had the remotest chance of seeing Sir Laurence on the stage," the filmmakers have decided "to preserve and enhance this *Othello* and more or less present it as one might have seen it at the National Theatre." Once again, film is relegated to a subordinate position, as Havelock-Allen's rhetoric makes clear: "We have put the best cinema resources at the service of great theatre" (qtd. by Manvell 117). There is the brief admission that film might enhance the production, but this usually translates to the sense that every viewer gets to occupy the very first row of seats or, for Othello's epileptic fit and his approach toward the sleeping Desdemona, the box closest to stage right.

The feeling of being solidly, even uncomfortably, in front is most pronounced during Iago's soliloquies. Through the supposedly impermeable screen, Burge is able to reproduce the feeling that the fourth wall of the proscenium arch stage—a convention Shakespeare predated—is constantly in danger of being violated, that we will be exposed as voyeurs in the theater. Frank Finlay's performance as Iago intensifies the feeling: he doesn't always face us in soliloquy, but when he does it's unnerving. Director of photography Geoffrey Unsworth shoots him in medium to extreme closeup from a low angle; Finlay tilts his head back slightly, guaranteeing that he always looks down at us. The widescreen format makes these instances of the screen's "look back" all the more disruptive. It also allows, in other scenes, audience members greater flexibility to choose where to cast their gaze. The full width of the stage (William Kellner's designs were based upon those of the theatrical production) is re-presented to the cinematic viewer: after Othello overhears Cassio's supposed "confession" and sees Bianca with the handkerchief, only he and Iago remain. Finlay and Olivier are at opposite ends of the stage and as they exchange lines viewers may focus either on the speaker or on the listener. In a later scene, Iago fills up the left side of the screen in closeup profile while we see at right, in the deeply focused background upstage, a diminutive Roderigo protesting he's had enough. The presentation allows both for choosing our own focus and for recognizing Roderigo's trivial place in the tragedy. The realization is all the more poignant, since Robert Lang's Roderigo is no conventional buffoon.

What remains to consider is Olivier's performance, the primary reason for the film. For many viewers, his Othello has bearing but not always dignity. Part of this impression may be the result of Iago's preemptive mockery from the start: Finlay parodies Olivier's artificially deepened, West Indian–accented voice before we get a chance to hear it ourselves. But part of it is Olivier's view that Othello is not only a victim but a flawed, tragically heroic figure. His primary flaws are common to acknowledged heroes, especially those praised for physical action—self-satisfied faith in one's abilities, a desire for decisive resolution of any dilemma. Olivier's Othello is, like Macbeth, more a warrior than a general; he is more like the Mark Antony of *Antony and Cleopatra* than of *Julius Caesar*. Olivier trained physically for the performance in order to enhance the athletic grace and power of his character. His sheer presence announces that Othello's powers are desperately needed by a somewhat effete Venice, represented by a doddering Duke whose voice has returned, as Jaques puts it in *As You Like It*, "to childish treble." Grandly proud, this Othello assumes skills he does not possess, such as being a shrewd judge of character. This makes him vulnerable to Iago, who wounds Othello's pride in order to turn him violently against Desdemona. At times, Olivier comes dangerously close to assuming racist stereotypes—suggesting parallels, for example, with 1960s black athletes—and was criticized at the time (as well as subsequently) for doing so (Hirsch 127). There is, however, along with all this, not only an operatic grandeur of a sort rarely seen on later stages but also a disarming self-referentiality in the performance. Olivier presents himself, as well as Othello, as a foolishly vain individual, easily led, powerfully trusting in appearances, indeed in makeup.

Tony Richardson's 1969 film of *Hamlet* is a valuable record of a performance—Nicol Williamson's—and a production, but film is not so clearly subordinated to the stage in this instance. From the outset, Richardson developed the production for both theatrical and cinematic presentation. He was drawn toward the Roundhouse Theatre in London (which was built as a switching station and repair depot in Victorian times) because of its challenge to conventional theatrical spaces. In his view, the typical theater encouraged conservative, even reactionary interpretations and actor-audience interactions. The Roundhouse structure is also well-suited for filmmaking; it can serve as a giant soundstage and also offers, as in its brick-lined corridors, some useful "location" shots. The production turned out to be equally non-naturalistic on stage and on screen. We are nowhere but the Roundhouse itself, which stands in for Elsinore. At times, we are completely nowhere, as the dark recesses of the space leave the actors alone in a "black void," as Neil Taylor has observed (188). No attempt is made to represent the Ghost of Hamlet's father; only blinding light and near-deafening sound briefly fill the void and highlight the reactions of those who indeed "see" the specter.

Nicol Williamson's Hamlet is not visually youthful, but his snarling delivery of the character's indictments of the corruption that surrounds him impressively reflects the spirit of the student movements of 1968. (The casting of Marianne Faithful—pop singer and companion to the Rolling Stones' Mick Jagger—as Ophelia provides another connection with that era's youth culture.) This Hamlet is an eternal and eternally world-weary graduate student, impatient with pretense yet naively hopeful that some ringing truth can be heard amid the hypocritical lies that pass for "sensible" discourse. Williamson here embodies the 1960s version of creative maladjustment, the idea that insanity is the appropriate response to insane conditions, adding further complexities to Hamlet's strategic assumption of "an antic disposition." Director Richardson concentrates almost exclusively on the main character's philosophical journey, reflecting this Hamlet's preoccupation with intellect and psychology. No wonder Anthony Hopkins's sensual Claudius offends Hamlet so. Through insistent mid-shots and closeups, Richardson crafts a surprisingly exciting drama of "talking heads," even in scenes such as Hamlet's confrontation with Gertrude. Gordon Jackson, as Horatio, visually echoes Williamson's Hamlet: both have thinning hair and compensatory beards, their receding hairlines recalling the famous "egghead" Shakespeare of the Droeshout portrait in the First Folio. Their heads are seen in profile throughout the graveyard scene—where Yorick's skull provides its foreshadowing of mortality—and at the very end of the film. After Hamlet's restless search, which Richardson has followed with characteristically mobile camerawork, we see Horatio lean over in closeup over the face of the dead prince. Horatio closes his friend's eyes after he utters the film's last lines, "Now cracks a noble heart. / Good night, sweet prince, and flights of angels sing thee to thy rest!" (5.2.359–60). The camera pulls in still closer as Horatio's head leaves the frame and we are left with Williamson's Hamlet in extreme closeup profile, finally at rest. Fortinbras does not intrude; the play is at an end with its hero. What is most fully documented is a Hamlet for that historical and cultural moment, a time which greatly valued relevance to its own social conditions and conflicts.

Al Pacino's *Looking for Richard* begins and ends not with lines from *Richard III* but from *The Tempest*—Prospero's speech of explanation about the magical entertainment he has conjured up in honor of his daughter Miranda's impending marriage to Ferdinand. "Our revels now are ended," he tells his future son-in-law. The "actors" they've just seen were spirits who "Are melted into air, into thin air" (4.1.148–50). But more material entities will also disappear: from "cloud-capp'd tow'rs" to "gorgeous palaces," from "solemn temples" to "the great globe itself," all "shall dissolve." At this point, however, we hear a change in Prospero's language. Where most published playtexts read "And like this insubstantial pageant faded / Leave not a rack behind" (155–56), the voice-over narration offers "Leave not a wisp behind." Most editions of the play also add an explanation that "rack" indeed means "a wisp of cloud," but performances usually do not have the luxury of providing that kind of helpful information. *Looking for Richard* will instead savor that luxury, as it later explores the linguistic shifts, historical background, and cultural contexts that so often keep Shakespeare remote from audiences and actors in the United States. At this point, the film simply substitutes the word that will make the passage more comprehensible to listeners new to the play or to Shakespeare's language more generally. The substitution tacitly signals Pacino's hopes to present and to document the processes by which Shakespeare's accessibility and intelligibility may be enhanced for his fellow Americans. His solution to these problems is to present Shakespeare, as Douglas Lanier has observed (1998, 41), by focusing "upon the *process* of performance" (his emphasis).

The barriers between an American "us"—represented and guided by Pacino—and Shakespeare constitute a recurring theme in what follows the opening passage from *The Tempest*. There is a brief exchange among the filmmakers (director-producer Pacino, co-producer Michael Hadge, line producer James Bulleit) over who gets to say "action"; that is, who functions as director, as auteur here. Pacino says he doesn't want to assume that authority and the next scene illustrates why, presenting a distinctly Shakespearean version of the proverbial actor's nightmare. At a tiny New York theater, Pacino is about to take the stage. The camera follows in cinéma vérité fashion as he fumbles along dark passageways until he comes to the curtain. Looking at us, he announces, "This is my entrance." We enter with him to discover only one person is in the audience, Shakespeare himself, looking decidedly skeptical about the performance that is about to begin. Who are we, then, to come to terms with him? Pacino turns aside and lets loose a classic Anglo-Saxon expletive: "Fuck!" It's not just Shakespeare who wonders about the American "us." Intercut with introductory titles are startlingly pertinent questions. One young woman from Europe is a bit embarrassed to ask Pacino if he will do Shakespeare with his "American accent," but she still asks. A disheveled gent in what turns out to be Stratford-upon-Avon is initially incredulous that Pacino would dare, on his unworthy scaffold, to stage so great an object as Shakespeare. He fires a challenge: "What the fuck do you know about Shakespeare?"

That is the question that haunts and provokes Pacino. What may have started as a film of *Richard III* becomes instead a film about Shakespeare as part of U. S. culture. The opening title illustrates the shift: king richard transforms into looking for richard. The responses of people on the streets of New York are interspersed with interviews with actors, directors, and scholars—all centering on the issue of American engagement with Shakespeare. F. Murray Abraham notes the trap many American readers (including actors) fall into of approaching Shakespeare too reverentially; Derek Jacobi agrees, observing that American actors are often "inhibited" by self-conscious attitudes over their abilities to perform the plays; John Gielgud ascribes the difficulties to a lack of familiarity with Shakespeare's age and, he implies, with English culture more generally. An eloquent street person in Manhattan proclaims his conviction that "we should speak like Shakespeare" because of the emotional honesty and empathy he associates with the plays. Other reactions on the streets are more predictable, ranging from Shakespeare is "boring" to problems with archaic language and the tangled dynastic power struggles behind this specific play. Early on, Pacino asks aloud why he picked *Richard III*. The difficulty is part of the answer, along with the irresistible appeal of the starring role for actors.

To overcome the difficulties, an array of study aids and strategies is assembled over the years spent making the film. The Cliffs Notes volume devoted to the play is consulted. A handy paperback edition replaces the formidable complete works first used. Pacino and Frederic Kimball (who often serves as the Sancho Panza figure in Pacino's Quixotic quest) search for late medieval atmosphere in the neo-Gothic setting of the Cloisters in Upper Manhattan, first seen in conjunction with the opening voice-over from *The Tempest*. They discuss changing another line, this time from

Richard's first soliloquy, to help the audience. Richard, still Duke of Gloucester, has started his campaign toward the throne. If his first plan has worked, then his brother George, who is Duke of Clarence, will be imprisoned by the king, elder brother to them both: "This day should Clarence closely be mew'd up / About a prophecy, which says that G / Of Edward's heirs the murtherer shall be" (1.1.38–40). Pacino and Kimball decide to change G to C, even though Clarence very soon explains the full significance of the prophecy's application to him, and even though the proposed change eliminates the dramatic irony of another G—Gloucester, Richard's present title—fulfilling the prophecy. The mistaken discussion is left in, but the subsequently filmed scene with Clarence (played by Alec Baldwin) shows why the change was not only unnecessary but dramatically unworkable. The process of *Looking*, complete with wrong turns, is documented.

If errancy receives documentation, so does genuine discovery and growth, as the actors negotiate their roles and their interaction. At a reading, Kimball suggests that the Woodville clan, aligned by marriage with King Edward, is a hapless crew; Elizabeth, Edward's queen, is merely being hysterical in her concerns over her husband's illness. Penelope Allen, who plays Elizabeth, gives an impassioned defense of her character's strength and political acuity. The point is taken and the version of the scene filmed in costume reflects her interpretation. Despite this concession, however, Pacino's film does little to recognize the sheer force of the female characters in Shakespeare's play. Elizabeth and Queen Margaret, widow of the monarch deposed by Edward and his brothers, appear only in this scene. Estelle Parsons as Margaret gleefully prophesies the collapse of the political alliances that Edward made possible and that Richard is busily undermining. But we don't see Margaret's bitter triumph when her prophetic curses come true. We see only briefly Elizabeth's grief at the murder of her children; Pacino shows none of her wary dealings with Richard when, before the play's decisive battle, he proposes a dynastic marriage between him and her daughter. Instead, we see her on a hilltop watching the battle itself. The potential strength of Lady Anne, widow of the deposed king's son, is also contained. Pacino decides they must "cast . . . someone young enough to believe Richard's rap" when he audaciously asks for her hand in act 1, scene 2. Winona Ryder is given the role in order to express inexperience and naiveté (see Figure 3). The resulting performance is filmed in closeup as an intimate exchange, not as a scene of political as well as emotional maneuvering on a London street. A decision, then, has been made

46

FIGURE 3. Al Pacino and Wynona Ryder prepare for a scene between a cunning Richard and a naive Lady Anne in *Looking for Richard* (1996). Photo courtesy of the Nostalgia Factory.

not so much between a political and a psychological reading of the scene but between a reading that allows for both and a reading that privileges one over the other.

The "nonfiction effect," however, allows for a competition between discourses—and I would argue that such an effect can be just as crucial in drama as it is in documentary. An instance of competing discourses has been evident in the scenes that first "explain" the passage about *G* and then "correct" that explanation. Another instance involves the role of the visual in Shakespeare. At a social gathering, a woman shows Pacino her copy of A. L. Rowse's *The Annotated Shakespeare*. Because the tome is so impressively bulky, so canonical in appearance, Pacino has some irreverent fun with the title, calling it "the Anointed Shakespeare." Somewhat overlooked in the exchange is the imbalance of power between the woman and Pacino himself as star. She holds her ground, though, pointing out that the edition includes examples of Victorian illustrations of the plays; it's a beautiful book, she insists, with "great pictures." With unmistakable irony, Pacino replies, "That's what I like about Shakespeare; it's the pictures. I love the pictures." The film, however, refuses to let this putdown be the last word. It cuts immediately to Elizabeth collapsing in tears upon King Edward's body, then to the same images as they appear on a film editing machine. The footage seen on the monitor then shows coins placed on Edward's eyes. Pacino and the other filmmakers are forced to consider, "Now what?" There is another quick cut this time to a forested area. As Pacino and Kimball walk among the trees, we hear Hadge and Bulleit quietly comment on the possible need for yet more visuals: "Freddy [Kimball] said something about burying the king. Is that in the play?" It is not explicitly acknowledged that what we have already seen is not in the play either: Edward dies offstage. Especially when making a film of Shakespeare, the physicality of the scenes and the language—their visual potential—has to be a major part of what one likes about him.

Another potential that is explored is the helpfulness of revisiting familiar parallels and visiting unfamiliar sites. The council meeting in which Lord Hastings is summarily arrested and condemned to death (act 3, scene 4) is described as "a gathering of dons," appropriating for the scene Pacino's own experience in Francis Ford Coppola's *Godfather* films. Method-influenced exercises involving improvisation also contribute to a sense of the familiar for Pacino's cast; we are especially privy to Kevin Spacey's development in the role of Buckingham. For the unfamiliar and even the uncanny, Pacino travels to England: he visits the reconstruction of Shakespeare's Globe Theatre, then in progress; he visits Drury Lane, wanting to encounter the ghosts of past performers in the role (this in preparation for act 5, scene 3, in which the ghosts of Richard's victims visit him on the eve of the battle at Bosworth Field); he and the film crew set off fire alarms in what traditionally has been thought to be Shakespeare's birthplace in Stratford. Finally, an implication that this project is "killing" Pacino signals that it's time to kill off Richard and end the film. Pacino's Richard is a long time dying, however.

First he is shot in the back by one of Richmond's archers, then another arrow pierces him. Richmond (played by Aidan Quinn) sees his adversary down on his knees and approaches to dispatch him. Despite one withered arm, along with his wounds, Richard fights back; there is more than a hint of *Monty Python and the Holy Grail* in this sequence. Richmond had previously been shown in reverent prayer—intercut with Richard's attempt at a rallying speech to his own troops—but here he rather uncharitably kicks Richard onto his back and treads upon the king's good arm. Pacino's Richard, paralyzed, snarls like Dracula anticipating the stake through his heart; Quinn's Richmond delivers the deathblow, a sword piercing Richard's chest. The film cuts to an extravagantly improvised death scene between Pacino and Kimball, back on the streets of New York. We return to the theater of the actor's nightmare, where Shakespeare shakes his head in disgust. As church bells resound, Pacino declares that Richard is dead. "Now we can rest," is Kimball's reply. This rewrite of Horatio's farewell to Hamlet suggests that another play—and its formidable role—has also been part of Pacino's quest. A series of quick cuts returns us to the battlefield, where Richmond proclaims that "the bloody dog is dead" over Richard's corpse and we hear Pacino say "I love the silence," and then to a rehearsal room where he reiterates, "I love the silence." We flashback to the interview with Gielgud, whose own performances as Hamlet were never filmed, but only see him chuckle with amusement. Then again to Pacino, "After silence, what else is there? What's it—what's the line?" Off-camera, a voice prompts him: "The rest is silence." Pacino repeats it and adds: "Whatever I'm saying, I know Shakespeare said it." Or something very near it. With Pacino still on the screen, we again hear the words "Our revels now are ended" and Prospero's speech continues, now with visuals drawn from the process of making *Looking for Richard*, but still with the explanatory *wisp* for Shakespeare's *rack*.

Looking for Richard provides a fascinating synthesis of documentary styles along with its insights into Shakespeare's place and displacement in contemporary U. S. culture. It presents "actual"—if somewhat staged—events such as Pacino's on-the-street interviews, talks to school groups, visits to Shakespearean shrines; it attempts to situate its viewers in the midst of the lively exchanges between actors coming to terms with their roles; it also records performances that would never have happened without the documentary project itself. The film is, in part, a record of having to find a substitute for performance: no full realization of *Richard III* occurs (or occured) on stage or screen. More importantly, however, the film catalogues abiding obstacles to the appreciation, interpretation, and production of Shakespeare and suggests methods for overcoming such obstacles. It also records how even this film depended on the personal bankability—as well as the personal conviction—of its director and star, Al Pacino. Again, this continues a long tradition in the documentary mode, starting with Herbert Beerbohm Tree and continuing with Sarah Bernhardt, taking on new significances in the framing of Leslie Howard's and Norma Shearer's film performances, and to some extent culminating in Laurence Olivier's Othello. In the next chapter, we will examine what happens with Shakespeare when performers do not appear in filmic documents but in star "vehicles," productions designed to deliver celebrity actors to broad consumer markets. As the saying goes, that's show business.

CHAPTER FOUR

◇

Shakespeare and the Screen Idol

CASSIUS: The fault, dear Brutus, is not in our stars
But in ourselves. . . .

—Shakespeare, *Julius Caesar*

Shakespeare has always been such stuff as economic dreams are made on. The playwright most probably did not see himself as primarily a playwright. He was, instead, first and foremost a shareholder in a theatrical company; in order to increase profits for himself and his fellow actor-investors, he continued to write plays because they increased audiences, attracted patrons, and decreased the need to rely on independent (and sometimes undependable) scribblers. Initially, at least one of the independents recognized the threat Shakespeare represented. In his posthumously published *Groats-worth of Wit*, Robert Greene famously sounds an alarm to his fellow playwrights that actors—"those Puppets (I meane) that spake from our mouths, those Anticks garnisht in our colours"—are now daring to write for themselves. In particular "there is an upstart Crow, beautified with our feathers . . . [who] supposes he is as well able to bombast out a blanke verse as the best of you" (qtd. Schoenbaum 115). The upstart's identity is made clear by Greene's parody of a Shakespearean line ("Tygers hart wrapt in a Players hyde," adapted from *Henry VI, Part Three*) and by his sneer that this player is

51

a Jack-of-all-trades ("an absolute Iohannes factotum") who considers himself "the onely Shake-scene in a countrey."

Shakespeare not only dared to master the intricacies of composing speeches and dialogues in iambic pentameter lines (already known as blank verse and established on the English stage by Christopher Marlowe) but also acknowledged how important his fellow actors were. He wrote parts with specific performers in mind. After Will Kempe retired from Shakespeare's company in 1598, Robert Armin became the principal comic actor of the troupe. Subsequent plays reveal a shift in the complexity of its jesters: Touchstone in *As You Like It*, Feste in *Twelfth Night*, and the Fool of *King Lear* (Skura 74). Shakespeare knew that audiences came less to hear his words than to hear his words from the mouths of Armin and of Richard Burbage, the company's leading tragedian. Star power paid off in Shakespeare's time and throughout the stage history of his plays: from Thomas Betterton in the seventeenth century, to David Garrick in the eighteenth, to Edmund Kean, Edwin Booth, Henry Irving, and Herbert Beerbohm Tree in the nineteenth century, people admired the virtuoso interpreters of Shakespeare much as they came to admire musical soloists.

As suggested earlier, film continued this tradition in documenting renowned stage performers in Shakespearean roles. But as the film industry developed its own constellation of stars, increasingly separate from the stage, it also established itself as a mass-market enterprise. Through the 1920s, film could be defined more and more by its commercial aspects, by its practitioners' skill in commodifying its products. The exchange of money for product was still presented more as access to individual performers rather than to individual stories. The rise of the narrative film was partly obscured by the rise of the star system, as packaged by the dominant studios. From the articles appearing in magazines devoted to the film industry to the size of the letters appearing on movie posters, it is clear that the players—not even the titles of the screenplays—really count in economic terms. What happens, then, when the play and the playwright also vie for top billing? Can Shakespeare be anything but "box-office poison" in an industry driven by audience appeal as established by popular performers? This chapter considers who it is that most benefits from the conjunction of Shakespeare, the star system, and that system's own perennial screen idol—the bottom line.

If John Ellis's analyses of the star-system in cinema are accurate, then any character played by a star performer is kept usually "to one side"

(103): that is, the star's general image is established and refined both in relation to the performer's roles and independent from those roles. While Shakespearean stage actors have historically been able to integrate inhabiting their roles and being recognizable as "themselves," the dynamics of the studio star-system make such integration problematic, if not impossible. The star image serves as "the invitation to cinema," as it was designed to do (Ellis 97)—attracting certain audiences, in the hopes of guaranteeing a basic level of box-office return. Confronting such audiences with their well-cultivated expectations, Shakespeare films that have fully engaged with the star-system face the unenviable tasks of sustaining the stars' general images while developing the complex roles that emerge from Shakespeare's language and dramaturgy. If the Shakespearean role is not close enough to the star's persona (even casting "against type" usually involves several components of the general image), the very audiences most attracted to the film will be the most disappointed. Given such difficulties, it is perhaps surprising that studios have made as many attempts at screen-idol Shakespeare as they have.

The list of studio actors who have been cast in Shakespearean roles is not overwhelming, largely because Shakespeare on screen has not been reliably profitable. Why, then, have certain actors, directors, and producers insisted on adding Shakespeare's plays to the distribution system that mass-market films have become? The case of the first synchronized-sound film version of a (more or less) complete Shakespeare play, the 1929 United Artists *Taming of the Shrew*, is instructive both for the filmmakers' motives and for the number of compromises they felt compelled to make. In this case, the producers included the stars—not surprising, given Mary Pickford's and Douglas Fairbanks's role in establishing United Artists with Charlie Chaplin in 1919. They were drawn toward Shakespeare because of their own stage experience and their desire to establish their credentials as speaking performers: there could be no better proof of abilities in sound films, it seemed, than successfully negotiating Shakespearean verse. They were drawn to this particular play even more for its visual potential: the sunlit streets of Padua; the sumptuous palazzo of Signor Baptista, Katherine's father (representing the dowry that makes her attractive to Petruchio); the knock-about farce implicit in many of the lines. Another reason to be particularly interested in the visual was economic, since in 1929, a great many theaters were not yet equipped with sound projectors. The vehicle for proving these actors' abilities with speech would have to be released in two versions—a talkie and a silent.

The design is indeed sumptuous, as realized by William Cameron Menzies, just before he started his own directing career, and Laurence Irving, grandson of famed actor-manager Henry Irving. The adaptation and direction, by Sam Taylor, ranges from the genially hearty to the manic. Taylor had found considerable success with Harold Lloyd's comedies and had worked with Pickford extensively. In his reworking of Shakespeare, he tried to find every opportunity to showcase Fairbanks's physical grace and swagger and to present Pickford, at long last, not as "America's Sweetheart" but as an attractive example of that problematic figure (for American men, anyway), the "New Woman." Shakespeare, then, is deliberately involved in the attempt to transform a star's general image. In addition, the subject matter seemed to be as appealing as the star attractions—bringing an independent female into domestic conformity. To make the message even more appealing, thereby developing a wider audience, the story's ending is staged so that however much Kate conforms we are invited to believe she is not really "tamed." Compromise here verges on contradiction.

The film begins by wearing its contradictions on its sleeve. It opens with a puppet show featuring the traditional characters (derived from the Italian commedia dell'arte) Punch and Judy. Here, Judy is the initial aggressor, attacking Punch with a stick. After Punch collapses under her blows, she draws near. He then kisses her, takes the stick from her, and returns the violent attack. She, in turn, responds with passionate kisses. On the soundtrack, we hear two falsetto voices—at times indistinguishable—exclaiming "Kiss me, kiss me"; "I'll tame you"; and "You're wonderful!" It is not immediately clear which puppet is saying which line, raising questions of who's being tamed and even of who's being praised. In response to this confusedly "happy" ending, a crowd of spectators applauds as the camera pulls back to reveal a street scene. Now hinting that we will go "behind the scenes," Karl Struss's camera then tracks past the puppet show, along a narrow, medieval street to Baptista's house. Once the screen dissolves to and goes through the doorway, we know that the first confrontation between Petruchio and Katherine will be quick in coming.

As Petruchio, Fairbanks retains the swashbuckling insouciance that held him in good stead throughout several adventure films, most recently (that same year) *The Iron Mask*, an adaptation of Dumas's *The Man in the Iron Mask*. He carries a whip at his very first appearance, though, suggesting defensiveness as much as self-confidence. Katherine responds in kind at their first meeting, asserting her superior status at the top of the stairs and brandishing her own whip. The two characters re-enact the puppet show, in a verbally abridged but visually expanded version of their encounter in act 2, scene 1. Pickford's Katherine concludes her warning, "best beware my sting" (2.1.210), with a slap of her suitor's face. As Fairbanks's Petruchio observes that Katherine is, contrary to all reports, "pleasant, gamesome, passing courteous" (245), his outraged bride-to-be punctuates each compliment with another slap. For his part, Petruchio is no gentler than she—pulling Kate onto his lap, nearly smothering her in enforced affection so that it appears to Baptista that they are already a happy couple. When Baptista inquires as to the progress of the courtship, Petruchio replies, "how but well?" (282). Having been released, Kate expresses her disagreement with a crack of her whip. After literally disarming her, Petruchio insists that they shall be wed that Sunday; Kate's father eagerly agrees. The betrothal is sealed with a kiss—Punch triumphs over Judy once again, if only temporarily—heralded by the imperative invitation, "kiss me, Kate" (324). He embraces her; she initially struggles, but either relents at his ardor or is simply stunned by it. While she is still dazed, Petruchio makes his exit—but he returns her whip to her. This enables her to express her wrath upon her father and his associate, Gremio, beating them out of the room. She'll wed, but we'll see who tames whom. Sam Taylor's version here borrows from an eighteenth-century adaptation of Shakespeare's play, that of David Garrick. As in Garrick's *Catharine and Petruchio*, the reluctant bride advises the audience that Katherine "will tame" Petruchio instead (Garrick 14). Unlike the developments in Garrick or in Shakespeare, the film finds a way to let this happen.

Shakespeare does not stage the actual wedding; perhaps fearing censure for impiety, he relies on Gremio to describe Petruchio's deliberately provocative behavior in church. Most filmmakers, if they feel any such qualms, soon get over them. Fairbanks's Petruchio does not go so far as to strike the priest, but he does wonderfully cavalier business with an apple: leaning on a pillar and then stepping forward for the ceremony, he munches happily and unconcernedly, handing the core to Gremio just in time for the actual vows. As in the account in Shakespeare's playtext, he substitutes a profane oath—"Ay, by god's wounds" (3.2.160)—for the traditional "I do." Pickford's Katherine, knowing this performance has been for her supposed benefit, thinks hard and squeezes her lips shut when asked if she will take this man for husband. Petruchio stamps on her foot to prompt her and her outcry is taken by the congregation as consent; all kneel in thanksgiving as the priest makes the sign of the cross over the couple, in a moment of surprisingly quiet blessing. Also surprising is Katherine's apparent willingness to make the best of this unpromising situation (see Figure 4).

The story continues as in the playtext, with Petruchio dragging his new bride away from the festivities her father has planned (though this Katherine cracks her whip in protest) and bringing her through mud, rain, and cold to his estate. Once they arrive, he plays the household tyrant—haranguing the servants and rejecting a splendid feast—who nevertheless presents his demands as reasonable and his foremost concern as Kate's welfare. He announces that they "will fast for company" and go directly to her "bridal chamber" (4.1.176–77). In the playtext, servants inform us that Petruchio intends to observe an erotic as well as culinary fast with Kate, "making a sermon of continency to her" (180–82). In the film, we enter the chamber to the strains of romantic music provided by household servants. Instead of either courting or preaching, Fairbanks's Petruchio sits at a card table, plays solitaire, and generally ignores Pickford's Katherine. Diana Henderson (152–53) has noted the personal background for this film, underscoring the contrast between the shrewd (it must be said) reconciliation negotiated by Kate and Petruchio and the growing estrangement between Pickford and Fairbanks. This staged rejection must have seemed disturbingly familiar to Pickford at the time of the filming. There is a surprising poignance to the scene as she drops the whip on her own and runs into the next room.

At this point, Petruchio sneaks back downstairs to sample the food and wine that have survived his tactical tantrum. His soliloquy to the audience that explains that all has been done as part of a campaign to "curb her mad and headstrong humor" (4.1.209) is here directed to his dog, Troilus. The name is slyly suggestive. The legendary figure of Troilus is an exemplar of devoted love to the lady Cressida, so his name could serve as a substitute for, say, Fido. Shakespeare's dramatic version of their story, *Troilus and Cressida*, provides a richly ambiguous look at his devotion and her infidelity—along with a scrupulously unheroic treatment of the Trojan War, which serves as the background for the legend. This background suggests that Petruchio's pragmatic cynicism toward love manifests itself even in his dog's name. Furthermore, this version allows Katherine to overhear his account of the whole scheme. She's had the same idea as Petruchio and has ventured out of the rooms upstairs to see

FIGURE 4. Douglas Fairbanks and Mary Pickford as the newly-married Petruchio and Katherine in *The Taming of the Shrew* (1929). Photo courtesy of Jerry Ohlinger's Movie Material.

what's left of the evening meal. At the top of the stairs, she stops and hears all. In response, she nods, smiling, and gives the first of three significant winks. For a while, then, the terms for this battle of the sexes change: she will try to make his conduct appear even more ridiculous by playing the role of an outrageously compliant wife.

The strategy works very well. Fairbanks's Petruchio gets more and more flustered as his attempts at asserting arbitrary command are received by Pickford's Katherine as anything but arbitrary. In a deft revision of act 4, scene 5, she agrees that the moon is anything he says—the sun, a candle, or indeed "the blessed moon" itself. Being thus disarmed he tries to find fault with the bedcovers, throwing them and the mattress onto the floor. Seeing this, Pickford settles on them, arranges them to her satisfaction, and fetchingly bats her eyes. Fairbanks's Petruchio, in full retreat, decides to sleep on a chair instead but finds it uncomfortable. In one last try to be unreasonable and to be seen as such, he yanks a pillow out from under her head, which bumps against the wall. A fight over the pillow ensues, complete with a shoving match, and then Katherine throws a stool at Petruchio (visually echoing Kate's barb in act 2, scene 1, that he's a "join'd stool"). It hits his head; he collapses. As soon as she sees she's knocked him out, she becomes deeply concerned and goes to revive him. Upon his regaining consciousness, she takes up her whip, smiles, and tosses it into the fire. While she comforts him, he continues—though weakly—to play the old game: "The sun is shining bright" now becomes a question. "Aye, the blessed sun," she agrees. Reassured, he cuddles more closely to her, as she winks knowingly at the audience.

A similarly ironic acceptance of patriarchal authority characterizes the closing scene, which includes Katherine's speech in defense of wifely subjection. She lectures her sister Bianca: "Thy husband is thy lord, thy life, thy keeper" (5.2.146). Petruchio nods approval, his bandaged head both undermining his authority, since we know she "really" won the battle, and justifying it, since she "freely" submits to his will. Pickford's Katherine concludes her own sermon not only with the words that women "are bound to serve, love, and obey" (5.2.164) but with the last significant wink—this time directed at Dorothy Jordan's Bianca, whose reaction indicates the message has been received. Henderson (154) persuasively argues that this gesture reveals "a conspiracy of 'unspoken thoughts,' a female subculture whose bond is unbroken" that operates "behind the patriarchal ventriloquizing" at work in the playtext. The enduring questions remain, however. Does ironic acceptance differ from other forms of assent? Does Shakespeare's playtext, in dramatizing the processes of "speaking for women," do more than ventriloquize? Pickford's own answers may be found in her decision to withdraw the film from circulation. After its initial release, it was not re-issued until 1966, with a new music score and remastered soundtrack. The reason was to capitalize on the interest generated by a new film version of the play, featuring a celebrated couple of another generation: Elizabeth Taylor and Richard Burton.

Only two predominantly star-driven versions of Shakespeare would appear on screen in the interim and their disappointing box-office receipts go far in explaining Hollywood's subsequent avoidance of "overt" Shakespeare productions. In 1935, Warner Brothers set itself the task of adapting for film Max Reinhardt's grand stage production of *A Midsummer Night's Dream*. Reinhardt had first realized his spectacular approach—almost the apotheosis of Victorian naturalism—with the Deutsches Theater in Berlin, from which so many luminaries of international film would later emerge. During his first year as director of the theater, in 1905, he mounted a stage interpretation of *Dream* that was not only impressively grand but also bravely challenging. Over the course of the nineteenth century, the fairy realm became increasingly tame and domesticated on stage as well as in popular imagination. Reinhardt returned to Shakespeare's sprites—literally, spirits—their elemental powers and their daemonic drive (Williams 210). Reinhardt went on to produce many more of Shakespeare's plays over the next decades, but he kept returning to *Dream*, taking a version of it on tour in the United States in the late 1920s. Emigrating from Germany in the early years of Hitler's ascendancy, he restaged *A Midsummer Night's Dream* in open-air productions first at such places as Oxford University and later at the Hollywood Bowl.

This revival led to the Warner Brothers project and many of its scenic elements are not only incorporated but embellished in the film version. The cast, however, reflects the dynamics of the motion picture studio more than that of the stage. Although Olivia de Havilland, an understudy for the stage Hermia who got the chance to appear in the role, made her film debut here, most of the other roles are assigned to established and immediately recognizable performers. These include Dick Powell as Lysander, James Cagney as Bottom, Joe E. Brown as Flute, and an eleven-year-old Mickey Rooney as Puck. (Also appearing, as the Changeling Boy who is the occasion of the feud between the monarchs of the fairy realm, is Kenneth Anger, the future director of *Scorpio Rising* and chronicler of *Hollywood Babylon*.) Some of the transpositions occasioned by the star-system work well, under the guidance of Reinhardt's co-director, William Dieterle. Powell and de Havilland, with their supporting players, are very much at home amidst lavish musical numbers and what are basically two related girl-meets-boy, girl-loses-boy, girl-gets-boy stories. Rooney as Puck is both amusing and disturbing; his screeching voice proclaims kinship with a natural world that is anything but tame. Cagney and Brown (along with the ever-giggling Hugh Herbert and a laconic Arthur Treacher) simply try too hard to make comedic what is already pretty funny stuff. Fearing that their roles were too removed from their general images (the characters are too far "to one side," in Ellis's phrase), they strive mightily to bridge the perceived gap. The comedy soars only at the end when Brown, as workman Flute in the role of tragic heroine Thisbe, emotes at the discovery of Pyramus's corpse—as portrayed by an obviously lively Cagney/Bottom. Allowing the character of Flute to assume another role, Thisbe, lets Brown in turn feel more assured and perform more confidently.

The fairy realm, for its part, delivers on the film's promise of spectacular entertainment. Jack Jorgens is right to notice that Reinhardt's vision is "a precursor of the 'darker Dream' which has fascinated modern critics and directors" and which was anticipated by "earlier illustrators, [like] William Blake and Henry Fuseli" (41); the film brings to life elements of their visions. The film and the productions upon which it is based are also precursors of lighter, more fanciful versions of *Dream* such as Benjamin Britten's operatic adaptation. Ian Hunter as Theseus is unremittingly benign (a quality also seen some years later in his Richard the Lionhearted for Warner Brothers' *The Adventures of Robin Hood*), by turns imposing, kindly, and even tender and tentative with Hippolyta. Titania is here played by Anita Louise, who commands a corps de ballet of attendant fairies, led by Danish dancer and choreographer Nina Theilade. Louise sings or intones all of her lines in bright falsetto. In Britten's opera of *A Midsummer Night's Dream*, the parts for most of the fairies, most notably Oberon, are scored for the upper reaches of the human voice; Puck is the only one who does not sing and even he does a kind of chanting partly indebted to Rooney. Especially in Oberon's train, many of the fairies are grotesques who have walked straight out of one of Fuseli's paintings. Victor Jory, already established as a screen "heavy," conveys Oberon's potential for malevolence; dressed in black, some of his attendants are bats, the "reremice" with which Titania orders her followers to battle. Special effects contribute to the sense of the unearthly: Titania's train of attendants blend into her gown's flowing train; both her followers and Oberon's dissolve into his cloak with the dawn and with their reconciliation. To reinforce how completely the supernaturals influence the lives of these mortals, a ghostly Puck materializes in Theseus's palace in order to make sure that Bottom and company are chosen to provide the evening's entertainment at play's end. Other visual elements from the film have reappeared elsewhere, from the decidedly dark *Dream* of the BBC Shakespeare series for television, with yet another forbidding Oberon, to the palace of the Sultan in Disney's animated feature *Aladdin*, the balcony of which is indebted to Reinhardt and his designers' vision of Theseus's court.

In promotional trailers, the studio had expressed its hope that *A Midsummer Night's Dream* would profoundly influence the making of motion pictures in the future. Although influential in other media and other art forms, this *Dream* had its greatest film impact in the area of special effects and in dissuading most studio executives from trying anything like it ever again. The very star-system that made the making of the film possible tended to work against its popularity: while the Warner Brothers celebrity ensemble does, for the most part, a creditable job, the stars are eclipsed to a considerable degree. Reinhardt's visuals celebrate themes and images in Shakespeare's language (even when that language is cut) far more than his featured performers. The next—and for a long time the last— attempt at star Shakespeare avoids that mistake. The Metro-Goldwyn-Mayer *Romeo and Juliet* (1936) is from first to last a showcase for its Juliet, Norma Shearer. Though rivaling Warner Brothers in the sumptuousness of its designs (here by Oliver Messel), the film keeps its focus on the female lead. Shearer, a gifted screen performer, had the studio's blessing guaranteed; her husband Irving Thalberg, still MGM's wunderkind, served as producer for the film. At thirty-five, Shearer was more than twice the age of the playtext's Juliet, a fact that raised concerns we have already seen expressed in the promotional short *Master Will Shakespeare* (see previous chapter). Nearly everybody in the cast skips a generation: young Romeo is played by a forty-two-year-old Leslie Howard; Mercutio by the already declining John Barrymore; Juliet's nurse by the venerable Edna May Oliver; her father by the still more venerable C. Aubrey Smith. Basil Rathbone is a convincingly volatile Tybalt, but even he appears to be a bit too old (and dignified) for such adolescent swagger as his character demands.

Shearer's Juliet initially provides the clearest examples of arrested development when she tries to skip and simper her way into Juliet's youth without also invoking the character's bold strength and precocious maturity until very late in the film. (In this, it must be said, she follows centuries of stage practice and textual revision.) Even so, the film regularly succeeds in merging the camera's gaze, as guided by William Daniels, with this Romeo's own. It is at its best, however, when it steps beyond the achievement of that visual synthesis.

The first glimpses of Juliet provided by the film, when she is counseled by her mother about marrying Paris, are formulaic: after being summoned by the Nurse, she appears as an emblematic Medieval maiden, feeding a pet deer that roams the remarkably spacious Capulet grounds. Talbot Jennings, the adapter, originally intended to show a more assertive Juliet, one who can assist the household's falconer at his task (Jennings 154–55). Similarly, Jennings's scenario follows the playtext's sequence, which presents Romeo in conversation with his kinsman Benvolio before we meet Juliet. In director George Cukor's—and producer Thalberg's—actual film, Juliet is more demure but she also takes pride of place: her scene comes first. Its stock representations are paralleled in our introduction to Romeo. We see him emulating a lovelorn shepherd (who sings in the background), bringing pastoral conventions almost parodistically to life. Howard's Romeo is languidly in unrequited love with Rosalind. The somewhat flat shots of the separate lovers—despite many, many close-ups—serve to underscore the lack of depth in their other relationships and also to set up the transforming power of Romeo's view of Juliet and her returned gaze.

The Capulets' ball is presented as a social debut for their daughter and heir. Despite the vast dimensions of the ballroom, all attention is easily directed to Juliet as soon as she enters. The dance, choreographed by Agnes de Mille, centers on Shearer in the role: the other women dancers arrange themselves around her and bow as she passes; the men dancers turn to salute her first. The camera and Romeo's gaze are irresistibly drawn toward her. (To help explain, though, why Romeo forgets Rosalind so quickly, Jennings and Cukor add a scene at the ball where she snubs him.) In something of a social ritual, Juliet receives a rose from one woman dancer and is supposed to hand it to Paris, her suitor. Before she can do so, her gaze meets Romeo's—and they are mutually entranced. Paris prompts her, taking the rose and leading her away, but she keeps looking back toward Romeo. For his part, Howard's Romeo follows her

every move in the dance, a human camera engaged in a long, long tracking shot. The shimmering gauze effect at work in our views of Shearer's
Juliet blend with the dizzying effects of love at work in Romeo. To reinforce this, the film intercuts his reactions to everything we see of her.

When he finally approaches her, he removes his mask briefly (not
wanting to be recognized by her kinsmen—though that has already happened without his knowledge). The sight of his face confirms her earlier
opinion and she agrees to dance with him. As all the other couples observe
the proprieties of a stately pavane, with hands never quite touching, they
make contact, palm to palm. Jennings's scenario has Juliet make the first
move, as "she drops her fingers into his upturned palm" (167), but this is
less clear in the actual film, since Shearer immediately begins to draw her
hand away after contact. Howard's Romeo prevents her from withdraw-
ing, which marks him as the more assertive. Cukor and his designers have
added a visual foreshadowing of Romeo's first conversation with Juliet
when he and his kinsmen are greeted by Capulet upon their arrival: they
hold artificial palm-fronds, made of paper, in imitation of pilgrims—
"palmers"—travelling to a holy shrine. Romeo and Juliet skillfully and
collaboratively improvise a love sonnet that puns on palms and palmers.
Jennings's scenario and the film punctuate the end of the sonnet by letting the lovers kiss after Romeo completes the couplet: "Then move not,
while my prayer's effect I take" (1.5.106). After Romeo immediately ini-
tiates yet another sonnet, the Juliet of Jennings's screenplay retreats
(though she contributes the next line) and Romeo must follow. In the
actual film, Shearer steps away at first but then returns to keep the sonnet
going. Juliet must not be too forward, but she is still an active participant
in the developing romance.

The sense of her agency is diminished, however, in the balcony
scene. Here, the voyeuristic aspect of film viewing dominates, in part
because the camera's gaze is so strongly identified with Romeo's from the
very start of the sequence—in which he, unseen, sees and hears Juliet. The
spectacles celebrated and excerpted in *Master Will Shakespeare*, the beau-
ties of the Capulets' garden and daughter, are presented from Romeo's
perspective. There is a huge reflecting pool—which will undergo a transformation of its own in Baz Luhrmann's film of the play—and groves of
trees, all of which guide our sight to the cynosure of Juliet's balcony.
When she emerges from her room, he agonizes over whether to reveal
himself or not. As she delivers her famous lines beginning "O Romeo,
Romeo!" (2.1.33), he's drawn closer and closer; the camera responds by

bringing Shearer into more and more extreme closeup. When he speaks, the voyeuristic spell is broken, but it is not, as before, replaced by a mutual exchange of gazes (see Figure 5).

The film's special concern with vision is evident in the death scene, as well. Romeo fights his way to the sight of Juliet in the tomb, pushing the grieving Paris backward "down steps and through the dusty passage-ways of the great vault" (Jennings 224). Once there, he declares her tomb to be not a grave, but a "lantern"—that is, a lanthorn, a tower room glassed in on all sides. Juliet's "beauty makes / This vault a feasting presence full of light" (5.3.85–86), a presence here indicating a hall suitable for festival, for receiving guests. The body of the sleeping Juliet is veiled and Romeo removes the covering. Once again, unseen by her, he feasts his eyes on her presence. Here, we are shown more his gaze than the object of it. Howard's Romeo is entranced by Juliet's face: he looks steadily at her as he makes his farewell and as he prepares to drink the poison that will allow him to join her in death. After he drinks, he bends to kiss her— "Thus with a kiss, I die" (120)—and his eyes remain open throughout. He resists closing them and losing the sight of his love, his wife, until he collapses onto the floor.

In contrast, the gaze of Shearer's Juliet does not focus exclusively on Romeo. Though she tenderly, mournfully admires him, she looks away at the sound of the approaching watch. She looks up as she prepares to stab herself and the camera pulls into extreme closeup as the blade penetrates; Cukor quietly underscores the eroticism of the Love and Death motif. Shearer closes her eyes at the wound and as she lowers her head we cannot tell if she reopens them to return, too late, Romeo's gaze. The MGM *Romeo and Juliet* both exemplifies and complicates Laura Mulvey's formula for "voyeuristic active/passive mechanisms" and their gendered significances in mass-market films (26). While Shearer's Juliet is most definitely the object of the camera's gaze and Howard's Romeo the on-screen representative for the film audience, Shearer at times returns the gaze in ways not limited to acknowledgment of the voyeur's presence. Most notably in the ballroom scene, her Juliet enters into an open and collaborative visual exchange with her Romeo. This dynamic, along with the retention of most of Juliet's lines, shows how both the star-system and the idea of the "women's film" helped the film suggest the capacity for significant action—in short, the agency—seen in the playtext's character.

The film did not fare well at the box office or with the critics— although Frank S. Nugent of the *New York Times* was the exception that

FIGURE 5. Leslie Howard and Norma Shearer in the Balcony Scene; a publicity shot for the MGM *Romeo and Juliet* (1936). Photo courtesy of the Nostalgia Factory.

proved the rule, since even his glowing review concluded with skepticism about its popular success. Nugent believes that "the screen is a perfect medium for Shakespeare; whether Shakespeare is the perfect scenarist for the screen remains uncertain" (2). Nugent was unimpressed with both the Pickford/Fairbanks *Taming of the Shrew* (scoffing at the "additional dialogue" by director Sam Taylor) and the Warner Brothers *Dream*, but he saw this production differently: he considered it to be "Shakespearean— not Hollywood." The studio tried hard to establish the film's authenticity. Professor William Strunk, Jr., of Cornell University served as textual adviser; all manner of period visuals (including borrowings from Renaissance painters Sandro Botticelli and Benozzo Gozzoli, among others) and quasi-authentic music (besides the inevitable Tchaikowsky) were incorporated into the overall texture of the film. *Master Will Shakespeare* insisted on the playwright's preference for this play and his approval of the medium and the leading lady. Random House published "A Motion Picture Edition" of *Romeo and Juliet*, combining publicity stills, playtext, film script, and short essays by the leading filmmakers and stars, with "A Preliminary Guide to the Study of the Screen Version." But either the production was guilty by association with the earlier films or the marketing campaign did too well in giving it Shakespeare's imprimatur. Nugent worried that "Shakespeare has become a literary exercise or a matter for a drama cult's admiration" (2). He may not have believed it but audiences, by their lukewarm response, seemed to think so. The studios were quick to concur.

Star-power Shakespeare remained largely absent from the screen for nearly three decades. Both Olivier and Welles tended to rely on stage performers for the bulk of their Shakespearean casts. Joseph Mankiewicz's *Julius Caesar* (1953) successfully mediated between stage and screen personalities, benefiting from the marquee appeal of names like Marlon Brando, Deborah Kerr, and Greer Garson. The political messages of the film still overshadow the director's shrewd exploitation of the studio system (see chapter seven). It was not until Franco Zeffirelli let Elizabeth Taylor and Richard Burton run amok through soundstages and countryside alike that Shakespeare again attracted a celebrity couple as performers; they in turn attracted a wide audience. Zeffirelli's 1966 *Taming of the Shrew* announces its carnivalesque approach very early on. As Lucentio, who will vie for the hand of Kate's sister Bianca, and his servant Tranio approach Padua on horseback, the city appears to glow, at the end of a rainbow (suggesting the gold Petruchio seeks?), amid a blissfully green landscape. Michael York's Lucentio is awe-struck as he rides and then walks along its streets, which are silent, if still filled with the sort of temptation his servant Tranio appreciates. All this, however, is merely the calm before a stormy festival. Attracted by a solemn service at the town's university—a sacred chorale in honor of the new school term—they enter a church. The ceremony concludes with a riotous celebration, a kind of academic mardi gras before the Lenten discipline of university studies, and Lucentio and Tranio are literally carried away by the crowd. The festival mood never ends in the film, as Zeffirelli insists on breaking loose from the "church of Shakespeare" piety that sapped the energies of the MGM *Romeo and Juliet*. In itself, the spirit suits the play admirably: Lucentio neglects his books in favor of the fair Bianca; character after character assumes stock roles or disguises or both; the leading characters, Petruchio and Katherine, refuse to have their energies contained by the niceties of polite Paduan society. Taylor's and Burton's notoriety as on-again, off-again lovers and spouses was also being exploited that year in the film version of Edward Albee's *Who's Afraid of Virginia Woolf?*. Zeffirelli, too, plays with public knowledge of the couple's battles—unlike the efforts of Pickford and Fairbanks during the filming of their *Taming of the Shrew* to keep hidden the tensions in their marriage.

Taylor and Burton, true to the star-system, are not just "playing themselves" in the roles of Katherine and Petruchio. Instead, Zeffirelli connects Shakespeare's characters with his stars' public personae to rewrite the play as Katherine's escape from being tamed. Burton's Petruchio, for all his claims to be wild only as a matter of policy, really is at odds with civilization. Like any devout participant in carnival, he vigorously expresses the energies that social norms and institutions endeavor to suppress or channel. There is a savage joy in his onslaughts against church, society, family, and all their trappings. He finds a kindred spirit in Taylor's Katherine, who not only chafes but storms against polite—and patriarchal—expectations for her life and conduct. Jack Jorgens rightly describes them as Zeffirelli's "Lord and Lady of Misrule," embodiments of the saturnalian impulses and customs embraced by much of Elizabethan society (75). They are cousins to Sir John Falstaff (especially in Orson Welles's admiring presentation; see chapter six) and to Sir Toby Belch of Shakespeare's *Twelfth Night* in their delight in raucous, even violent humor and in the unbounded body; Burton's Petruchio shares plump Jack's devotion to the bottle and Taylor's Kate barely keeps her décolletage contained.

The courtship and the wedding ceremony become tours de force of physical comedy. Where Pickford and Fairbanks cracked whips at one another, Taylor and Burton as Kate and Petruchio smash utensils, railings, furniture, windows, and even walls in their attempts to impose their wills, each upon the other. This Kate does, however, use the Italian equivalent of a hickory switch to interrogate Bianca, while this Petruchio does indulge in a bit of Fairbanks-style trapeze work. Petruchio will have Kate ("will you, nill you, I will marry you") and Kate will have none of it. She imposes one barrier after another; he either circumvents or destroys them. She endeavors to put distance between herself and this new suitor, going so far as to walk along the rooftops of her father's house. He doggedly follows, for the sake of preserving her life—and her claim to the largest dowry. The conflict of wills escalates in intensity, energy, and destructiveness: it results in the two of them falling through Baptista's roof. The comedy, in short, goes well beyond the slapstick physicality even of Pickford and Fairbanks.

Zeffirelli's wedding also sets out to overgo the depiction found in the earlier film. Fairbanks's Petruchio is devil-may-care; Burton's is, simply, up yours. Other kinds of chases and competitions are at work in the ceremony. Katherine arrives at the appointed time, resplendently dressed. When Petruchio appears, very late, in his motley, he finds himself first being pushed away by the bride when he tries to kiss her and then having to pursue Kate down the aisle to the altar. The congregation hurriedly follows. Petruchio drinks a profane toast with the sacramental wine, indeed "cuffs" the outraged but timorous priest, nods off, has a coughing fit before saying "Marry, I will" (a nice pun), and even pretends to have misplaced the ring. In revenge, Kate bides her time, hoping to trump her adversary by vowing not to wed him. When asked if she will accept Petruchio as her husband, Taylor's Katherine begins to say "I will not," but Burton's strategically timed kiss lands as soon as "I will" is uttered.

The stress on competition—on regendering one-upmanship—is appropriate to the play's conclusion. The speech in praise of wifely submission, after all, wins a considerable bet for Petruchio. In Zeffirelli's version, Kate has the satisfaction of exposing her demure sister's machinations: Bianca has waited until after the marriage to reveal fully her own brand of independence. Kate also challenges Petruchio to stop playing games, as Taylor gives special stress on obedience to a husband's "honest will" (5.2.163). The sexual connotations of *will* are made honest as well:

Kate's lingering look at a group of children announces what she hopes will result from both the fulfillment of mutual desire and the establishment of domestic order. Burton's Petruchio is stunned and lifts the kneeling Katherine to her feet. But in response to Petruchio's admiring invitation, once again, to "kiss me, Kate," Taylor initially accedes only to retreat—impulsively, but with more than a hint of invitation for him to follow. This time, she has decided to leave her father's house, not Petruchio; despite the protestations of obedience, she remains assertive and now she's gone. Burton delivers his last lines so as to indicate his character's eagerness to pursue his wife and to continue the contest; he almost fights his way through the throngs. "And being a winner," he finally boasts to the other guests, "God give you good night." The victory, though sweet, has been short-lived and off he runs. His hope of winning again and his understanding that he has gained far more than he expected combine to make for an inclusively celebratory conclusion. Zeffirelli extends that prayer to all its auditors: after his servant Grumio has shut the door and let the couple escape in some semblance of peace, the screen fades to black and "God give you good night" appears.

Zeffirelli's next Shakespeare film, the wildly successful *Romeo and Juliet* (1968), would scrupulously avoid casting big-name performers in the major roles. That would not be the case for his 1990 *Hamlet* featuring Mel Gibson as the title character and Glenn Close as Queen Gertrude, his mother. These actors had been strongly associated with other roles: Gibson as the star of action adventures such as the *Mad Max* and *Lethal Weapon* films; Close as the noble but haunted Sarah in *The Big Chill* and the scarifying Alex Forrest in *Fatal Attraction*. Zeffirelli, much as he alluded to Burton's and Taylor's reputation in *Taming*, shrewdly exploits these associations as he advances his interpretation of these characters and the play overall. He jettisons the first scene of the playtext, along with its overview of the sociopolitical turmoil in which Denmark is embroiled. We are instead allowed to witness the interment of Hamlet Senior, late King of Denmark, in the medieval castle's crypt. In part this is because Zeffirelli's interest in realistic settings has not diminished; it is also because he wants to withhold sight of the Ghost from the audience until later. Close's two previous roles coalesce in the film's presentation of Gertrude, leaving us uncertain as to her complicity in her husband's death. Her show of grief is intense, as she removes a jeweled flower from her hair, sets it on the massive stone that covers the tomb, and then prostrates herself on the stone. She exchanges a look, though, with Claudius, her brother-in-law and husband-to-be, and her sobs end abruptly. Is this Sarah, sobbing in the shower after the funeral of her college friend and houseguest, or is this Alex, libidinous and murderous? What follows, however, brings to mind Norma Shearer as Juliet: we see Gertrude girlishly happy on the occasion of her marriage with Claudius, giggling with her ladies-in-waiting.

This is certainly too much visual information for Gibson's Hamlet to process. He carefully notes how his mother's and uncle's glances meet over the very body of his father; he is embarrassed as well as appalled by Gertrude's giddiness. The decision to assume the disguise of madness comes as a relief to him. The "antic disposition" lasts much longer in this production than usual: during the fateful duel, Hamlet undercuts his apology to Laertes by clowning through the swordplay. We are not far removed from Martin Riggs, rogue cop in the *Lethal Weapon* films, inwardly melancholy with grief, outwardly manic. What triggers, in effect, the eager adoption of such behavior is the encounter with the Ghost and arguably the strongest performance in the film. Paul Scofield stands out among a supporting cast of British actors who more than ably fulfill the secondary roles—but whose roles are, for the most part, diminished in scope. Alan Bates presents a Claudius who is not nearly as clever as he thinks; Ian Holm's Polonius is a petty tyrant, who almost deserves Hamlet's errant blade; Helena Bonham Carter's Ophelia sorely lacks the resources to endure the tragedies that befall her. Scofield offers, appropriately enough, a haunting performance—but also one that is unencumbered by the standard cinematic trappings and signs of the supernatural. For Zeffirelli, the father's unsettling presence is enough.

There is more than a little autobiography in this. The director, born out of wedlock, has written about the infrequent times in his early childhood when his father would visit his mistress, Zeffirelli's mother. All three would share the bed in which father and mother made love (Zeffirelli 6). "References to the primal scene," Donaldson (1990, 147) notes, recur in other Zeffirelli films, such as *Romeo and Juliet* and even *Endless Love* (1981); in the latter, roles are rewritten as a mother watches her daughter's lovemaking with a young man. Donaldson describes Zeffirelli's father as "mostly absent and then confusingly and vividly present" (1990, 148), but also devoted to his son's education. Ottorino Corsi, the father, wanted English to be part of that training and Shakespeare, almost as a matter of course, played a pivotal role. The Ghost of his father appears to Hamlet only twice: first on the castle battlements and later in Gertrude's private room (the actual meaning of the term "closet"). In death Hamlet Senior is compellingly absent and then compellingly present, asking his son to take action against Claudius and, significantly, to take no action against Gertrude.

Scofield's infinitely sad, infinitely gentle Ghost is far removed from the shadowy, devouring presence in Olivier's film (see chapter six) and the piercing, transcendent light we have seen in Richardson's film. Zeffirelli takes his cue from Hamlet's line to Horatio: "[He] was a man, take him for all in all" (1.2.187). After leaving his companions and following the Ghost, Gibson's Hamlet comes upon him quietly seated. Zeffirelli is able to convey more strongly a sense of horror and pity through closeups of Scofield's craggy, careworn face, and by trusting in the actor's delivery of the lines, than by special effects (which he forgoes) or even his star's reactions to the Ghost's story. Scofield sits in loco parentis not only in suggestions of Zeffirelli's father but in suggestions of other approaches to Shakespeare: his own appearances as Hamlet on stage—beginning in 1950—and his harrowing King Lear in Peter Brook's film of the play (see chapter seven). The Ghost's simple garb is reminiscent not only of penitential, purgatorial sackcloth but also of Scofield's costume at the end of Brook's *King Lear*, after the character has stripped himself of the gorgeous "lendings" of what the privileged classes may wear. Gibson's Hamlet is haunted by alternatives and he finds comfort in what is familiar to both actor and his intended audience.

The scene between Close's Gertrude and Gibson's Hamlet verges on the primal. Zeffirelli follows the twentieth-century tradition of a very Freudian reading (as seen in Olivier's version) by making the setting not only Gertrude's bedroom but especially her bed. After his impulsive murder of Polonius, Hamlet confronts his mother with the choice she has made to "step from this to this" (3.4.71), from Hamlet Senior to Claudius. Gibson forces Close down onto the bed, lying on top of her. He begins to act out the desire he finds so appalling, pressing against her as he declaims against living "In the rank sweat of an enseamed bed, / Stew'd in corruption, honeying and making love / Over the nasty sty" (92–94). At this point, Zeffirelli omits lines declaiming against Claudius and skips directly to the Ghost's entrance. Abashed, nearly caught in the act of Oedipal desire, Hamlet leaves the bed to face his father—whom Gertrude cannot see or hear. Zeffirelli seems to chasten himself as well as his star performers with Scofield's quiet but disconcerting presence to Gibson and absence from Close.

The director began his career in the theater, refusing to follow the career path his father had chosen for him, architecture. Film offered a way both to assert independence and, through its grander visual designs, to accede to the father's wishes. Olivier's film of *Henry V* helped to confirm Zeffirelli's decision (Donaldson 1990, 148)—despite its implicit critique of the stage—and Zeffirelli's later films show an abiding interest in buildings: from the seemingly endless interiors of Baptista's palazzo in *Taming of the Shrew*, to the Veronese cityscapes of *Romeo and Juliet*, to the weighty bulk of the castle in *Hamlet*. Film also demands to be taken on its own terms, however much freedom the medium offers the filmmaker in defining them. Zeffirelli opts for the star-system as his major definition in two Shakespeare films. In the first, he can both revel in architecture and authenticity and demolish them; he shares in the carnivalesque with his stars as they all rewrite the playtext. In the second, he genuinely wonders whether it may have been better to obey the father's will after all; despite Hamlet's delays in exacting revenge, despite the late flashes of comedy in Gibson's performance, the playtext demands that tragedy will out and even Zeffirelli's abridged version follows its instructions.

Who, then, profits from star-system Shakespeare? Ironically (if appropriately) enough, it has not been the studios—although they have sought both to make their stars an economic safety net for Shakespeare and to make Shakespeare a participant in the star-system itself. Ironically (and sadly) enough, it has not been Shakespeare, either, whose perennial status as "box-office poison" stems from his playtexts' incompatibility with the usual insistence on stars' general image. Finally, it has not been the stars themselves, whose sometimes valiant efforts have been regularly met with puzzlement from their admirers and with derision from Shakespeare's admirers. On occasion, however, directors have benefited from the resources underwritten by hoped-for attendance figures. When cinematic vision, Shakespearean roles, and stars' personae come into alignment, if only briefly, filmmakers can achieve startling and significant results: Reinhardt's dark forest and Zeffirelli's cityscapes endure in the memory and recur in the work of their successors. In the next chapter, I will examine the achievements of filmmakers who have bypassed the studio system and still found in Shakespeare not only visual resources but also a kindred spirit in imagination.

CHAPTER FIVE

◇

Shakespeare the Filmmaker

THESEUS: Such tricks hath strong imagination . . .

—Shakespeare, *A Midsummer Night's Dream*

Laurence Olivier's 1944 film of *Henry V* initially stages its version of the playtext in a reconstructed Globe Theatre. The first scenes present unruly spectators entertaining themselves at the expense of the actors. We are meant to see in these early sequences the severe limitations of the stage, especially the Elizabethan variety. Olivier wanted the audience not only to feel superior toward the actors (an attitude which helps make the comic treatment possible) but also to empathize with the poor players, to share their and Shakespeare's supposed frustration at being constrained within the girdle of these walls.

Olivier aimed at a sense of release in moving from the Globe to the stylized set representing Southampton:

> I wanted the film audience to get a restless feeling of being crabbed and confined in the Globe's wooden O, irritated by the silly actors speaking in their exaggerated way, so that when we at last leave the place, with a flourish of William Walton's music, and I speak my lines beginning with "Now sits the wind fair, and we will aboard" realistically and with a modern tone, there's a tremendous feeling of relief and anticipation. (Olivier 1986, 188)

In the imagined salt air of a Denham Studios soundstage, both the film's audience and the play's language gain a kind of freedom from the director, just as the king announces that he will release "the man committed yesterday / That railed against our person" (2. 2. 40–41). Now at representational liberty, Olivier and his designers entertain themselves and their audiences with a dizzying array of settings. Some, like the beachhead at Harfleur, are acceptably naturalistic in 1940s general-release film terms (see Figure 6); others, like those for the French court, invoke the vivid colors and pre-perspectival views found in medieval illuminations. In a deft visual pun, Shakespeare's Duke of Berri is shown perusing the famed *Book of Hours* the historical duke commissioned that also contains the illustrations upon which the set design is based. For the battle scenes, Olivier moves to exterior shots for the effect of heightened realism—even though the portrayal of warfare that follows is, at times, as fanciful as the earlier sets.

When the screenplay for Olivier's *Henry V* was published in connection with a re-release of the film, the director insisted that he had been more true to the play by being less faithful to the stage: "Shakespeare, in a way, 'wrote for the films.' His splitting up of the action into a multitude of small scenes is almost an anticipation of film technique, and more than one of his plays chafe against the cramping restrictions of the stage" (Olivier 1984, v). From Southampton he cuts immediately to a naturalistic set for the Boar's Head Tavern; the tracking shot takes us to and through the window in order to witness some of Sir John Falstaff's death throes. After the moving account of the old knight's death by Mistress Quickly (played by Freda Jackson) and the departure of his erstwhile followers for Staines, the film presents the actor who portrays a living prologue, still in Elizabethan dress, floating through mists and fogs. Set free from the constraints of time and space, he flies toward the French court, urging us to "Follow, follow!" (3.Prol.17). To avoid adopting the art of imaginative collaboration between performers and audience that is invoked by the play's opening lines, Olivier decides that Shakespeare wanted to show something as close to "the warlike Harry, like himself" (1.Prol.5) as was technically possible (Buhler 1995, 57).

Olivier was by no means the first filmmaker to adopt such an attitude (as seen in *Master Will Shakespeare*), though his *Henry V* may well be the first Shakespearean film to thematize it. He was able to draw upon an established tradition in Shakespearean film: asserting the peculiar powers of the cinema as distinct from those of the theater. For example, William Ranous and Charles Kent had produced several silent adaptations of

FIGURE 6. Laurence Olivier leads a charge toward (relative) film realism in his *Henry V* (1944). Photo courtesy of the Nostalgia Factory.

Shakespeare plays for the New York–based Vitagraph company from 1908 to 1911 (Uricchio and Pearson 59–63), most of which availed themselves of exterior locations. Much of the Vitagraph *A Midsummer Night's Dream* (1909) was filmed in New York City's Central Park. *Twelfth Night* (1910) shows Viola's brother Sebastian being rescued very early on; the remains of an actual shipwreck become the backdrop for the shot. These are highly compressed retellings—usually one reel (roughly ten minutes) for each film—that often drastically rewrite the plays. In *A Midsummer Night's Dream*, Kent transforms Oberon, King of the Fairies, into a character named Penelope, a sprite who is both mischievous and matronly. Even so, there is a sense that the translation from the stage provides, at times, greater access to Shakespearean intentions. The fairies do disappear and reappear, thanks to the rough magic of early special effects. In one of Ranous's first Vitagraph offerings, the director makes a shrewd link between Shakespeare's playtext and his own film version simply by using the prologue to *Romeo and Juliet* for the opening title card. Here is the full story, packed into fourteen lines; see what we can do, Ranous suggests, in eleven minutes.

Ranous's successor in Shakespearean presentation for American film audiences was Edwin Thanhouser. In 1916, he produced *King Lear* featuring the veteran stage actor Frederick B. Warde in the title role. The film was directed by Warde's son, Ernest, who also appears as Lear's Fool. While inviting audiences to trust in Frederick Warde's theatrical reputation, Thanhouser and the younger Warde announce in the film's opening images that cinematic Shakespeare ultimately draws its inspiration from the playtext. The opening shot reveals a man, seated, reading in his study; subsequent closeups reveal that the book he reads is a copy of *King Lear*. From the page we shift to the stage and beyond, as we see Warde Senior in modern dress dissolve into Warde as Lear himself. The special effects reinforce the idea that film can be, in its way, a more "direct" translation of Shakespearean writ. Words come to life and Warde becomes his character, all through techniques possible only in the cinematic medium. What follows is a valiant attempt to capture the play's intricacies of plot and relationships in five reels.

Some of the details of character interaction are communicated by means of reaction shots, at times done in extreme closeup. As a result, the audience can see the malevolent side of Regan and Goneril (played by Edith Kiestal and Ina Hammer) almost immediately; Kent's devastation at banishment is similarly communicated merely by J. H. Gilmour's facial expressions. Gestures are significant without being overdone: when Lear confronts his two elder daughters, the hand that still holds a sceptre trembles. The shaking indicates both Lear's rage and his incapacity. A moment later, Lear staggers away. Outside he looks heavenward and a storm answers; shots of a real storm are intercut with views of the gates being closed against Lear and of a blazing hearth within the castle. Montage provides an analogue to the language's vivid contrasts between luxury and poverty. Similarly, Edmund (played by Hector Dion) is able to achieve much of the effect of a Shakespearean aside just by gazing at the camera. Most compelling of all is the film's conclusion, after Lear appears with the body of Cordelia. He emerges from their prison into harsh sunlight, holding the cord that had been used to strangle her. A title card supplies the appropriate line, "I know when one is dead, and when one lives" (5.3.261), and then the film shows Lear's own death. The final image, however, is of Cordelia, not of Lear. We are left with the sight that was too much for him to bear, as the camera wordlessly communicates what, in the Folio version of the play, are his final words: "Look there, look there!" (312).

As seen in the efforts of the Vitagraph filmmakers (and of the Clarendon Company in Britain, whose 1908 *The Tempest* explores the use both of special-effects cuts and of exterior shots), such an approach exploits—and sometimes advertises—the medium's illusionistic powers and its more radical plasticity. When Renato Castellani attempted to realize *Romeo and Juliet* as film in 1954, he followed the example of silent filmmakers, as had Olivier. A 1911 Film d'Arte production entitled *Giuletta e Romeo* had made effective use of location shots in Verona (reinforcing the blend of fantasy and reality at work in such tourist attractions as Juliet's tomb and balcony); in his search for a setting that would convey a sense of historical authenticity, Castellani used not only Verona locations but also sites in Siena and Venice (Jorgensen 1972, 109). Unlike the earlier film, Castellani's *Giuletta e Romeo* follows the Shakespearean story quite closely—and retains much of the text. Castellani nonetheless suggests that film might bring audiences closer to Shakespeare than even his words can.

Again, the first scene asserts film's capacity to provide access not only to Shakespeare's words, but also to his mind. The opening credits have appeared in lettering indebted to the typeface used in the First Folio edition of Shakespeare's plays, so it comes as no surprise to find the Chorus in an Elizabethan-style room, where he holds a copy of the

Folio itself. As the Chorus, John Gielgud performs a number of important services: he helps to validate what follows by offering his own theatrical approval and by delivering the sonnet authoritatively (some of the authority is provided by his being made-up to resemble Shakespeare). At the end of the play's opening sonnet ("What here shall miss, our toil shall strive to mend"), he reaches out directly to the audience, imploring our indulgence.

After this literal gesture toward the audience, the camera takes over and draws us into Verona itself: it enables us to enter the gate and be in the midst of the trouble brewing between the households of the Montagues and Capulets. Castellani establishes the violence that blazes out the more fiercely for being confined within the city's walls. After Abram, one of the Montague servants, is clubbed to death, Lord Montague leads his men through the narrow streets in an assault upon the Capulets' house. At several points, the camera considers the mob scene from above, as if we were looking from one of the neighboring houses threatened by the two families' civil brawls. The Prince's soldiers must fight their way through the melee in order to separate the parties. Instead of having the Prince command the combatants to disarm themselves on the spot, Castellani moves the rest of the scene into a hall of justice, where Montague and Capulet "throw" their weapons down in a ceremonial act of submission to Veronese authority.

Castellani's inventiveness and his eye for meaningful spectacle is impressive—enough so to have earned an award at the Venice Film Festival. But his energies seem to flag as soon as his attention is drawn to the title characters: Benvolio's meeting with a listlessly lovelorn Romeo occurs on a lazy, hazy riverbank; Lady Capulet is bored not only during the Nurse's prattle but in her own conference with her daughter about Count Paris. The director tries to enliven things by intercutting the negotiations between Paris himself and Juliet's father, who receives a vigorous interpretation by Sebastian Cabot, and by having Romeo actually follow Rosalind and her escorts into the Capulets' feast. The overall strategy is to highlight the obstacles between the lovers, stressing the violence of the feud and the authority of Lord Capulet. This couple is denied even the textual intimacy of a complete sonnet, much less an actual kiss, at their first meeting. The Nurse interrupts them after Romeo's request—"grant thou, lest faith turn to despair" (1.5.106). Such emphasis on separation, on frustration, could conceivably have led to a highly charged drama and an even more poignant ending. The lovers miss a final scene, in Shakespeare's playtext, by mere seconds; if most of their earlier scenes are also marked by intrusion or deferral, the sense of sheer waste could be intensified. Laurence Harvey's Romeo, though, communicates insufficient ardor to sustain much emotional tension and Susan Shentall's Juliet receives something of a hagiographic treatment from the filmmakers. She becomes in earnest the statue of a "saint" alluded to in the witty sonnet that the characters share in the playtext—and that Castellani cuts short.

Juliet is constantly framed by architectural elements. Before the balcony scene, she appears kneeling before a small, candlelit shrine. When she is surprised by Romeo, she is a figure in a central arch looming above the balcony railing—as though occupying a physical niche in her father's house. Much of their dialogue is whispered, curiously enough, across the Capulets' courtyard: Castellani allows little in the way of physical intimacy. The transition to the next scene continues the sense of separation. Juliet's "Good night, good night" is delivered off-screen, as we follow Romeo's departure. We immediately fade to Friar Laurence gathering herbs, and as his speech progresses the shots pull away further and further, until he is dwarfed by the city's stone walls. The monastery in which he lives provides a problematic sanctuary for the lovers, as even their exchange of vows is marked by separation. In an awkward echo of the story of Pyramus and Thisby, one of the play's ancient sources (as it is for *A Midsummer Night's Dream*), Romeo and Juliet stand on opposite sides of a wall and join their hands through a barred window. After Friar Laurence pronounces the Latin prayers that sanction their marriage, they kiss through the bars. Romeo pulls away, she briefly holds on. The camera switches to her point of view, regarding her new husband through the barriers that cannot be removed or overcome.

Yet more obstacles are presented visually and, at times, with chilling poignance. In the play, Friar John seeks an associate in Mantua to help in carrying word to Romeo that Juliet is not dead; that miscalculation leads to both friars being detained for fear of the plague. Castellani shows John alone deciding to minister to a dying man. Before he can perform the act of charity and continue on his way, officials seal the doors and shutters. The film highlights the play's fascination with good intentions gone awry—from Benvolio's early attempt to keep the peace (and further indicated by his name, which means "good will") to Romeo's own "I thought all for the best" (3.1.95). Intending to make a good end with his beloved, Romeo returns to Verona. In the cathedral, he breaks a massive candleholder and uses it to pry open the entrance to the Capulet family's crypt.

When the grieving Paris accuses him of malicious impiety, Harvey's Romeo achieves a level of passion: shaking with rage at yet another obstacle, he still warns Paris, "tempt not a desperate man. . . . Put not another sin upon my head, / By urging me to fury" (5.3.59–63). Paris refuses to give ground, and Romeo clubs him with the candleholder (recalling the death of Abram early in the film). The arbitrary violence intensifies for the lovers' deaths, too. Castellani changes the means of Romeo's suicide from poison to a dagger and intercuts Friar Laurence's arrival at the cathedral with the self-inflicted blow. Shentall's Juliet takes the time to regard, once more, her husband; this time, the barrier is death itself. She caresses his hair and returns the kiss he had given her. Impatient to join with him, she stabs herself insistently, jerking the blade deeper. Though the scene quickly changes to the doors of the cathedral, Castellani suggests that enough time has passed for the Prince to prepare another ceremonial statement: not only have the families been summoned but also the church's prelates, who intone "miserere"—have mercy—at the film's conclusion. The same singing had been heard during the opening credits. As the prelates descend into the cathedral's crypt, however, they appear to be swallowed up by the kind of ponderous (though beautiful) cityscape that Castellani has depicted as a primary obstacle to all attempts at mercy and concord.

Other kinds of institutional obstacles provide the subject and many of the occasions for Liz White's *Othello*, which was filmed over the course of four years, from 1962 to 1966. Stage history in general—and not just the history of this play—led White to mount an all-black production: cast and crew, as well as director, were all African-Americans. In the face of discrimination against actors of color, White crafted her own offstage career as a dresser and established a summer repertory theater on Martha's Vineyard. After a successful stage production of *Othello* by that company, White decided to experiment with a film version with many of the same cast members. White also made use of the Shearer estate, the summer theater's site, which had historically served as a resort for blacks and a refuge from the exclusionary practices of mainstream American society. National identity plays a significant role in White's reconfiguration of the conflicts at work between Othello and "Venetian" society. As Peter Donaldson has observed, Yaphet Kotto "plays Othello as a young, passionate, and emotionally sensitive African" who stands in contrast to the other actors, who "sustain a tone of urban American sophistication" in their portrayals (1990, 129). (Kotto would achieve some fame as the sometimes imperious, sometimes volcanic "Gee"—Inspector Giardello—on the television series *Homicide*; *Othello* was his first major film role.) The drama occurs as a result of cultural tension: specifically these Venetians' denial of racial kinship with Othello in the interests of protecting their identity as "less black" than he is. In the playtext, Othello's fall is sealed when he internalizes the social codes that mark him as outsider and Desdemona's love for him as "monstrous"; in White's film, that fall is embodied by all the characters.

At the same time, White delights in celebrating blackness and in the potentials for an African-American culture that embraces both terms: Shakespeare, while often a problematic inheritance from years of oppression, can nevertheless provide opportunities for individual and societal self-awareness. White pits Othello's healthy racial pride—the playtext's "Haply [i. e., perhaps], for I am black" becomes "Happily, I am black"—against his blithe unconcern for Iago's dogged service; Richard Dixon's Iago regularly assumes the stereotype of the black porter, hauling the general's luggage and shining his shoes. This Iago both admires and resents Othello's flamboyant otherness and tellingly plays upon his distaste for what seems to him Western European decadence. Iago's plots seek for dominance as well as for revenge: the ensign bestrides the stricken Othello after the playtext's epileptic fit (White extends the seizure into two episodes). The campaign is fought over and upon the bodies of women, and White's version never overlooks this aspect of the tragedy. Audrey Dixon's Desdemona adopts African dress when she feels Othello's increased emotional distance; in return, he abandons such garb in his preparations for murder. The film's Emilia makes a strong, defiant accusation of both Othello and Iago not in the quiet of the bedchamber but in the exterior space of a courtyard; she announces and suffers in public the cost this struggle exacts on women.

These developments are presented in daringly free style by cinematographer Charles Dorkins, whose camera readily follows the performers through corridors and along coastline terrain. Dorkins's past experience had been with documentary films; here he combines cinéma vérité mobility with startling shifts of tonal effect from lush exterior color to pale blue light. As filmmaker and editor, White herself offers stark counterpoints through frequent intercutting: considering his own image in a mirror, after Iago has successfully planted the seeds of doubt, Othello sees not only himself but Desdemona and Brabantio near the time of the marriage and after its discovery. As he prepares to exact vengeance on himself for Desdemona's murder, Othello is provided with a series of flashbacks of their tragically brief times of happiness and intimacy. There is no easy flow of images, as tracking shots labor to keep pace with the characters and even memories are interrupted by the present moment. White's film captures the sense of a history's troubling impact on today and of the effort required in achieving any level of self-awareness.

White's *Othello* was not screened publicly until 1980 and even now has been seen mostly (and infrequently) at film festivals. Donaldson relates that the director was not interested in having her *Othello* labeled an art film (1990, 128). Her belief was that it spoke clearly to everyday concerns of anyone interested in African-American culture. For that reason, she contacted major studios during the heyday of the "blaxploitation" films of the 1970s, such as the original *Shaft*; if such sendups and reinscriptions of stereotypes could attract audiences, surely Shakespeare's—and White's revision thereof—could too. The studio executives were unpersuaded; perhaps they felt that "Black Shakespeare" was both too counterculture and too elite-culture (too African and too American, to borrow from the film's own terms?) for the mass market.

The next major effort in filmic Shakespeare exhibited no qualms about being both high-culture and counter culture; it certainly seemed at ease in "the aura of art," as Dudley Andrew has expressed it. The director, Peter Hall, had long been associated with the Royal Shakespeare Company; he was, in fact, one of the architects of the transformation of the Shakespeare Memorial Theatre at Stratford-upon-Avon into the RSC. One of the hallmarks of the new regime was a taste for topicality and for increased experimentation; another was political awareness. Even though later writers would question the depths or even the existence of the RSC's radicalism (Sinfield 185–94), in the 1960s Hall was largely believed when he announced: "I am a radical, and I could not work in the theatre if I were not. The theatre must question everything and disturb its audience" (Addenbrooke 66). His film of *A Midsummer Night's Dream* may not have been politically radical—especially in its gender politics—but it possessed an anarchic energy appropriate to its time; it was released in 1969. It still possesses a power to disturb expectations, including stylistic ones.

Hall delights in juxtaposing discordant scenic and technical elements (see Occhiogrosso 175–76). The opening scene unfolds in a neo-classical entrance hall; the actors, with assertive anachronism, appear in costumes that could be described as Mod if not for their muted colors. This is not "authentic" Shakespeare, for all the authority that the RSC already carried, but it does capture the dizzying displacements of time in the playtext, where mythical Greece and early modern England coalesce. The disjunctions continue with an abrupt shift to a naturalistic setting for the mechanicals, who wear early twentieth-century working-class clothing. Appropriately enough, given Bottom's eventual absorption into the fairy realm, the workshop where Quince (played with long-suffering earnestness by Sebastian Shaw) assigns the roles for Pyramus and Thisbe serves as bridge and contrast to Hall's wood. The mechanicals and their milieu are clearly more connected than the denizens of Theseus's court with nature and the physical world in general; so too are Hall's fairies, who harken back to Reinhardt's startling rediscovery that Shakespeare's play is indeed haunted by elemental spirits. Oberon, Titania, and Puck are inhabitants of the "Green World" ably described by Harry Berger, Jr. (25–40), both unsettling and productively challenging. Their nearly naked bodies bear the color of the forest's vegetation as they immerse themselves in earth, water, and wood. Quince's workshop is also caught up in quotidian concerns. These men cannot easily break free of the necessary burden of earning their bread—something the two courts, those of Theseus and of Oberon, disdain. Where Quince and company are filmed in a realistic (or even social realist) manner, the fairies are presented with a panoply of non-illusionistic techniques; Hall has found a filmic equivalent to the play's alternations between prose and verse speech. The division between Oberon and Titania finds an analogue in a breathtakingly fragmented approach: Hall and his editor, Jack Harris, cut back and forth between the two characters, each glimpse taken in a fraction of a second. When Lysander and Hermia resolve to flee Athens, they are relatively isolated, sitting in a small boat on a pond that seems to be part of Theseus' estate; they hail Helena, whom they see on shore, and immediately appear beside her for their conversation about Demetrius. In his scenes, Puck appears, disappears, and reappears with the help of jump cuts that refuse to disguise themselves: far from trying to "fool" the audience, Hall's *Dream* endeavors to announce itself as film. The medium's ability to transcend time, to collapse or extend space, to bring drastic extremes into close proximity—this becomes the basis of the magic both within the play and of the play.

The film also announces itself unmistakably as Shakespeare by means of careful attention to the language—a trademark of the RSC, thanks in part to John Barton's work with the troupe. An accomplished cast delivers both verse and prose with unusual clarity: Ian Richardson as

Oberon, Judi Dench as Titania, Ian Holm as Puck, David Warner as Lysander, Helen Mirren as Hermia, and Diana Rigg as Helena, among others. Paul Rogers's Bottom enacts the power of language during the mechanicals' performance. After taking excruciating care to provide illusionistic aids for their audience (actors portraying a Wall and Moonshine) and reassurances that these are merely illusions (the Lion is, after all, just good old Snug the joiner), one of their special effects fails them at a critical juncture: Moonshine's candle goes out just after Pyramus has thanked the moon "for shining now so bright" (5.1.257). Bottom, however, simply intensifies his vocal performance, and his passionate insistence that there are still "gracious, golden, glittering gleams" wins applause from the usually heckling audience of courtiers. Verbal language can win "strong imagination" to its will; in Hall's *Dream*, it shares its power with the multiple languages of film.

Roman Polanski's adaptation of *Macbeth*, in contrast, tries to translate the richness of Shakespeare's words more directly into images and techniques. The imagery of this play's language is oppressively violent and Polanski cinematically matches that violence. Castellani's 1954 *Giuletta e Romeo* had been criticized for the supposed prettiness of its settings; *Roman Polanski's Film of "The Tragedy of Macbeth,"* as it was titled for its 1971 release, would be condemned for brutality of vision. Part of the problem in the film's reception was a highly charged context. First, the choice of murderous materials invited comparisons with the death of Polanski's wife, Sharon Tate, at the hands of the Manson "Family." Second, the bare bodies that appear on screen were seen as a cynical nod to Hugh Hefner's Playboy Productions, which financed the film (Hefner was the film's executive producer). Finally, the involvement of drama critic Kenneth Tynan as co-writer of the screenplay (especially in light of Tynan's role in the development of the "sexual revolution" musical *Oh, Calcutta!*) was taken as a sign of the director's own incomprehension where Shakespeare was concerned. Polanski, however, knew exactly what he was doing with the playtext as well as with the filmic medium. Starting with a series of sketches—a storyboard, in effect (Kliman 1998, 131–32)—he gradually realized a vision of a world in which Macbeth's actions are the unacknowledged norm. This is not the whole of Shakespeare's vision in the play, but much of the play's energy stems from how seriously Shakespeare treats his character's despairing conjecture that life is nothing more than "a tale / Told by an idiot, full of sound and fury, / Signifying nothing" (5.5.26–28).

The opening sequence establishes a setting in which nothing indeed flourishes: the sun rises over tidelands, hurrying aloft only to set and rise in endless repetition. The frame is then split by a stick held by one of the witches; she traces a circle in the moist but barren sand both to begin their spell and to confirm the sense of inescapable closure. No thing, no being, may escape the meaningless cycle of outrage and requital. "Tomorrow, and tomorrow, and tomorrow," muses Macbeth after being informed of his wife's death, "Creeps in this petty pace from day to day / To the last syllable of recorded time" (5.5.19–21). Polanski helps to take us beyond time's last syllable by telling so much of his story without words. The witches dig out the sand and place in the hole a noose and a severed hand; in the hand they place a dagger. Herbs are sprinkled over the grisly relics, which are then buried. Only after the physical rites are complete do we hear the first words of the play: "When shall we three meet again?" Unsettlingly, the answer is presented as meaningless, since all human choice is either sharply circumscribed or utterly illusory. Macbeth will be a mere pawn in the subsequent events: it will not matter whose hand wields the dagger that slays King Duncan. The witches, too, have assumed their dark craft by default. Two are old women, clearly outcasts from society; one is blind, seemingly born without eyes, but she is the one who draws the circle and leads the spell. The third is young, but plagued by a disfiguring eczema. There is no place for them to go but the heath, upon which they will encounter Macbeth. The young witch leads the blind one along and pulls a cart as they walk away from the camera, heading left as the remaining witch trudges right. Polanski holds the shot for nearly a full minute, before mists fully envelop the women. The appearance of agency is there, but the destination—first the heath, then oblivion—is the same no matter which path has been chosen.

King Duncan's reign is presented as callous and bloody. In the face of rebellion, those loyal to the present wearer of the crown are implacable in their wrath. The Captain who reports what Macbeth has done in battle wins approving laughter for describing how the title character "unseam'd" Macdonwald "from the nave to th' chops" (1.2.22). The Thane of Cawdor, who has been captured in the rebellion, sees all too clearly that only might makes right in this world. Where Shakespeare's Cawdor dies offstage, both stoic and repentant, Polanski's Cawdor is a tough-minded old thug who mockingly announces "long live the King" before leaping to his death, strangled by the chains around his neck. Malcolm, soon to be proclaimed the heir apparent, still marvels that "Nothing in his life / Became him like the leaving it: he died / As one that had been studied in his death, / To throw away the dearest thing he ow'd / As 'twere a careless trifle" (1.4.7–11). Here, it is Cawdor's defiance, not his penitence, that wins admiration. The irony of Cawdor's "prayer" is compounded by what immediately follows, as in the playtext: the arrival of Macbeth and Banquo, who have heard the witches' prophecies and learned of their initial confirmation. Similarly, Macbeth's dismay at the designation of Malcolm as heir (not the Scottish custom) and therefore Prince of Cumberland (which was the customary title for a designated successor) inevitably follows from Shakespeare's play. Polanski, however, adds the response of Duncan's younger son, Donalbain, who appears just as outraged as Macbeth. Plenty is rotten in the state of Scotland, but Duncan believes he knows what is needed not only to maintain power but to keep it in his immediate family. Surely his sternness with the rebels will deter any future unrest.

Lady Macbeth, of course, has other plans, which we already know. Before Duncan's announcement about Malcolm, the director has intercut the beginning of act 1, scene 5, showing her elation and resolve upon reading her husband's letter about the witches. In Francesca Annis's portrayal, she is young, vigorous, lusty—very much the equal of Jon Finch's Macbeth. Both characters are presented as far more complex inside than out: their major speeches are largely given in voice-over, as internal monologues (a strategy pioneered in Shakespearean film by Olivier in his *Henry V* and *Hamlet*). In one audacious scene, Polanski has Macbeth consider that "If it were done when 'tis done, then 'twere well / It were done quickly" (1.7.1–2) while seated next to his royal guest at the feast in Duncan's honor. Still more of their characters are presented visually. As Duncan and his train approach across the fields, Lady Macbeth watches from high above (lending further irony to Duncan's praise that the "castle hath a pleasant seat"). She sees and becomes a bird of prey hovering before its attack; in voice-over she identifies herself with the raven "That croaks the fatal entrance of Duncan / Under my battlements" (1.5.39–40). When Macbeth hesitates in agreeing to her plan, she keeps insisting even as the festivities take place around them. Such scruples on his part are sorely undermined when Malcolm pulls rank and expects Macbeth to serve him wine. Despite this, Finch's Macbeth remains plagued by conscience even in the king's bedchamber: it is not clear that he will carry out the murder. Only when Duncan awakes and recognizes the intruder does Macbeth strike. Knowledge of what would ensue after capture—the kind of retribution Macbeth himself had enacted— decides the issue. He kills in order to avoid being discovered.

The play constantly returns to an ancient example of dramatic irony: attempts to protect oneself—from attack, from the dictates of fortune—often increase one's vulnerability. Lady Macbeth's recourse to "a little water" in order to hide her guilt and that of her husband leads to her obsession with being cleansed of the signs of culpability. Macbeth's efforts to remove all possible threats to his reign merely intensify the opposition against him. Duncan wishes both to ensure his safety and to honor his chief protectors by visiting Macbeth's castle. Polanski multiplies these examples: Duncan's faith in the virtue of deterrence forces his murderer's hand; Lady Macduff trusts in the advice she receives from Ross, who here bribes her servant so the gates are open wide for Macbeth's henchmen; Macbeth not only arms himself physically long before battle but uses the prophecies he thinks he has received as psychological armor.

The nature of Macbeth's prophetic visions is made more problematic by his direct participation in the spell that brings them. In the midst of a witches' coven, Macbeth drinks down a cup of the disgusting brew and then gazes into the caldron. He sees his own face and hears his own voice warn him about Macduff; his reply, "Thou hast harp'd my fear aright" (4.1.74), seems astonishingly naive. When he immediately asks for "one word more," the apparition tumbles into the abyss, visually presaging Macbeth's fate: his head will indeed fall. The other visions are similarly apt; only the words prevaricate, to echo the Porter's speech. As Macbeth is told that "none of woman born / Shall harm" him, he sees a caesarian birth without realizing it. He concludes, at first, that Macduff shall live—and Polanski's Macbeth indeed spares his killer—but then decides to "make assurance double sure" and plot his death. He envisions himself plunging a sword through the armor of an adversary, but the armor turns out to be empty. Later, Macbeth will kill an armed warrior, but it is not Macduff. While appearances may indeed be deceiving, some visions are false only by nature of the interpretations placed upon them.

There is no illusion, for example, to the vulnerability of flesh and blood. The human body, in this film, cries out for compassion and finds none: Macbeth early on describes pity as "like a naked newborn babe" (1.7.21) and Polanski equates nakedness with victimization. The nudity of the witches during the coven is as much a sign of their marginality as it is of their malignity. Lady Macduff has just finished bathing her son before an entire troop of assassins attacks her absent husband's castle; in trying to avoid her own rape and murder she enters a chamber filled with the naked bodies of her family and household, already slain. Lady

Macbeth's sleepwalking reveals her body as well as her mind: neither has much in the way of defense against violence and death. Her death here is a suicide; she has apparently leaped from the battlements from which she surveyed Duncan's approach. The discovery of her remains provokes sharp but evanescent grief from her attendants; soon they join in the mass desertion from the castle. Someone covers her face with a blanket, but her bare legs remain visible—and only briefly noticed by the invading soldiers. Finally, Macbeth himself is mortally wounded through the arm-holes of his supposedly impregnable armor. In one-on-one combat, he had Macduff at his mercy, with his sword's point ready to pierce Macduff's throat. Earlier, he had delivered death wounds to one of the rebels against the king and then to Duncan himself exactly in that most vulnerable of places. Here, Macbeth not only warns Macduff but spares him when he says "my soul is too much charg'd / With blood of thine already" (5.8.5–6). That final scruple, perhaps indulged in because of his insistent faith that he is invincible, hastens Macbeth's inevitable death.

The new regime of Malcolm may not be bothered by any scruples, however. The Prince of Cumberland receives the bloodstained crown from Ross—who in Polanski's rendering becomes the emblem of political expedience and brutality. Here, Ross has been Cawdor's captor and then one of Macbeth's ardent supporters. Without fully believing in the official account of the king's murder, he participates in the ceremony making Macbeth Duncan's successor. He observes and assists Banquo's assassination and then helps to eliminate the less than successful (and inconveniently knowledgeable) murderers. After helping to make the slaughter of Macduff's family possible, he feigns outrage while informing Macduff what has happened: he has gone to the side of Macbeth's enemies not out of principle but because of disappointed hopes for advancement. With supporters such as these, Malcolm has established his reign on shaky ground, in terms of ethics and pragmatics alike. The trouble ahead is further suggested by the film's last sequence, where we see Donalbain, the new king's younger brother, enter the witches' cave. Polanski's images have completely undercut the hopeful words uttered by Macduff, that "the time is free" (5.9.21).

The achievement of Polanski's "rereading" of *Macbeth* is all the more remarkable given how restrained its techniques are. Unlike Hall's *Dream*, this film generally avoids the kinds of editing that call attention to the constructed quality of the medium. While Polanski deftly borrows images from past directors like Yutkevich and Welles (especially their use of reflections), he generally does not emulate their striking, non-illusionistic angles. Instead, it is the imagistic—even symbolic—power of film that Polanski here exploits. Perhaps the most disturbing of all the images, though, is suggested by means of unconventional editing and point of view. After Macbeth's first vision has come to pass with his decapitation, Macduff calls Malcolm's attention to "Th'usurper's cursed head." Polanski's photographer, Gilbert Taylor, shows us the severed head in closeup, and in grisly, naturalistic detail. The eyes are open—and may still retain the ability to see. As Malcolm crowns himself, the frame goes red and Polanski intercuts quick views of the head stuck on a pike with low-angle shots of jeering soldiers. Our point of view, then, is provided by Macbeth's eyes: we see what they might—or do—even after death. The chance of escaping the fatalistic circle, of entering an afterlife, is presented as no less nightmarish than this life. In a final twist, the film's ambivalence toward language (an ambivalence Shakespeare clearly shares in this play, among others) receives confirmation through the words of the closing credits. We learn that while Hugh Hefner's involvement in financing the film was represented by "Playboy Productions," Polanski established a different institutional identity through his own production company, "Caliban Films, Limited." In *The Tempest*, Caliban asserts: "You taught me language, and my profit on't / Is I know how to curse" (1.2.366–67).

Christine Edzard's startling *As You Like It*, released in 1992, offers another self-consciously filmic approach to Shakespeare. Edzard updates the play's witty critique of pastoral idealism—the longing to escape to an idyllic existence in Nature—by transforming its court scenes to glimpses of late twentieth-century corporate power and its country scenes to a landscape blighted by corporate practices. As Amelia Marriette (76) rightly observes, Edzard's settings and techniques pave the way for Baz Luhrmann's *William Shakespeare's Romeo+Juliet* (1996). In Luhrmann's case, however, the director almost constantly gestures beyond film toward other media, especially video. The "Sycamore Grove" where Romeo pines for Rosalind is here a ruined movie theater (not far from the long-closed stage theater, the Globe); one of the play's pivotal events, Mercutio's death, later unfolds on its abandoned stage. Just as the play uses the formal conventions of the sonnet as a framing device, Luhrmann's film uses the television news broadcast to contain not only the narrative but also the medium of film. This *Romeo and Juliet* will be filtered through the conventions and technologies of broadcast and cable television. As the film camera zooms in on a TV set tuned to the local news, the anchorwoman gives her report, the play's prologue, nearly in full (unlike most earlier versions and unlike the published screenplay); at the film's end, the camera pulls away from the monitor as the news anchor reads the play's final lines, originally assigned to the Prince, which follow the structure of a sonnet's conclusion. The prologue here omits only the final couplet about the audience attending "with patient ears." Careful listening is optional, since the first six lines of the sonnet are immediately repeated by an unseen narrator on the soundtrack. Phrases from the sonnet appear on screen, followed by explanatory visuals and additional graphics which further explain the situation and introduce the characters—not, as in the MGM film version, the actors portraying them. Such devices are not absolutely necessary, given how familiar the story remains. Instead, Luhrmann uses these old conventions to establish his strategies of adaptation. His opening visuals give previews not only of what will happen—as does Shakespeare's sonnet—but also of how these events will be presented: irreverent updates (Count Paris becomes "Dave Paris, the Governor's son"), energetic intercutting and camerawork (there are no fewer than seventy separate edits in the sequence and many, many pans and zooms within these brief glimpses), and a postoperatic style deeply indebted to music videos.

When we join Sampson, Gregory, and Benvolio—"the Montague boys" (one has the family/corporate name tattooed on the back of his shaved head)—en route to their confrontation with the Capulets, we have fully entered the hyperkinetic world of the popular music video. Raucous music blares as they drive through town, screaming insults concerning the Capulets. They pull into a gasoline station and Benvolio tries to calm his comrades down. He is given part of Gregory's line, "The quarrel is between our masters," here suggesting it is none of their business. Gregory completes it—"and us their men"—and thereby asserts his stake in the feud. Benvolio shakes his head ruefully and leaves, apparently to prepay for the gas. The mini-drama that ensues upon the arrival of some of the Capulets draws from sources ranging from John Ford's cowboy movies and their spaghetti-western derivatives to Alfred Hitchcock's *The Birds*. Elsewhere, Luhrmann, with co-writer Craig Pearce and designer Catherine Martin (both of whom had worked on Luhrmann's directorial debut, *Strictly Ballroom*), return to the use of water in previous film versions of the play—the reflecting pool in MGM's vision of the Capulets' garden, the water trough where Zeffirelli's Mercutio tries to cool off—and amplify these images a hundredfold. Romeo first spies Juliet through an aquarium; they both wind up in the Capulets' swimming pool during what is usually known as the balcony scene; when Tybalt dies, he falls into a pool at the foot of a religious monument while torrential rains fall. This kind of eclectic recycling from entertainment classics is a hallmark of the music video. Once more, Luhrmann goes a step further and borrows directly from MTV "classics"; he conflates any number of Michael Jackson videos, including "Beat It" (with a glance at Benvolio's role as would-be peace-maker) and "I'm Bad" in his version of the opening skirmish. The ethnic differences between the Montagues and the Capulets derive from a source the film shares with "I'm Bad": *West Side Story*, with its Anglo Jets and Puerto Rican Sharks standing in for the play's noble families. The visual assault of religious icons that pervades the film is drawn from Madonna's "Like a Prayer," among other sources, and culminates in the Capulet tomb where Juliet lies in state and where Romeo and she will die in earnest: the scene is illuminated by countless blue neon crosses.

The style and imagery of the Capulets' ball is permeated by the music video format. Previous film versions have taken advantage of the scene's potential for music or spectacle: in the MGM film, as we recall, the ball was a showcase for Juliet and for the actress who portrayed her; in Zeffirelli's 1968 version, all action stops as we and the guests hear a minstrel sing "What Is a Youth" (which, with new lyrics, became an international pop music hit as "A Time for Us"). Here, all eyes initially are on Harold Perrineau's Mercutio in full drag queen regalia, lip-synching to Kym Mazelle's disco-style vocals for "Young Hearts Run Free," one of several songs specially commissioned for the soundtrack by composer and producer Nellee Hooper. The soundtrack album, in fact, became a success even before the film's release. As a result the music and lyrics of the complete songs—most of which are heard only briefly in the film—provided intriguing intertexts for younger audience members. Eventually, the audience's eyes and those of Leonardo DiCaprio's Romeo light upon Claire Danes as Juliet. Her costume glances back at earlier versions and at the play's own language but also to the nascent music video tradition. Mercutio's costume does this as well: the flamboyance of John Barrymore's interpretation and the homoerotic longings of John McEnery's character in Zeffirelli's version converge so that Mercutio, in this scene, becomes Queen Mab. Juliet's simple gown and modest wings echo Castellani's interest in religious imagery; she is both the "saint" of Romeo's playful idolatry and the "bright angel" Romeo desires to speak again at the start of the balcony scene. In addition, Claire Danes had made a memorable appearance in Soul Asylum's 1995 video, "Just Like Anyone," as a hunchbacked teenager who sprouts wings and takes flight from her high-school prom. The video, in turn, had capitalized on Danes's appearances as Angela Chase in the recently canceled television series, "My So-Called Life." Luhrmann trumps all the previous appropriations, absorbing them all into the hypertext of his *Romeo+Juliet.*

Almost predictably, then, Danes as Juliet was the winner of the 1997 MTV Movie Award for Best Actress. It was certainly predictable that the televised award ceremonies include a parody of the balcony scene, featuring host Mike Myers in his "Austin Powers, International Man of Mystery" persona playing Romeo to MTV personality Jenny McCarthy's Juliet. What may be less predictable, however, is the emotional impact that Luhrmann's death scene can have on audiences amidst the film's extravagant techniques and knowing plays on words, images, and their commercial value. For example, the playtext's constant references to "swords" are visually explained by turning the different types of blades into brand names for guns: early on, Montague (not, as in the play, Capulet) asks for his "Longsword," here a semi-automatic weapon. Friar Laurence's letter to Romeo, advising him that Juliet is still alive, is not entrusted to Friar John but to a courier service, "Post Post Haste"; the result is the same as in the playtext. Luhrmann also considers Shakespeare as more than just cultural capital. The cityscape of Verona Beach, the film's setting, is dominated by billboards and business signs, many of which incorporate a Shakespearean echo. Prospero Whiskey, one ad proclaims, is "Such stuff as dreams are made on." It's not clear whether one should expect to buy it from "The Merchant of Verona Beach" or at "Rosencrantzky's" grill. Such sly asides mark an awareness of the marketing strategies involved with attracting a wider audience for the film—and betray some self-critique over them.

Luhrmann's sense of the play's stage history is similarly self-aware. For much of the eighteenth century, *Romeo and Juliet* was performed only in the form of adaptations by Theophilus Cibber and, more famously, David Garrick. Both versions provide something that Shakespeare, in the opinion of his adapters, must have simply overlooked: a final exchange of dialogue between Romeo and Juliet. Juliet awakens after Romeo has taken the apothecary's poison, but before his death—allowing for, it was hoped, a more poignant scene than the one provided by the Bard. Luhrmann and Pearce synthesize Shakespeare and his adapters, retaining Shakespeare's language but allowing a brief, anguished reunion in consciousness. Even with all the carefully cultivated knowingness of this production—and most audience members quickly realize "this isn't how the play goes"—it realizes considerable pathos in presenting the lovers' deaths. In part this comes from heightening the characters' awareness of what is occurring: they share in the audience's understanding of how cruelly close they have come to happiness. Juliet awakens after Romeo has taken his parting kiss and is preparing to drink the poison; not realizing his intentions, she strokes his cheek tenderly as he drinks instead of snatching the vial away. Her touch tells him everything in a flash: she is alive and he is doomed. She quickly understands, too, and selections from the playtext's words are addressed to a dying Romeo, not an already departed one:

> JULIET
> O Romeo, what's here?
> *Romeo's clear wide eyes stare back. He is completely still but for the sound of weak breaths desperately drawn across motionless lips. Juliet finds the broken vial beside him.*
> JULIET (continued)
> Drunk all, and left no friendly drop to help me after. I will kiss thy lips. Haply some poison yet doth hang on them.
> *She delicately kisses Romeo's lips.*
> JULIET (continued) (*a heartbroken whisper*)
> Thy lips are warm.

In reply, Romeo's last words are whispered to a living and despairing Juliet: "Thus with a kiss I die" (Pearce and Luhrmann 158; adapted from 5.3.120, 161–67). The quiet delivery of the lines and the extreme close-ups heighten the impression of intimacy; the combined illusion is that they know what we know and we feel what they feel.

In 1955, Paul Jorgensen published a somewhat lonely defense of Castellani's *Giulietta e Romeo*. What critics had overlooked, he argued, was the director's "emotional intent" (1972, 108) in setting the story amidst the physical splendor and massiveness of period architecture: Castellani hoped to "make one feel the warm, hurried anguish of living love contrasted with the cold, immobile beauty of art" (111). While I still feel that Castellani's film conveys coldness and immobility far better than it does warmth or haste, Jorgensen's reminder of the play's potential for emotional power is an important one. Emotion and artifice, though, do not have to conflict; they can support and sustain each other. The strategies of filmmaking, like the strategies of Early Modern stagecraft, have complex affective goals that are meant to co-exist with overt, often stylized technique. Shakespeare's stage audiences were moved not in spite of his reliance on sonnet structure or rhyme or other Elizabethan conventions, but often because of it; his film audiences can be moved as a result of his filmic adapters' techniques, as well as dazzled by them.

CHAPTER SIX

—— ◇ ——

The Revenge of the Actor-Manager

> PUCK: What, a play toward? I'll be an auditor,
> An actor, too, if I see cause.
>
> —Shakespeare,
> *A Midsummer Night's Dream*

In 1949, A. Nicholas Vardac published his comprehensive study, *Stage to Screen: Theatrical Method from Garrick to Griffith.* Vardac traces the development of what he terms "the realistic-romantic cycle" from its origins in David Garrick's eighteenth-century experiments in naturalistic representation to its apotheosis in the "spectacle filmings" associated with D. W. Griffith. At the time, Vardac wondered if "pictorial theater" and its traditions had simply exhausted themselves (250–51); he did not foresee how developing technologies—for the camera and, later, the computer—would extend the life, if not always the vitality, of the blockbuster spectacle. He also overlooked how other aspects of recent Western theatrical tradition could be incorporated into film and its creation.

Garrick was one of the first in a long line of actor-managers: star performers who essentially ruled over their production companies offstage as well as on. They decided the interpretive strategies, such as pictorial realism, that held sway through the eighteenth and nineteenth centuries. By the 1820s, William Charles Macready had initiated an archeological approach that privileged historically accurate costumes and sets; in the performance of Shakespeare, he also pioneered the restoration of scenes and language from the earliest playtexts. That set of practices was continued in mid-century by Charles Kean—whose career was haunted by the memory of his legendarily charismatic father, Edmund—and at the century's end by Henry Irving. The waning of the tradition during the Second World War is captured on stage and screen in Ronald Harwood's *The Dresser*, which is based on his experiences as part of Donald Wolfit's company. Even as the actor-managers faded from the stage, their functions were appropriated by actors who were determined to bring Shakespeare successfully to film. Like those of their stage counterparts, the careers of these directors often have been marked by fierce competition (Macready's feud with Edwin Forrest led to the 1849 Astor Place Riots) and by anxiety toward forebears. Laurence Olivier constantly looks back at the theater; Orson Welles constantly glances at Olivier as a rival claimant to the Shakespearean mantle. Kenneth Branagh attempts to negotiate a separate identity with these formidable predecessors and in opposition to them. The three directors offer a wonderfully rich latter-day analogue to the Early Modern social phenomenon of emulation (Weinbrot 123–27). The term today suggests only a most flattering form of imitation, but in Shakespeare's day the word captured a complex mixture of fierce admiration, deep resentment, and ardent competition with the rival (who could be friend or kin) one passionately wanted to be like and to overshadow.

Olivier's success—critical, commercial, and patriotic—with *Henry V* stole a march on Welles, who had long been absorbed by Shakespeare. While Olivier had labored to establish his Shakespearean credentials through the 1930s, Welles had breezily asserted himself to be John Barrymore's successor as America's prime exponent of theatrical Shakespeare. After receiving an invitation from John Houseman to direct the Harlem branch of the Federal Theater, a New Deal program, Welles staged a "voodoo" *Macbeth* with an all-black cast; it was controversial at the time (especially with the African-American press) and remains so. The first production for his own troupe, the Mercury Theater, was an artfully truncated, modern-dress *Julius Caesar* that drew parallels between ancient Roman politics and the rise of fascism in twentieth-century Europe. A version was performed on radio as well, in which he reprised his performance as Brutus. Partly because of financial problems involved with *Five Kings*, his attempt to compress Shakespeare's two historical tetralogies into two evenings of theater, he agreed to move from Broadway to Hollywood in 1939. RKO Pictures offered him artistic control along with considerable resources. The first result, in 1941, was *Citizen Kane*; Welles's achievement, along with that of his co-writer, Herman Mankiewicz, eventually came to be recognized as one of the greatest works in U. S. filmmaking. Only Part One of *Five Kings* had been staged, for a short run, but its retelling of the rise of the house of Lancaster amidst civil strife included Welles' debut as Falstaff. He would return to that role after years of being overshadowed by an actor whose film success was secured by the story and the role of Falstaff's young, ambitious, and royal companion—King Henry the Fifth of England, formerly Prince Hal, the triumph of Lancastrian rule.

Before *Henry V*, Olivier, too, had been drawn to Hollywood—not once but three times. Unsuccessful sojourns in 1931 and 1933 had been followed by returns to the London stage, where he determined, in his own words, "to be the greatest actor of all time" (Olivier 1986, 141). Such an ambition could only be achieved with the help and challenge of Shakespearean roles. His performance as Romeo in 1935 was daringly naturalistic in vocal delivery, but won little in the way of critical praise; the contrast with other cast members' more traditional verse-speaking was too great to be accepted from that character. Later in the season, he switched roles with John Gielgud, who had been playing Mercutio; the exchange had been planned from the beginning. At once, Olivier's comparatively brash style seemed to fit. With Gielgud and Peggy Ashcroft in the title roles, the production won unqualified acclaim and ran through March 1936. That same year, he appeared in a film version of *As You Like It* (see chapter seven). Olivier's performance was generally well-received, despite what was perceived as serious flaws in the production. In 1937, he went on to successes on screen with *Fire Over England* and on the Shakespearean stage as Sir Toby Belch in *Twelfth Night* and with starring roles in both *Hamlet* and *Henry V*. His 1938 return to Hollywood, for *Wuthering Heights*, initiated a stormily productive period which included Alfred Hitchcock's film of *Rebecca* (1939) and George Cukor's film of *Pride and Prejudice* (1940); it also included the flowering of his romance with Vivien Leigh and the start of their deeply troubled marriage. The propaganda needs of Britain presented the opportunity to combine the worlds of stage and screen in *Henry V*, which was filmed in 1943–44 and released in England a mere four months after D-day, bringing the two incursions into France into an uncanny relationship. The film's U. S. release in 1946 led to a Special Academy Award the next year in recognition of Olivier's "outstanding achievement as actor, producer, and director."

Meanwhile, Welles's star had fallen considerably. The technical and artistic achievements of *Citizen Kane* and *The Magnificent Ambersons* (1942) were not answered with wide audiences; RKO seized control of the latter film and clumsily re-edited it. The studio then pulled the plug on his ambitious documentary project, *It's All True*, and terminated its deal with Welles. In a curious parallel with Olivier's career, he appeared in *Jane Eyre*, another film adaptation of one of the Brontë sisters' novels, for David O. Selznick. After this, RKO agreed to distribute Welles's *The Stranger* (1946) and its moderate success led Columbia Pictures to finance *The Lady from Shanghai*, especially since it would feature Welles's then-wife, Rita Hayworth. The results were commercially disastrous, despite attempts at reshooting and re-editing that delayed the film's release until 1948. Nevertheless, Republic Pictures approached Welles with the opportunity to film a low-budget production of a Shakespearean play. Welles's choice for his debut as director of Shakespeare, as it had been with the Federal Theater, was *Macbeth*.

Although many of the details of the film had been developed during a more recent production, for the Utah Centennial Festival, its overall conception owes much to the "voodoo" *Macbeth* (France 34). Welles's opening narration reframes Shakespeare's tragedy as the conflict between malign, chaotic, demonic forces and the hope of a social order predicated on Christian principles. The representatives of these polarities are the witches—here called "the Three" and including a male—on the one side and a new figure—called "Holy Father"—on the other, created from lines given to various characters in Shakespeare's playtext. Macbeth himself is caught between these adversaries. In an early scene, a clay effigy of Macbeth is shaped by the Three and crowned by them; they quickly disperse as some of Duncan's troops draw near, carrying tall, thin crosses. The Holy Father later serves as the prime instigator of the insurrection against Macbeth: with a massive stone cross in the background, he (instead of Ross) informs Macduff of his family's slaughter and he (not Malcolm) urges that "Macbeth / Is ripe for shaking" (4.3.237–38). When Macbeth confronts the army raised against him, he recognizes the Holy Father's responsibility. He hurls a vicious weapon—which somehow combines a spear with spiked mace—and kills the priest, immediately provoking the decisive battle.

Clearly the storyline of an ambitious man's downfall appealed to Welles: meditations on the corrupting influence of power recur in Welles's films from *Citizen Kane* to *Touch of Evil* and beyond. Critics have also pondered the extent to which Welles tried both to realize and to exploit that story in his own life (Thomson 335). The difference between self-regard and self-knowledge is a thematic concern in several of Welles's films, regularly figured by mirrors. When Kane is left alone in Xanadu, we see him stagger down a hallway past a pair of reflecting mirrors: his image repeats endlessly, underscoring the character's narcissism and isolation. The memorable climax of *The Lady from Shanghai* takes place in the hall of mirrors in an amusement park fun house; deceptive images multiply in dizzying fashion until they shatter from gunshots and something like the truth is revealed. Welles's Macbeth crowns himself in front of a warped mirror, even as he muses that "To be thus is nothing" (3.1.47). Critics hastened to agree, irked not only by the film's technical flaws—such as a frequently incomprehensible soundtrack—but also by what was seen as Welles's egotism. Michael Anderegg (74–78) has noted the sharp contrasts, for example, between *Life* magazine's coverage of Welles's alleged meddling with Shakespeare and its celebration of Olivier's perceived service to both the text and the public.

Olivier's *Hamlet* was widely hailed. There were criticisms of the attempts at a guiding interpretation, both implicit—as influenced by Ernest Jones's Freudian reading of the play—and explicit, as Olivier himself declares in opening voice-over that "This is the tragedy of a man who could not make up his mind." There was understandable comment on the drastic cuts of the playtext: not only does Fortinbras disappear but so do Rosencrantz and Guildenstern. Even so, the film attracted sizeable audiences and earned Olivier an Oscar for Best Actor and the British Academy's award for Best Picture. The second honor may seem curious (or even a commentary on the state of the British film industry in the immediate postwar era), but there is much to admire from a technical viewpoint in Olivier's *Hamlet*. The camerawork, under the direction of Desmond Dickinson, is highly mobile. The sets, designed by Roger Furse (who had worked on the costumes for *Henry V*), allow for striking tableaux in themselves, but are all the more effective in conjunction with the cinematography. After the first scene with the Ghost, the audience is given an introductory "tour" of Elsinore: we see the passages, chambers, and doorways that will be associated with various characters that suggest what these characters mean to Hamlet himself.

Many such elements, though, were hallmarks of the "Welles tradition" that was earning disapproval under that name. *Citizen Kane* shows a fascination both with what the camera can do and with what architecture—especially thresholds and windows—reveals about character. The sequence with Susan (played by Dorothy Comingore) increasingly focuses on her being swallowed up by Xanadu and pivots on her leaving Kane, framed by a doorway as she resolutely walks down a corridor and out of his life. It ends with the camera—guided by the masterful Gregg Toland—sweeping back through the skylight of the nightclub where she continues to perform. The film opens and closes with shots of Kane's would-be castle, shrouded first with mist and then, at the end, by smoke from all of Kane's possessions—including "Rosebud"—not considered worth selling. At the start, after pulling in to see curious fragments of Kane's estate (the zoo, an artificial canal, ancient relics from Egypt), the camera enters the castle and we see Kane's death. At the end, a crane shot pulls back farther and farther in a self-consciously doomed attempt to suggest the sum of Kane's life. Olivier's *Hamlet* also begins and ends with its main character's demise, with the prince's body first appearing on the battlements of Elsinore and much later, after the catastrophic duel with Laertes, carried ceremoniously to the same spot. But while Olivier's exploration of Hamlet in and through Elsinore suggests that the film has fully plumbed its occupants' mystery, Welles's glimpses at Xanadu are deliberately denied any such claim to definitive insight.

Welles's *Othello* is in many ways a direct assault on Olivier as well as an attempt to justify Welles's own approaches to filmmaking and to Shakespearean adaptation. His *Macbeth* had suffered in comparison to Olivier's *Henry V* to such a degree that Hollywood interest in Welles's *Othello* was withdrawn back in 1948, initiating years of duplicitous, start-and-stop, sometimes manic fundraising efforts that marked the production. The results are overwhelming and audacious. Reclaiming the "frame" elements shared by *Citizen Kane* and his rival's *Hamlet*, Welles opens the film with the funeral procession of Othello and Desdemona. Olivier's final sequence is announced by a severe closeup on the dead Hamlet's face, upside down to our view; the camera then pulls back to show his body supported by the soldiers that Horatio, somewhat inappropriately, nominates for the prince's cortege. The film ends with silhouettes of the procession carrying Hamlet up to the tower where he had encountered the Ghost and pondered "To be or not to be." Welles's *Othello* begins where Olivier's *Hamlet* leaves off: the contemplation of the tragic hero in closeup, again upside down; the pallbearers here accompanied by bishops, priests, and monks, some of whom carry an oversized cross (recalling, briefly, his *Macbeth*). Again we see the procession in sil-houette, with dark figures on a stone staircase appearing starkly against the sky. Quickly, however, Welles shifts focus to the man responsible for Othello's downfall and the deaths of Desdemona, Emilia, and Roderigo. Iago, in chains, is dragged through the city's streets and thrown into a cage which is then suspended high in the air. He looks down on the results of his handiwork, which now includes a closed coffin—Emilia's—along with the bodies of Othello and Desdemona. The bars of the cage constitute a major part of Iago's vision of the world and of our perception of him. Welles completely integrates images of bars and other barriers into his vision of the play.

Welles combines the visual elements of obstacles—bars, pillars, gates, and slats—with those of access—most notably, mirrors. When Micheál MacLiammóir's Iago first suggests Desdemona's infidelity to Othello, he positions himself at a window opening onto the chamber where the Moor stands. Iago's room is at a lower level and, with his face framed by the window's stone bars, he gazes up at Othello as if in sub-servient fealty to his general. On the window sill is a small mirror in which Welles, as Othello, considers the unsettling image his ensign, in all duty, has posited. Shaken, he turns away from the window and goes to another mirror, this one on a chamber wall. Despite this "independent" perspective, Othello has already (even before Iago's promptings?) inter-nalized the message that Desdemona's desires for him must be "unnatu-ral"; every time he returns to the mirror, as he does after the ensuing scene with Desdemona, he finds confirmation for his suspicions (Hurwitz 337). Also, every time he looks through bars, he receives a distorted view of things: he overhears Cassio and Bianca while positioned at a small, barred window; he sees Desdemona behind bars as he approaches in preparation to kill her.

Welles's Othello dies in isolation, locking himself away with Desde-mona's corpse; he cannot attack Iago from behind the iron gates, so he immediately unleashes his rage upon himself. His life is already ebbing away when Iago flatly declares, "What you know, you know" (5.2.303), and when he delivers his own eulogy. The effect is strangely similar to that achieved in *Hamlet*: the hero almost reluctantly remains among the living in order to ensure that his understanding of events is shared after his death. Going from Hamlet's urgent requests to Horatio—"Report me and my cause aright"; "tell my story" (*Hamlet* 5.2.339, 349)—to Othello's "Speak of me as I am"; "Set you down this" (*Othello* 5.2.342, 351) is not very far. Welles collapses the distance altogether. The film then comes full circle, signaled by a round opening in the roof of the chamber where Othello and Desdemona lie. Some members of the Venetian delegation, unable to break through the bars Othello had closed against them, go to the next floor and find a hatch overhead. Stunned by the events, they watch Othello as he returns their gaze and tells his story. After he collapses on the bed, they seal the opening. At the closing of the circle, the screen returns to the funeral procession that had opened the film. The camera moves from silhouettes dark against a bright Mediterranean sky to one of the fortress's walls and pans down.

Welles's *Othello* caused a sensation at the 1952 Cannes festival, earning the Palme d'Or, its grand prize; his command of filmic language was unmistakably in evidence. Welles himself, though happy with the film, was dissatisfied with his grasp of the character, preferring the 1951 stage performances he gave in London (Thomson 313). At the same time, Olivier increasingly concentrated on the stage, even joining the Shakespeare Memorial Theatre at Stratford-upon-Avon for the 1955 season. He did not abandon the notion of Shakespearean film or even the idea of competing with Welles: he tried unsuccessfully to finance a filmed *Macbeth*, a play which constituted one of the triumphs of the Stratford season. When he did realize his next Shakespearean project, though, the resulting film marked a retreat to the stage. His *Richard III* is not only an exercise in sheer theatricality, but a celebration of it. Along with the rejection of the stage in *Henry V*, Olivier had offered viewers an appreciation of its history, starting with the reconstructed Globe and then moving to realizations of nineteenth-century style sets, before the grand assertions of naturalistic filmmaking for the exterior battle shots. No stage could contain the charge of the French cavalry across "the vasty fields of France," but theatricality serves as a useful foil nevertheless. It is appropriate, then, that Hal's own foil, Falstaff, is played by a beloved stage figure: George Robey, a music-hall veteran who had specialized in historical sendups (Oliver Cromwell in particular) and then triumphed in legitimate theater as Falstaff in productions of *Henry IV, Part One*. For *Richard III* Olivier invokes stage history from the very beginning—the credits list the play's adaptors over the centuries, including David Garrick and Colley Cibber—and provides, in the coronation of Richard's brother Edward, the kind of historical tableau much beloved by nineteenth-century actor-managers. Olivier's Richard does not hesitate to address the camera directly, reinforcing a sense of the theatrical rather than the cinematic. Even the casting pays homage to the stage, with John Gielgud as Clarence and Ralph Richardson as Buckingham, while Roger Furse's designs are far more stylized than those for *Hamlet*. The Battle of Bosworth Field is done with naturalistic exterior shots, but generally repeats what Olivier had done stylistically with Agincourt in the earlier film. Olivier is already becoming English stage history; his *Richard III* is first and foremost a record of his performance in the role. As such, and as Branagh would dramatize later, it would define for generations "real" Shakespearean acting. For the 1965 *Othello* (see chapter three), Olivier would not be involved behind the camera. Instead, he would be the theatrical subject of a film documentary.

Even so, in appearing as Othello, there remained elements of rivalry with Welles. While preparing his 1951 stage production, Welles had visited Olivier and Vivien Leigh to discuss the play. Welles's film Iago, as played by MacLiammóir, is sexually impotent; he attacks Othello out of bitterness and envy, but also out of unacknowledged desire for him. Olivier had worked on a similar interpretation as Iago in an unsuccessful 1938 production. Welles then went on to observe that Olivier himself shouldn't attempt the leading role in the play: the deep voice was lacking (Thomson 313). Could Welles have also been suggesting something about Olivier's own power to convey the virility that Iago envied? As we have seen, Olivier's performance wanted to answer unequivocally any doubts about voice, sensuality, or acting.

In contrast, Welles was dogged with questions on all those points as his career progressed. Even his plans to revisit the Mercury *Julius Caesar* were trumped by his old colleague and rival, John Houseman, and his production for MGM (see chapter seven). As for his debate with Olivier, Welles did have the last filmic word in *Chimes at Midnight*, which takes an insistently unheroic view of the future Henry V as it celebrates young Hal's supposed foil, Falstaff. In Wellesian fashion, the film builds upon earlier work: just as the film *Macbeth* shared themes with the "voodoo" production, *Chimes at Midnight* revisits material used in the first part of *Five Kings*. But much more is going on, even as much less of the Shakespearean material is used. *Five Kings* had kept its focus on Hal and followed his career through the victory at Agincourt and the courtship of Katherine. *Chimes* never really leaves Falstaff, played by Welles himself, until Hal, the new King Henry, rejects him and we see the old man's subsequent death.

Falstaff's story, Welles asserts, is more important to Shakespeare than Hal's. The film does not flirt with the absurd, as does Tom Stoppard's play and film of *Rosencrantz and Guildenstern Are Dead*, by forcing minor characters into central roles; Welles uses Shakespeare's own scenes and language to make his case. Stage history supports it, too: *Henry IV, Part One* was, until the latter part of the twentieth century, almost always valued for the roles of Hotspur and Falstaff. When there were two starring performers in a company, such as Olivier and Ralph Richardson at the Old Vic in 1946, they split these roles. Hotspur represents a medieval conception of honor (even if he is notably unchivalrous with his wife, also named Kate) which is waning fast; Falstaff, in such a view, is Harry Percy's carnivalesque inversion and double, seeking the privileges of honor without doing anything to earn them. With Hotspur's scenes drastically reduced, Welles's Falstaff can take on a greater significance. That significance has changed, as well as increased, in Welles's interpretation. Troubling elements of Falstaff's character, such as his selfish exploitation of associates and subordinates, virtually disappear. Perhaps, in identifying so strongly with the role, Welles simply did not see them as vices or even flaws. What remains is the vital, celebratory aspect of Falstaff and what he comes to represent, all of which is exploited and abandoned by Prince Hal (played by Keith Baxter; see Figure 7), as Welles explained in an interview given shortly after the film's release:

> Falstaff is a man defending a force—the old England—which is going down. What is difficult about Falstaff, I believe, is that he is the greatest conception of a good man, the most completely good man, in all drama. . . . The film was not intended as a lament for Falstaff, but for the death of Merrie England. Merrie England as a conception, a myth, which has been very real to the English-speaking world, and is to some extent expressed in other countries of the Medieval epoch: the age of chivalry, of simplicity, of Maytime and all that. It is more than Falstaff who is dying. It's the old England, dying and betrayed. (qtd. in Lyons 261–62)

In early stages of development, that betrayal was to have been marked by the assassination of Richard II (Lyons 264), after Hal's father has seized the throne. Welles eventually decided that the new political climate could be communicated sufficiently through a voiceover from Holinshed's *Chronicles*, read by Ralph Richardson, and the depiction of Henry IV, played with icy disdain by John Gielgud. A new breed has taken over, as the old order passes: in that interview, Juan Cobos and

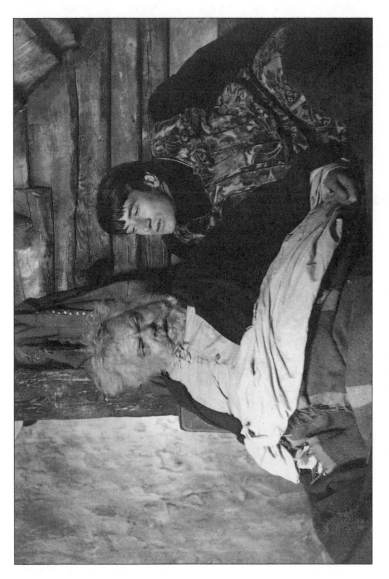

FIGURE 7. Orson Welles as Falstaff, the "most completely good man," and Keith Baxter as Prince Hal, his friend and betrayer, in Welles's *Chimes at Midnight* (1966). Photo courtesy of Jerry Ohlinger's Movie Material.

Miguel Rubio observed to Welles that he had presented the same story, in effect, in *The Magnificent Ambersons.*

He also presents a very different story from the one Olivier had told. Both Olivier's *Henry V* and Welles's *Chimes at Midnight* pivot on a battle, but the presentation of warfare contrasts sharply. Olivier captures the color and pageantry of a medieval tournament, beginning with a French nobleman being lowered by a winch onto his horse amid bright banners. A few, more realistic elements do emerge. The mud of Agincourt appears briefly; the technological importance of the English longbow is presented (something Shakespeare avoids); atrocities visited upon noncombatants by the French are depicted (although Shakespeare highlights the sav-ageries committed on both sides). Despite all this, the myth of Merrie England is alive and well in the presentation of English soldiers surpris-ing French horsemen by dropping from tree branches like Robin Hood's men. Finally, the battle in Olivier's presentation is decided by one-on-one combat between the English king and the Constable of France. Henry loses his sword, but with his armored fist knocks the Constable off his horse. There is no need for the king to ask the French herald if he comes again to inquire for ransom or whether the English have actually won: "I tell thee, truly, / I know not if the day be ours or no" (*Henry V* 4.7.83–84). Olivier's Henry already knows, when the joust is over, that the battle and the war are won. Welles, in his presentation of the Battle of Shrewsbury from *Henry IV, Part One*, begins with a brief visual quotation from Olivier, as knights are lowered by ropes onto their saddled horses. But there are no bright colors in Welles's black-and-white film; there is no bright music to match William Walton's score for Olivier. Throughout the battle, we hear trumpet, drum, and unearthly singing constantly over-whelmed by physical sounds of war (Lyons 142). One of the knights is Hotspur himself. He vows that he and Hal will "Meet, and ne'er part til one drop down a corse" (4.1.122) and his words become a dire prophecy not only for himself but for all the warriors descending from branches and scaffolds. Or nearly all, since Falstaff's vast weight leads to his taking an ignominious tumble to the ground; later, he plays dead—"counterfeits" is his term—in order to escape death that day.

Bridget Gellert Lyons has sagely connected Welles's battle sequence with "the changed perspective of the 1960s, when antiwar feeling and representations of all war as absurd were common" (14). It is important to note that Welles is not debunking Olivier exclusively here, just as it is important to note that Olivier truly believed his presentation of Henry's "Famous Victories" could inspire his fellow citizens in the cause of their nation's survival. But Welles is also blaming Olivier for promoting a false view of war and of Shakespeare. He provides a corrective both wordlessly and with Shakespeare's language. Five minutes of film time pass between Hotspur's vow and Hal's reproach to Falstaff: "What, stand'st thou idle here?" (5.3.39). In that time the only words we hear are the combatants' battle cries. The sights, presented by over two hundred separate cuts, eloquently communicate the senseless horrors of war. There is no sense of direction, no clear sense of whose soldiers these are. Welles provides brief glimpses of hand-to-hand combat, but these encounters are anything but chivalrous and they result not in victory but in agony. Shakespeare does provide a one-on-one fight between Hal and Hotspur, but Welles presents the prince's survival as a matter of luck, not Providence—not even honor.

Welles's Falstaff, lying nearby, cannot continue to counterfeit convincingly as his labored breath is visible in the chilly air. Hal is affronted by the imposture and leaves. In this version, though, Falstaff's extravagant claim to have killed Hotspur is given at least partial credence by Henry IV, who still distrusts his son. Falstaff's greedy appetite for life and for the pleasures that status affords—"I look to be either earl or duke, I assure you" (adapted from 5.5.142–43)—turns the prince completely against him. Weaving passages together from all the plays featuring Falstaff, then, Welles makes the old knight a tragic figure. He would never quite abandon his hopes of filming *King Lear* (in 1953, he had collaborated with director Peter Brook in a controversial television production), but likely realized that the tragedy of Falstaff, more sinned against than sinning, might be as close as he could get to the stormy heath on film (Howard 132).

When Kenneth Branagh chose a model for his career as Shakespearean director, he understandably followed the celebrated and successful Olivier instead of the constantly frustrated Welles, always scrambling for cash. He acknowledged his indebtedness to Olivier in *Henry V* from the start, expressing the terms of the interrelation of the two film versions in this way:

> Although Olivier's film had been welcomed and celebrated as part of the war effort, its seeming nationalistic and militaristic emphases had created a great deal of suspicion and doubt about the value of *Henry V* for a late twentieth-century audience. (Branagh 1989, 9)

Branagh's "post-Vietnam," "post-Falklands" adaptation deliberately enters into debate with Olivier's on a number of levels (see Kliman 1989), although here he concedes that many of the differences are matters of emphasis and even, as Branagh says, of "seeming." The terms of conversation include a strong element of personal ambition—not only the king's, but Olivier's and Branagh's own. Branagh has recalled how the gradual allaying of his "personal paranoia about having to 'prove myself' as an actor . . . helped [his] playing the role immeasurably over the long months of the Stratford season," in which he first played the role for the Royal Shakespeare Company (Jackson and Smallwood, 102). But that same resolve to prove oneself is clearly a central component of Branagh's conception of the role, and a strong factor in his directorial debut with the film version.

The terms of debate include the kind of realism with which war is represented, and here Branagh uses Welles against Olivier. Olivier's movement to naturalistic cinema still idealizes the conditions of battle, especially the medieval variety; Branagh's slide into the mud also embraces looting the fallen and combat that is not one-on-one. As in *Chimes at Midnight*, the battle lines dissolve during the course of the battle: medieval warfare, bereft of any chivalric ideal, quickly degenerates into savagery. There is, however, a tension between the dehumanizing effects of war—as captured by Welles—and the use of humanizing closeups by Branagh. We see the faces of the English warriors registering fear at the advance of the French cavalry; Branagh makes sure that we know who each of these characters is by the time we get to these effective reaction shots. In Welles, even Falstaff's humanity is lost for a time in the chaos, as he appears something of a tank-like figure in his rotund armor. The parallel in Branagh's film is Brian Blessed's Exeter, yet another surrogate father for Henry. Exeter, by contrast, keeps his dignity and something of his humanity even as he displays savage glee in smashing his opponents. The battle's frame of reference reassumes its bearings shortly after the king is informed, here, that the English have indeed won. In part, this affirms that there was a clear victory. But Branagh also needs his audience to have a sense of clear sides in the battle in order to make his most direct reply to Olivier. In the earlier film of *Henry V*, the actual battle is preceded by the impressively long single-take shot of the cavalry charge; the duration of the shot and the quickening pulse of William Walton's score add suspense and excitement. In Branagh's rebuttal, the long single-take shot follows the battle and shows the aftermath of the mud-drenched, bloody exchange. Henry himself carries the tavern boy, killed behind the lines, across the length of the battlefield; as he slowly trudges, we see some of the human costs—connected to characters known and unknown—of Harry's military campaign. Olivier's shot follows the galloping horses from right to left, while Branagh's reverses direction. King Henry wins, but the fruits of victory are, for now, anything but sweet.

Following Welles, Branagh is more overtly concerned with the costs of this enterprise than Olivier is: what is lost; who is, indeed, sacrificed. Welles describes Hal as a character "who must betray the good man [i.e. Falstaff] in order to become a hero, a famous English hero. The terrible price of power which the Prince has to pay" (Lyons 262). Branagh takes the opportunity to explore the payments at some length. We see, through the king's eyes, the execution of Bardolph for petty—if sacrilegious— looting, and Branagh's casting of the popular situation comedy actor Richard Briers in the role adds for English viewers (and many PBS fans) a poignance to Bardolph's passing which can rival that provided by Olivier's use of George Robey as Falstaff. Later, as the Duke of Burgundy describes the effects of war upon France, we visually recall, with Branagh's Henry, all those who have been lost along the way to victory. Not only does York, the slain leader of the vanguard, appear in flashback as part of Henry's "sacrifices" (as the French king similarly recalls the fallen Constable), but so does the conspirator Scroop, along with Bardolph, Falstaff, Nym, Mistress Quickly, and again the tavern boy.

Branagh's own account of what the king feels at the end of the scene at the Field of the Dead spells out the hollowness and culpability he intended to convey:

> We cut close on his blood-stained and exhausted face, the dreadful price they have all had to pay for this so-called victory clearly etched into his whole being. His head drops as if in shame. (Branagh 1989, 114)

But, as Donald Hedrick has observed (50–53), Henry's guilt has already been washed clean in the mud of the land he has conquered; he has suffered along with his troops, has apparently paid more than his share of "the dreadful price" to which Branagh refers. Henry grieves at Bardolph's death, even as he approves it; after his anguished prayer before the battle at Agincourt, we are told in the screenplay, "he has done and felt all he can" (Branagh 1989, 93). At first, Patrick Doyle's music makes an intentionally ironic comment on the glories to be found on the battlefield, especially in contrast to Walton's more martial score. Its last strains carry into the next scene, however, and seem far less ironic in the context of the state room in which both peace and marriage will be shrewdly but good-naturedly negotiated. By the same token, Branagh's inclusion of the full epilogue which points out the collapse of the new Anglo-French union fails to deliver the bitter impact that it can. Members of the audience can fail altogether to absorb the import of the words; for others, Derek Jacobi's world- and war-weary delivery of those last lines as Chorus transform the "ironies of the Epilogue [to] those of mortality and mutability, not social critique" (Donaldson 1991, 63). Branagh's reassessment of Henry's character and policies is not as radically skeptical in impact as he might have intended.

Branagh's choices of emphasis and inclusion often do, however, challenge Olivier's. Where the earlier film makes the king's extant drinking companions only occasionally more than comic caricatures, Branagh's version supplies a grittily realistic look at the tavern world, at the violence and rivalry that always lurked beneath its genial surface, and at the inescapable effects of its excesses. But this exposé is literally softened in the flashback scenes featuring Falstaff, which are shot in a sentimentally hazy and golden light, and figuratively softened by the emphasis on age's debilitating visitations on Bardolph, Nym, and Pistol. As a consequence of this strategy, however, nearly all the comic scenes smack more of pathos than humor. Robert Stephens's Pistol never succeeds, however briefly, in persuading anyone (much less Fluellen) of his martial abilities. As lone survivor of the demimonde, he delivers his last soliloquy on the battlefield, grieving and bitter by turns—not waggishly defiant, as was Robert Newton in Olivier's film, after being comically chastised by Fluellen. Welles's sense of Falstaff as embodying the myth of Merrie Olde England becomes Branagh's view of the tavern world. Following Welles, Branagh places special emphasis on Shakespeare's foreshadowing of Hal's eventual rejection of Falstaff: "Banish plump Jack and banish all the world" says the old knight in *Henry IV, Part One*; Hal's reply is "I do. I will" (2.4.481). In the playtext (and in Welles) the two characters are playing roles. Falstaff is speaking in the person of Hal, who assumes the role of his severe father. In Branagh, though, there is no such mediation, so Branagh's Hal refuses to answer Falstaff aloud and we hear the reply only in voice-over. Falstaff, as played by Robbie Coltrane, understands anyway. "We have heard the chimes at midnight" (addressed to Shallow in *Henry IV, Part Two*) is now part of Falstaff's shocked, pleading response to Hal's silent warning. As Welles had observed, "the thing that most concerns me about the film and my own performance is that I am not as funny as I expected to be. That was part of what preoccupied me all through the shooting: the more I studied the part, the less funny he seemed to be" (Lyons 261). Branagh quietly pays homage to Welles in his presentation of Falstaff as a doomed figure.

After Branagh's Henry successfully deals with the traitors (a scene that Olivier's film avoids), the script observes that "[t]his latest test has been passed with flying colours . . . but at a great personal cost, which we can read on the strained features." When he is confronted with Bardolph's disobedience, we are meant to see that

> a public trial of strength is provided for the King. Watched by his sodden soldiers, he must enforce his decree that any form of theft or pillage of the French countryside will be punished by death. Any favouritism or sentiment shown here will be disastrous for discipline amongst these poor soldiers. The cost to the King is enormous as he gives the nod to Exeter. . . . (Branagh 1989, 71)

Of course, the cost to Bardolph is considerable too, but our focus is on Henry's response to this and all other "challenges." Welles's fatalism and skepticism are kept at bay: a more positive attitude must be maintained in the character, the production, and behind the scenes as well.

Ever since Branagh presented his film version of *Henry V*, it seemed likely that he would produce a *Hamlet* for the screen. The parallels with Laurence Olivier's film *Henry V* were too strong not to suggest a comparable future career. Yet one of the tasks that Branagh has set for himself in his own career is to bring himself and other actors out from under Olivier's shadow. *A Midwinter's Tale* (titled *In the Bleak Midwinter* in U.K. release), the film Branagh made just before his *Hamlet*, depicts a stage production of Shakespeare's play. It also continues Branagh's engagement with Olivier's work, career, and enduring presence in British theater and film. The central character is Joe (Michael Maloney), a long-suffering and long-out-of-work actor, who decides to renew his dramatic vocation by staging (and, actor-manager-style, starring in) a production of *Hamlet* in his hometown, the village of Hope. As he explains this slightly mad scheme to his agent—from whom he's asking seed money and emotional approval—he finds Olivier a useful, if at times humiliating, name to conjure with:

If everything had gone according to Laurence Olivier's book I would have known triumph, disappointment and married a beautiful woman. Instead I've known tedium, humiliation and got shacked up with the psycho from hell. (Branagh 1995, 2)

Joe, of course, conveniently forgets the tedium and humiliation that Olivier regularly faced and may also rather callously glance at the illness that destroyed Vivien Leigh's life (Edwards 214–15). At the same time, Joe himself is in a strongly depressed state. The point is not the inaccuracy of Joe's account but the paradoxical necessity and impossibility (which Leigh faced, as well) of matching the perceived triumphalism of Olivier's career.

Joe has lots of company in being burdened by Olivier's example. During auditions, one hapless actor is incapable of doing Richard III in any way other than cabaret Olivier:

CLOSE-UP *on the contorted face of a young actor in hunch-back mode giving the full dalek-ian version of Olivier's Richard III.*
          YOUNG ACTOR:
     "Now is the winter of our discontent
     Made glorious summer by this son of York."
          JOE (*rushing to the actor, all concern*):
     I don't feel you've made it quite your own, you know
     . . . Listen, let's just drop the voice, silly idea I know, and drop
     the hunch and the gestures OK?
          YOUNG ACTOR (*eager*):
     OK. Fine.
Joe goes back to his desk.
          JOE:
     Then let's just see what happens. Whenever you want, in your
     own time.
After great loosening-up preparations, he does it exactly the same way.
(Branagh 1995, 7)

The actor is physically weighed down by Olivier's precedent. The constraints, if felt at all, seem utterly natural to the actor, who declares that "something really freed up" in his second attempt. Later in the proceedings, "a fervent young Scotsman"—played by Branagh's longtime film composer Patrick Doyle—retains an almost impenetrable Glaswegian delivery, but still tries "to impersonate Olivier's hunchback" (11). As Joe and Branagh try to shake loose the fetters of Sir Laurence's example, they reject these actors from the developing ensemble.

Visually, however, Joe's production and the film overall owe quite a bit to Olivier. While Branagh prepared for his own, widescreen, color version of the play, he explored aspects of Olivier's film on a decidedly smaller scale in the black and white of *Midwinter*. The site of the production, a neglected village church, allows Branagh to provide visual echoes of Olivier's Elsinore: there are a number of shots through archways, usually involving the actress playing Ophelia and reminiscent of Olivier's constant framing of that character's entrances and exits. The treatment of the castle as a psychological map to the protagonist's mind in Olivier's film (Jorgens 210; Donaldson 1990, 31–48) finds a witty analogue in Branagh's use of the space just in front of the altar as Joe's office, his inner sanctum. Joe's designer, a chronically procrastinating (Hamlet-like?) woman named Fadge, presents a concept strongly reminiscent of some of Roger Furse's work for Olivier. The battlements of Olivier's Elsinore are shrouded in fog; the Ghost appears out of an indistinct mist. Fadge's design is more immediately inspired by a read-through during which the company eventually produces a cloud of cigarette smoke, but the effect in the opening scene is similar to that in Olivier's film.

The direct impact of Olivier's version upon both Joe and Branagh, though, is effectively displaced in Joe's account of what the play means to him, in the program notes for the premiere screenings of Branagh's *Hamlet*, and in the introduction to Branagh's published screenplay for it. While Joe attests to the power of the first production he ever saw, he never lets us know which production it was or even whether it was on stage or film. A slightly more direct, if also more breathless, version of Joe's rationale appears in the notes Branagh wrote for the program brochure distributed for *Hamlet* in first-run theaters. In those notes, Branagh declares the film to be "the passionate expression of a dream" that has gripped him "since first watching *Hamlet* on British television" at the age of eleven. He remembers being struck by

> Sex, violence, swordfights, the ghost of a dead father, a journey into madness, the politics of a country and a family at war—a quite extraordinary story. For me, *Hamlet* still produces the feeling of excitement that overwhelmed me all those years ago, when I first saw the play. (Branagh 1996a, 4)

If this description of *Hamlet* sounds vaguely familiar even to those who have not read this brochure and who have not seen *Midwinter*, it may be because something very similar has been said as an introduction to Olivier's film version. Joan Plowright—Olivier's third wife and frequent co-star—appears as a schoolteacher about to screen the earlier film in the Arnold Schwarzenegger feature, *Last Action Hero* (1994). Before showing the sequence in which Claudius tries to repent and Hamlet fails to exact revenge, Plowright's character tries to get her students' attention:

> Treachery, conspiracy, sex, swordfights, madness, ghosts—and in the end, everybody dies. Shakespeare's *Hamlet* couldn't be more exciting. And though it may seem that he is incapable of taking any action, he is in fact one of the first action heroes. (transcribed from the soundtrack)

Danny, the young hero of the film, gives the clip a try, despite the datedness of the acting style and the black-and-white film. He is soon exasperated by this Hamlet's inaction and fantasizes about a film production of the play featuring his favorite character, Jack Slater, played by Schwarzenegger. In the imaginary trailer, Jack-Hamlet hurls Claudius out of a stained-glass window, fires a revolver at Polonius (the actor here made up to resemble Felix Aylmer in Olivier's film), uses semi-automatic weapons on the guards, and eventually blows Elsinore—looking much as it did in Furse's design—to smithereens (Mallin 127–30).

Barnardo's opening salvos with a machine-gun in Joe's production in *Midwinter* may owe a debt to *Last Action Hero*; certainly Branagh's own *Hamlet*, with its assertive and sexually active hero, attempts to do better than Olivier's version in holding the attention of audience members who prefer Schwarzenegger to Shakespeare. At Danny's age, Branagh too was skeptical toward all the literary fuss: he thought "Shakespeare was for swots" (Branagh 1996b, xi). What helped persuade him otherwise was going, still at fifteen, to see Derek Jacobi in an Oxford production of the play. He knew Jacobi primarily as a television actor, from the serialization of *I, Claudius*, and his interest led to Branagh's first "independent" visit to a theater. At least in retrospect, the play changed Branagh's life:

> In the production and in Jacobi's performance I had been taken on an emotional rollercoaster. It made me reflect on my relationships with my parents, the prospects of an adolescent love affair. (1996b, xii)

The memory of that production informs more in *A Midwinter's Tale* than Joe's recollections of his first *Hamlet*: it also informs his approach as a director. Time and again, Joe asks his fellow actors to connect the play with their own lives. For his part, Joe regularly blurs the boundaries between the play and his life, as well as the boundaries between his career and Olivier's. During a serious shortfall of ready cash, Joe takes Hamlet's early outcry as his own: "O God, God / How weary, stale, flat, and unprofitable / Seem to me all the uses of this world!" (1.2.132–34). Branagh intends the scene to be unreadable initially: the screenplay indicates that this "seems like another rehearsal scene," but at this point Branagh, like Prince Hamlet, seeks authenticity: he "know[s] not 'seems'" (1.2.76). Joe is truly losing his fight against depression. Molly, his sister, tries to kid him out of it: "That's not bad, Sir Laurence." The Olivier reference sparks a sardonic reply: "Well, understand how he feels, Vivien" (Branagh 1995, 64).

Though Joe eventually stages a version with more or less standard cuts, he insists on starting the rehearsal period with a reading of the full text. Even the edited version that follows suggests the sometimes dizzying complexity of the "full text" version of Branagh's own *Hamlet*: a conflation of what appears in all the earliest printed versions of the play. Not only do we have Rosencrantz and Guildenstern (dispatched altogether by Olivier and Alan Dent, his text editor, before the action ever starts) played by a single actor, we also have Reynaldo's scene with Polonius. Tom, the actor appearing as Reynaldo and in several other roles, adopts a somewhat strange take on the character: that he's "foxy," since his name comes from the French folk figure Reynard, the Fox. Some of this survives in how Branagh directed Gerard Depardieu in the same role. Most remarkably, Joe's abridged version nevertheless highlights Fortinbras. We hear Tom (played by Nicholas Farrell) assume a Norwegian accent as Fortinbras orders the Captain to "greet the Danish king" (4.4.1); we also hear, at the end of nearly every run-through and of the opening night triumph, his final command, "Go, bid the soldiers shoot." An even stronger emphasis on the oft-deleted role in Branagh's *Hamlet* has led Robert Willson, Jr., with tongue-in-cheek, to advocate retitling the film *The Revenge of Fortinbras* (Willson 1997, 7). The exchange with the Captain in itself suggests that some version of the "How all occasions do inform against me" soliloquy will survive Joe's editing. Sure enough, we find Joe delivering part of it to a rapt audience during the first performance:

> What is a man,
> If his chief good and market of his time
> Be but to sleep and feed? A beast, no more
> (Branagh 1995, 109; 4.4.33–35)

Branagh's *Hamlet* makes the speech a kind of turning point—and a convenient semi-climax to allow for an intermission break—by delivering it as a slightly ironized analogue to Olivier's St. Crispin Day speech in the film of *Henry V.* In both excerpts, the camera pulls back farther and farther in order to reveal the context—the English troops closely attending the King's rallying speech, the Norwegian troops oblivious to Hamlet's words—and to allow for a louder delivery and grander gestures. The published screenplay indicates that Branagh intended a contrast between the personal importance (and potential cost) of such resolve and its insignificance in the larger scheme of things:

> *HAMLET raises his arms with a great cry—*
> HAMLET (*continuing*)
> My thoughts be bloody or be nothing worth.
> *The huge scream of resolution hangs in the air as we pull further back and see the now tiny figure in the vast landscape, the music reaches its climax, and we fade to black.* (Branagh 1996b, 122)

The sense of climax is increased not only by the rapidity of Branagh's delivery, but also by the rate at which the camera pulls back and up. The overall pace of the film is brisk (there are all those words to get through, after all)—and a similarly swift approach characterizes the majority of scenes, whether comic or no, in *Midwinter.*

Branagh makes much of a theatrical community's ability to serve as a surrogate family. When Joe is offered a lucrative film role just before the play's opening, he tries to rationalize cancelling the run: "It's Christmas Eve; for Christ's sake, you should all be with your families." Nina, the actress playing Ophelia, is having none of it:

> We're with our family. That's what actors do. That's what people do in what's left of Hope. They hang on, they stick it out. (Branagh 1995, 96)

Olivier's *Hamlet* boasted something of an ensemble, since several of its actors had appeared in *Henry V.* Felix Aylmer, its Polonius, was the previous film's Archbishop of Canterbury; Esmond Knight, here Barnardo, had been the Welsh captain, Fluellen; Niall MacGinnis, the sea captain who brings news of Hamlet to Horatio, had been the Irish captain, Macmorris; Harcourt Williams, the First Player that Hamlet addresses, was Olivier's hapless French king. Welles, too, was intrigued by the notion of acting companies. Several veterans of the Mercury Theater, which he founded with John Houseman, performed in his radio and film productions. Jeanette Nolan, his Lady Macbeth, had worked with him on the "March of Time" and "Suspense" broadcasts; his Iago, Micheál MacLiammóir, had helped to hire the teenaged Welles as an actor for Ireland's Dublin Gate Theatre in 1931 (and appeared as Edgar in the television *King Lear*). Similarly, Branagh has tried to sustain a community based upon shared theatrical and cinematic experience, both from within his Renaissance Theatre company and from outside. Patrick Doyle has surpassed the number of Shakespearean filmscores that William Walton composed for Olivier. Branagh's stage debut in *Henry V* introduced him to his film's Exeter, Brian Blessed—who later appeared, a bit unconvincingly, as Antonio in *Much Ado About Nothing* and also, very appropriately, as Old Hamlet. *A Midwinter's Tale* indeed suggests a repertoire company preparing not only a stage *Hamlet* but the subsequent filmed one as well. Michael Maloney, Joe/Hamlet, previously appeared as the Dauphin in *Henry V* and becomes Laertes to make room for Branagh's own Hamlet. Nicholas Farrell, Tom/Laertes in *Midwinter*, shifts to Horatio. Richard Briers, Wakefield/Claudius, is Polonius in the later film; a stalwart of Branagh's stage company, he also made film appearances as Bardolph in *Henry V* and Leonato in *Much Ado*. When Branagh finds theatrical father-figures, he sticks with them: Jacobi, the Chorus for *Henry V* and the later film's Claudius, also directed Branagh for a stage production of *Hamlet*.

The conflation of theatrical and biological families (something that Emma Thompson experienced and to which Branagh paid tribute in casting her mother, Phyllida Law, in *Peter's Friends* and in *Much Ado About Nothing*) culminates in the company of players that visits Elsinore in Branagh's *Hamlet*. Charlton Heston appears as the First Player, here a biological paterfamilias of the troupe; Heston's actor-manager on tour is presented as an Americanized and far more able version of Mr. Crummles, the character in Charles Dickens's *Nicholas Nickleby* who leads a family-based theatrical company performing *Romeo and Juliet*. The First Player's daughter, apparently, plays the younger female roles, so Branagh's prince rather incongruously delivers the lines about a boy player's voice change to her:

Then to the child actress, whom he picks up in his arms.
>   HAMLET (*continuing*)
>   What, my young lady and mistress,
> *He checks out her footwear.*
>   HAMLET (*continuing*)
>   By'r Lady, your ladyship is nearer heaven than when I saw you
>   last by the altitude of a chopine. Pray God your voice, like a
>   piece of uncurrent gold, be not cracked within the ring.
>   (Branagh 1996b, 66–67; 2.2.424–28)

The Victorian setting of the film precludes any consideration of how gender roles may be destabilized by the theatrical convention of boy players. Olivier's *Hamlet*—like his *Henry V*—insists on retaining the convention. It survives in *Midwinter* only through a cross-gendered Gertrude and through Joe's sister Molly, who briefly appears in her brother's stead as Hamlet (see Buhler 1997, 50–51).

There remain a few more acknowledgments of Olivier's *Hamlet* along the way in Branagh's own film version: for example, the bleached hair and the restlessly moving camera. Elements borrowed from *Richard III* are also evident. The brilliant color and pageantry, especially in the entrance of Claudius and Gertrude with the entire court as a royal wedding party, recall the earlier film's opening sequence. The carefully cultivated—and usually restrained—"star-studded" cast similarly echoes Olivier's attempt to challenge himself with some of his theatrical peers: along with the aforementioned Jacobi and Depardieu, we see Billy Crystal and Robin Williams in comic roles (although Williams's Osric takes on untraditional seriousness), and Julie Christie as Gertrude. Welles, though, almost literally haunts Branagh's *Hamlet* in the person of Brian Blessed. A monumental statue of Old Hamlet comes to life, like the Commendatore in Mozart's *Don Giovanni*, before Horatio and the guards. The image of a massive figure, in armor, recalls Blessed as Exeter in *Henry V* and that figure's suggestion of the ponderous presence of Welles's Falstaff at Shrewsbury. Despite its "great mass," the statue swoops over the amazed bystanders and then away from them, as we see when the camera first adopts the Ghost's point of view (Branagh 1996b, 5–6). Bars and other barriers, a constant visual motif in Welles's *Othello*, regularly appear in connection with the Ghost and his domain, the "undiscovered country" (as Hamlet describes it in his most famous soliloquy) of death: Hamlet and his comrades look through the bars of a castle gate when the

Ghost beckons the prince to follow him; later, Ophelia is locked away from her father's corpse after Polonius is slain by Hamlet.

Time and again, this ghostly vision imposes its view of things upon the audience and ultimately upon young Hamlet. When Branagh's prince is finally confronted by his father's spirit, the camera initially reassumes the Ghost's perspective but then quickly cuts to the Ghost's eyes, described in the published screenplay as "piercing blue" and a strangely pale color (supplied by contact lenses) on-screen. The eyes and words shape Hamlet's imagination, as in Olivier's version: we see the prince's own vision of Old Hamlet's death. In an earlier scene, he tells Horatio: "My father, methinks I see my father." When a startled Horatio asks where, he replies: "In my mind's eye" (1.2.184–85). It is the mind's eye which creates and contemplates what he believes his father desires him to see. The audience follows suit, as we have already: when the Ghost fears that the coming morn will call him away before he can deliver his message, he turns directly toward the camera. "Brief let me be," he insists (1.5.59) and Blessed's voice races us through Old Hamlet's account, commenting on the otherwise silent version the screen offers. His judgment is also delivered directly to us: "O, horrible, O, horrible, most horrible!" (1.5.80). Then quick cuts move back and forth between Blessed's blue eyes and Branagh's, in extreme closeup. The capacity for vision is physically exchanged.

Blessed's breath, visible in the cold night air, drifts past his helmet. There is a suggestion that this Ghost is too, too solid to be an emissary from the next world, that it is counterfeiting and about to be found out, much like Welles's Falstaff. But no, young Hamlet reaches for his father's armored hand and the Ghost evaporates like its wintry breath. When the Ghost returns, however, its vision will have triumphed—and Welles's vision will assert itself. After Polonius's death, Hamlet continues to chide Gertrude for her marriage with Claudius. As in the playtext and in other versions, Old Hamlet interrupts his son's verbal assault. Following the stage direction given in the First Quarto, Branagh's Ghost appears—while in the intimate space of Gertrude's private chamber—in his dressing gown. But the costume for Blessed looks more like a shroud, or like the monastic robes assumed by Falstaff and company for the Gad's Hill robbery in *Chimes at Midnight*. When we see the Ghost's weary eyes in that setting, we discover that the walls of Gertrude's chamber have been painted the same pale shade of blue. At the scene's conclusion, Hamlet drags the body of Polonius away, leaving a vast, dark pool of blood. The shot is taken from a very low angle, with the blood foremost and the sobbing Gertrude behind it. This *Kane*-like shot is positioned to reveal the unearthly blue once more.

One more visual recollection of Welles should be noted. When Fortinbras makes his conquest of Elsinore, his assaulting army smashes all the windows in the great hall—a room dominated by mirrors. Into one of these mirrors, and indeed through it, Branagh delivers his version of the "To be or not to be" speech not only to himself in soliloquy and to us, but also to Claudius and Polonius who are keeping watch on him. After Hamlet realizes that Ophelia is a party to this surveillance, he presses her face against the one-way glass. The subsequent allusion to *The Lady from Shanghai*, when the windows are shattered, indicates that Ophelia, like the title character in Welles's film, has been caught up in a deceit and destroyed by it. This scene is Branagh's second borrowing from that particular film. His wry tribute to film noir, *Dead Again* (1991), boasts several homages to Welles, including a *Citizen Kane*-style interview with an aging friend of the objects of a detective's inquiries. The outlandish conclusion involves giant, scissors-shaped "sculptures"—all of which are polished to a bright, mirror-like sheen. In Branagh's *Hamlet*, all of Elsinore has been a hall of mirrors, one apparently of Old Hamlet's making. Young Fortinbras revenges his father's death and defeat at Old Hamlet's hand by breaking all the illusions of his reign and his dynasty. Branagh suggests that Hamlet is a faithful son to a possibly faithless father. The film's last image is not of Young Hamlet in state (here, too, Branagh subverts his predecessors by letting us face the dead prince); it is of the monumental statue being broken to pieces by Fortinbras's men. The Wellesian head hits the ground, to "obliterate the name HAMLET. For ever. As we . . . fade to black" (Branagh 1996b, 173). The old story is told once more, about the old order passing, but this time with little regret.

Branagh has attempted to establish a new order, to revive the actor-manager traditions, to reconcile high art with popular, mass-market audiences. Each attempt to break the mold has, both wittingly and unwittingly, reinscribed the past. Olivier, like Welles, had incredible difficulties in financing his Shakespeare films. *Richard III*, while it earned respect, was a box-office disappointment; its lasting impact on actors and audiences came in classrooms, such as the one presided over by Joan Plowright in *Last Action Hero*. Welles, too, had planned to reach a universal audience on the screen, on the airwaves, on the stage, and even on the page. *Everybody's Shakespeare* was a series of edited playtexts for which a youthful Welles supplied illustrations and a single introductory essay, "On Staging Shakespeare and Shakespeare's Stage," to be reprinted with each volume. Once Welles achieved fame, the series was retitled *The Mercury Shakespeare*, after his theatrical company, and enjoyed a fairly wide readership. In his essay, Welles counsels would-be actors to "give Shakespeare a chance" and simply trust the lines, even though these versions are already cut and though Welles himself would grandly rearrange lines, scenes, and plays. In his *Hamlet*, Branagh takes the advice seriously, while trying to compete with Welles and Olivier on so many levels, and mounts his "all the words" version of the play, running four hours. By contrast, Branagh's latest Shakespeare film, an abridgement of *Love's Labours Lost* (2000) in the style of a 1930s musical, cuts much of the dialogue and runs barely one hour and a half despite the addition of several songs by the Gershwins, Cole Porter, and others.

Love's Labours Lost shows that Branagh continues to be deeply susceptible to the influence of earlier *auteurs*: in this case, he has borrowed from the recent work of Woody Allen, who similarly integrated 1930s songs, performed by his actors, in his *Everyone Says I Love You*, released in 1996. (Branagh does an unsettlingly accurate imitation of Allen in the role of a media reporter in Allen's 1998 film *Celebrity*; comedic touches in *A Midwinter's Tale* echo Allen's work in *Manhattan* and *Zelig*.) For *Love's Labours Lost*, Branagh continued to rely upon members of his theatrical family. Geraldine McEwen appears as Holofernia (adapted from Shakespeare's pedant *par excellence*, Holofernes), having portrayed Princess Katherine's attendant in *Henry V*. Richard Briers returns, this time as Sir Nathaniel, the local curate, and in keeping with the spirit of *Everyone Says I Love You*, Branagh concocts a budding romance between Holofernia and Nathaniel. Timothy Spall, Branagh's film Rosencrantz, is cast as Don Armado; Richard Clifford, Duke of Orleans in *Henry V* and Conrade in Branagh's *Much Ado About Nothing*, is Boyet, chief adviser to the ladies of the French court; Jimmy Yuill, who provided a music-minded Friar Francis in *Much Ado* and the filmscore for *A Midwinter's Tale*, is Constable Dull, who demonstrates surprising talent as accompanist on piano and as leader of the local orchestra, the Dull Tones.

In his film productions, Branagh regularly includes well-known performers with tangential Shakespeare experience, such as Keanu Reeves's appearance in *Much Ado* after being featured in Gus Van Sant's *My Own Private Idaho* (with its debts to Welles' *Chimes at Midnight*). Here, Alicia Silverstone portrays the Princess whose presence undermines the King of

Navarre's resolve to spend three years in cloistered study. As Cher in Amy Heckerling's 1995 *Clueless* (itself a rewrite of Jane Austen's *Emma*), Silverstone had been able to identify a quote from *Hamlet* not because Cher knew Shakespeare so well, but because she could "remember Mel Gibson accurately." Other performers have more extensive backgrounds in Shakespeare and in musical comedy. The accomplished young stage actor Adrian Lester is a convincing song-and-dance man in the role of Dumaine. He had previously won an Olivier Award for Best Actor in a Musical for his work as Bobby in the London revival of Stephen Sondheim's *Company*. Lester had also captivated audiences as Rosalind in Cheek By Jowl's all-male production of *As You Like It* in the early 1990s. More recently, he has starred as Hamlet in Peter Brook's radically revisionist staging. Veteran Broadway performer Nathan Lane ably negotiates the transformation of local yokel Costard into a vaudeville star.

Many of Branagh's translations work very well here: the kingdom of Navarre becomes an Oxford-style college (the French ladies arrive by river, on punts); the sadness at play's end, brought by news of the French king's death, is at first intensified by linking it with the fall of France during the early stages of the Second World War. But Branagh is uncomfortable with the play's uncertain conclusion, which defers any happy reunion of its young couples into a never-seen future. Instead, he opts for a Hollywood-style happy ending at war's end. He has also been chastened by the response to his *Hamlet* and that film's abundance of words, words, words: he reacts by taking one of Shakespeare's most language-enraptured plays, cutting most of it, and replacing some of the text with musical production numbers.

The publicity department of Castle Rock had been skeptical about Branagh's *Hamlet*, much as Danny in *Last Action Hero* was toward Olivier's version. A lengthy trailer for Branagh's version runs before the feature on commercial videotapes for Oliver Parker's *Othello*, in which Branagh appears as Iago (see chapter two). In the trailer, we see and hear Branagh expressing pride in this full-text version and then retelling his early experiences with the play. In both cases, the captions for following segments glance backward at what Branagh has just said. The sequence that follows Branagh's comments on his "full version" introduces Polonius; using a title card that reads "Brevity is the soul of wit," however appropriate textually, suggests some resistance to the idea that a four-hour film will attract a wide audience. After Branagh talks about wanting to share the excitement *Hamlet* has inspired in him and his fellow actors, the next segment presents the character of Gertrude with the opening title-card: "The lady doth protest too much." The first run's lack of success marked Branagh's *Hamlet* for quick video release, in the less expensive pan-and-scan format. His filmic father-figures, the always opportunistic actor-managers, may have had some measure of revenge after all.

CHAPTER SEVEN

◇

Transgressive, in Theory

HAMLET: It is but foolery, but it is such a kind of [gain-] giving as would perhaps trouble a woman.

—Shakespeare, *Hamlet*

Shakespearean playtexts present a number of opportunities for transgressive cultural gestures. As social systems set boundaries to behavior, they
point to "the terrain of their [the boundaries'] possible transgression": the
violation of the rules, then, is part of "the complete horizon of a society's
symbolic values" (Détienne ix). The larger public theaters of Elizabethan
London physically demonstrate this dynamic. For the most part, they
were built in "the Liberties," lands not directly under the control of the
city fathers (Mullaney 42–44); they also invited citizens to leave off productive work, visit the precincts where other questionable activities
occured, and witness actors defying norms of behavior. Depending on the
roles they assumed, the players would violate rules of conduct proper to
status, class, gender, age, religion, or occupation.

Similarly, Shakespeare's plays allow filmmakers to violate cinematic conventions; as we have seen, the ubiquitous asides and soliloquies of Elizabethan theater give ample means to break the literal fourth
wall that is the movie or video screen. This is more than a stylistic variation, since the illusionistic approach to film can tend to naturalize

social and political conventions. Filmmakers may also choose to transgress film industry conventions: rather than conform to the dictates of genre, they may choose to mix them. Shakespeare's plays, with their insistence on complicating the same generic boundaries they have helped to construct (tragedy and comedy, romance and realism) do more than permit such "misbehavior"; they almost demand it. Finally, social and political conventions are constantly called either into question or into productive play time and again. Shakespeare's theater relies upon cross-dressing, explores a range of sexualities, and considers the arbitrariness of gender roles. It draws upon the mystery and mystification attendant upon social hierarchies and political systems, reveals some of the processes by which those systems are constructed and sustained, and sometimes questions them to the very core. Shakespeare films may readily choose to follow suit.

These opportunities present themselves most vividly when filmmakers situate themselves in collaboration with the Shakespearean playtext, rather than in subversion against it. The cultural significance invested in Shakespeare lends additional authorization for all manner of transgressive enterprises, even borrowing a given social system's investment in deviation. To borrow (and the economic language is deliberate here) from the language of *Twelfth Night*, such films are like the "allowed fool" that has been licensed by his patron not to follow cultural norms—especially in the areas of speaking both nonsense and the utter (if not always plain) truth to his social betters. An example of such supposed folly involving gender issues is what may be the second Shakespeare film ever made, a 1900 vignette featuring the widely acclaimed French tragedienne Sarah Bernhardt in the title role of *Hamlet*. Commentators at that time and since questioned the suitability of the performer for that role: her personality and nationality, as well as her sex, have been thought disqualifications. Bernhardt decisively challenges all such preconceptions about her abilities and about the role. Some of the earliest engagements with Shakespearean transgressivity, then, are to be found not in versions of plays that overtly deal with such issues (such as the cross-gender comedies) but in film productions of *Hamlet*, the critical history of which constantly circles around notions of "proper" masculine and feminine traits.

In filming the duel scene from *Hamlet* in 1900, director Clément Maurice was primarily concerned with the new medium's documentary capabilities. What he documented, though, was a compelling challenge to norms of theatrical presentation—Bernhardt's performance as Hamlet.

Stage historian Gerda Taranow, in her recent study of the 1899 stage production, stresses the consistently innovative nature of Bernhardt's approach. The actress broke away from the romantic notion of an incapacitated hero and returned instead to the "determined avenger whose roots were to be found in the Elizabethan theater" (xvii); she commissioned a new translation more firmly grounded in Shakespeare's playtexts. Bernhardt was not breaking entirely new ground in tackling the role itself, since several actresses (Taranow's count is over fifty) had portrayed Hamlet, along with other male Shakespearean characters. Usually, the roles had been selected for their supposedly feminine nature: Romeo, memorably enacted by Charlotte Cushman in the early nineteenth century, was as likely a candidate for a woman actor as the "irresolute" Prince of Denmark. Bernhardt, anticipating John Barrymore's self-consciously virile stage interpretations (1923 to 1925), stressed Hamlet's capacity for ingenious strategizing and often impulsive action.

This is reflected in the film record of the fencing contest between Laertes and Hamlet, as conceived, directed, and enacted by Bernhardt. The duel is staged with scrupulous attention to the ceremonies and rules of fencing: Bernhardt and her character both acquit themselves as accomplished in the masculine art of swordplay. The film goes yet further by showing Hamlet increasing in aggressive intensity before receiving the wound from Laertes's unbated weapon. Bernhardt's production suggests that Laertes is provoked by Hamlet's skill into following through with his and Claudius's plot against the prince. Her Hamlet quickly calculates the significance of the injury—and communicates that understanding to the audience by a series of glances (Taranow 181)—and disarms Laertes by striking his opponent's sword from his hand. The exchange of weapons is preceded by a long pause (much admired or condemned by critics) which establishes Hamlet's defiance and determination; Bernhardt's Hamlet then presents his sword to Laertes and gestures to an attendant to fetch the fallen blade. This Hamlet is determined to exact retribution while time permits. Bernhardt's prince shows the increasing effects of the poison, adding further desperation and violence to his assault on Laertes. After Hamlet has answered his adversary's blow, the film skips over the deaths of Gertrude and Claudius and shows instead the prince's demise. Bernhardt's Hamlet dies on his feet, supported by courtiers (likely including Horatio) who then gently lower his body to the ground.

The reasons for selecting this scene for cinematic preservation are clear: the sheer excitement of the physicality and the familiarity of the sequence of events (which makes actual dialogue less important) would make the sequence ideal for large audiences at an international exhibition. Along with these practical concerns, however, Bernhardt must have sensed that this scene best captured the defiant spirit of her production of the play. This was a *Hamlet* against the grain of nineteenth-century stage practice and criticism; this was also an actress resisting the received categories of role (off-stage as well as on-stage) and conduct. The next actress to portray Hamlet on-screen would instead take accepted norms of behavior and the romantic view of the prince to amazing extremes. Asta Nielsen's Hamlet is a woman who has been a male impersonator since childhood—all to fulfill the political ambitions of Gertrude, who here takes on more than a little of Lady Macbeth's character. The 1920 German production of *Hamlet: The Drama of Vengeance* derives many of these ideas from Edward P. Vining's book *The Mystery of Hamlet*, published in 1881. After considering the differences between the quarto and folio versions of the play, Vining had advanced the theory that Shakespeare, in his process of revision, presents "a gradual evolution of the feminine element in Hamlet's character" (Thompson 59). This culminates in the story of a woman who necessarily feels that the time is out of joint, because she has been forced to play a masculine role for which she is inherently unsuited. Ann Thompson accurately describes Vining's study as "a rich storehouse of information on Victorian gender stereotyping," and for that reason resists dismissing it "as mere eccentricity" (219): Vining speaks for his culture as well as for himself. The film itself both reinforces such stereotypes and, at least briefly, challenges them. As directors Svend Gade and Heinz Schall craft the narrative, they show a sensitive young woman—suddenly there's nothing wrong with Hamlet being so sensitive—struggle with the coarseness not only of the Danish court but also of university life at Wittenberg.

Wittenberg is very important in this version, since it is where Hamlet meets the unacknowledged love of her life, Horatio. The scenes between the two characters echo passages in *Twelfth Night* and *As You Like It*, and certainly Vining's theories and this film have been influenced by the gender confusion at work in these comedies. The film introduces this lighter note only to shift abruptly to Hamlet Senior's death, staged by Claudius with a real adder, rather than merely a reported one. When Nielsen's Hamlet returns home from Wittenberg, she is horrified by the reckless debauchery of the festival in celebration of Gertrude's and Claudius's wedding. Hamlet takes refuge in the burial vault and visually expresses her belief that death, with her father, is a consummation devoutly to be wished: she tries, without success, to open the cenotaph, as if to join her father in the dust. Later in the film, this Hamlet will not leap into Ophelia's grave. The psychosexual significances multiply as Hamlet's father speaks from beyond—"If thou didst thy dear father love," reads the title card—to demand revenge, as a concerned Horatio visits the tomb only to deepen his friend's despair, and as Hamlet stumbles upon evidence early on as to Claudius's guilt. Following a tip from a gardener on the castle grounds, Hamlet visits the dungeon where her uncle had selected the poisonous snake that dispatched his brother and rival. She is unable to lift the cistern lid that would reveal where the serpents are hidden, but she finds instead Claudius's dagger. The title card, again borrowing from the playtext, shows her knowledge of what actually occurred: "A dagger! O my prophetic soul—Mine uncle!" Her physical incapacity to open either the tomb (and identify with her dead father) or the cistern (with its phallic serpents) foreshadows her inability to act upon the clear evidence that Claudius is responsible for her father's death. She confides in Horatio and assumes an "antic disposition" in order to observe her uncle and, like an allowed fool, to confront him in jesting and riddling ways.

Hamlet's folly suggests a cure to Polonius. Here, Ophelia's love is presented to a reluctant Hamlet as a healthful diversion from "his" madness. Hamlet remains aloof, much to Ophelia's disappointment, but Horatio does not. When Horatio indicates his interest in Ophelia, Nielsen's Hamlet then decides to "make love to her," but only to "part her from Horatio." Aware that she is being watched by Polonius and Claudius, Hamlet convincingly portrays the ardent, male lover. Left alone, though, she is near despair at the deception: "How long—how long, O God— must I live my mother's lie?" A combination of filial duty, youthful hopes, and womanly weakness keeps her from suicide and revenge; a title card (which may reflect her own thoughts) declares her to be "Too weak to kill, and too young to die."

The story continues, with an on-again, off-again courtship between Hamlet and Ophelia, with the staging of "The Mousetrap" and Hamlet's decision not to strike down Claudius at prayer, and with several confrontations between Hamlet and a Gertrude increasingly desperate to keep safe the secret of her child's sexual identity. After Polonius is killed, Horatio tries to comfort Ophelia, but to no avail as she descends into unfeigned madness. Even so (and in part because of her vulnerability),

Horatio remains devoted to her. Nielsen's Hamlet challenges Heinz Stieda's Horatio on his emotional attachment. Could his love for Ophelia be "greater than thy love for me?" "Aye," comes Horatio's reply, "it is a man's love—for a woman." Hamlet nevertheless sustains her resolve to avenge her father's death; she may also seek to punish her mother for the disappointments attendant on her disguise. At the Norwegian court, Hamlet turns the tables on Rosencrantz and Guildenstern with the help of another Wittenberg schoolmate, Fortinbras. She then enlists Fortinbras's aid in plans for an armed campaign against Gertrude and Claudius.

First, however, she will exact private vengeance on her uncle. Returning to Elsinore, she traps an inebriated Claudius in a chamber that she sets ablaze. Ophelia has already become an indirect victim of Hamlet's campaign; mad with grief over her father's death, she cannot save herself from drowning. At Ophelia's funeral, it is Horatio who rushes to the grave, but Hamlet remains the recipient of Laertes's threats; after Gertrude discovers what has happened to her new husband, she devises the plot involving the duel with poisoned swords. This portrait of power-hungry womanhood would not be out of place in *The First Blast of the Trumpet Against the Monstrous Regiment of Women*, John Knox's 1558 tirade against Mary, Queen of Scots, Mary Tudor, and against female rulership generally. (Mary Tudor's successor and half-sister, Elizabeth of England, never quite forgave Knox for the work.) Nielsen's Hamlet agrees to the match, despite her inability, almost inviting death. As she chooses the sword, she gestures "about my heart—but it is no matter." Not surprisingly, Gertrude's death is poetic justice, the result of a servant's mistake, not an attack by her daughter. As Hamlet watches her mother's death throes, Laertes takes the opportunity to stab his adversary. Only as Hamlet dies does she receive the full attention of her beloved, Horatio. The Liebestod theme—the conflation of love and death now so strongly identified with Wagner's music for *Tristan und Isolde* (its strains can be heard at Juliet's death in Luhrmann's Romeo + Juliet)—grows stronger as Horatio embraces his friend, who cries "I die, Horatio." On the ground, Horatio replies, "Hamlet, my beloved Hamlet," to the departed prince. At this point, the filmmakers include what Lawrence Danson has called "the greatest scene of anagnorisis [Aristotle's term for discovery] Shakespeare never wrote" (48): Horatio's hand falls to Hamlet's breast and he realizes that his friend was, indeed, a woman. The title cards aim at pathos: "Death reveals thy tragic secret. Now I understand what bound me to that matchless form and feature. Your true heart was a woman's.

Too late—beloved—'tis too late." He kisses her, weeping, while Nielsen looks not only transported but ecstatic in death.

Fortinbras arrives, with his army, too late to help Hamlet to the throne of Denmark. As in the play, a funeral procession concludes the action; as in Olivier's film (and in Welles's borrowings from it for his *Othello*), there is a closeup of Hamlet's face as the hero is carried off. Nielsen's androgynous beauty is compelling, as is her performance throughout. As a result, critics have argued both about the tone of the conclusion and about the sexual politics of the film overall. Nielsen is too powerful an actress for the film to be rejected out of hand; even Danson, who finds Horatio's "discovery" scene ludicrous, recognizes a "bold—characteristically Weimar—polymorphous indulgence" (48) in the camera's exploration of her bisexual appeal. Despite this, the film's participation in efforts not to challenge the romantic reading of Hamlet's character but to "explain" it by means of naturalized gender roles work against both the pathos and the intelligence found especially in Nielsen's performance. The film, much more than the revised *Dr. Caligari* with its explanatory frame story, plays things too safe, works far too hard to "set things right" by its ostensibly tragic conclusion.

In 1936, director Paul Czinner decided on *As You Like It* as a star vehicle for the internationally known actress (and German émigré), Elisabeth Bergner. Bergner and Czinner were married, as were Norma Shearer and Irving Thalberg, star and studio head for MGM's *Romeo and Juliet* of that same year. The talents brought to bear on the project were impressive. Laurence Olivier plays Orlando to Bergner's Rosalind/Ganymede. In the role of Rosalind's uncle, Duke Frederick, who drives his niece and his daughter into the Forest of Arden, Felix Aylmer combines a suitably threatening manner with hints of his character's eventual remorse and conversion (which are only described, not shown, in the play). William Walton provides the filmscore; Olivier would repeatedly enlist Aylmer and Walton for his own efforts at Shakespeare on screen. J. M. Barrie, author of *Peter Pan*, and (uncredited) Carl Meyer, scenarist for both *Dr. Caligari* and *The Last Laugh*, assisted Robert Cullen in the adaptation of *As You Like It*. At the center, though, is a miscalculated interpretation of Rosalind's character: Bergner's performance, intended to be reassuringly feminine, quickly becomes irritating in the context. While in male drag as Ganymede, this Rosalind is anxious to telegraph her "true nature" and accordingly exhibits a wide array of coquettish mannerisms. Audience reaction and critical response was negative, even if much of the commentary focused on Bergner's accent, rather than her acting. While as viewers, English moviegoers may have been more ready for gender-bending than Czinner believed (the careers of both Marlene Dietrich and Greta Garbo continued to play with such definitions), as auditors they were strongly resistent to alien incursions on the language of their national poet.

Nearly five decades later, Kenneth Branagh aimed beyond the British film market in producing his 1993 *Much Ado About Nothing*. For his second effort in Shakespearean filmmaking (and the one in which he seems least haunted by the precedents of both Olivier and Welles), Branagh sought out U. S. performers with a range of American inflections and attitudes. He wanted "Different accents, different looks." In his introduction to the published screenplay for the film, he avers that he "had no set number of American actors" in mind, that he "was also interested in one or two Italian and French actors." As it turned out, though, the mix of American and British accents would suffice.

> In the end the choices became simple. I asked film actors whom I admired and whose career choices had been adventurous enough to suggest they would not be intimidated. In all cases I explained that I did not want artificial "Shakespeare voices," that they must perform in their own accents. . . . (Branagh 1993, x)

How this sensible advice translates into Michael Keaton's vocal performance as Dogberry is well worth exploring. While unconcerned about accents, Branagh was deeply concerned about what mass-market audiences would accept as comedy. Smarting from the "bitter experience" of "having played one of the great unfunny Shakespearean clowns—Touchstone in *As You Like It*," Branagh wanted to make sure that Keaton's Dogberry would not suffer the same fate (xv). So the director and actor agreed that the character "should be not only a verbal but a physical malaprop . . . a universal type, beautifully pompous, and, in our version, dangerous too" (xiii). The danger matters more than the humor, since the psychological economy of the play demands an excess of male aggression: most of the male characters have just returned from war and their capacity for violence when they believe their honor has been challenged is great. Branagh displaces this violence onto Dogberry in the interests of increasing audience acceptance of the other male characters—and thereby its acceptance of the film's ending as, indeed, a happy one.

Czinner's film unsuccessfully (and perhaps unnecessarily) tries to reassure viewers that Rosalind's sexual ambiguity posed no real threat to established gender roles; it tries to do this by removing as much of that ambiguity as possible. Branagh's film, it seems, has successfully reassured viewers that the men of *Much Ado* do not threaten women or women's sensibilities in the wake of recent re-examinations of gender roles. Emma Thompson's Beatrice, far from being at odds with urban, male-dominated society, is at the very core of a rural utopia. Branagh converts the city of Messina, in Sicily, to a Tuscan estate. Thompson's voice is heard first on the soundtrack, as she reads aloud Balthasar's rather cynical song about the need for women to accept male inconstancy. Here, it is meant as a public rationale for Beatrice's suspicions toward men and matrimony. Leonato and the other men of his house respond with a combination of rueful assent (yes, we menfolk are like that) and good-humored indulgence (yes, that's Beatrice, after all). The calculated disarming of audience suspicions continues with the film's title shot: *Much Ado About Nothing* self-deprecatingly appears on screen as the returning warriors on horseback re-enact *The Magnificent Seven*. Robert Sean Leonard's Claudio is ardent and vulnerable, largely unconcerned with Hero's dowry, and is given what he thinks is ocular proof of her infidelity. Denzel Washington's Don Pedro is solicitous and empathetic; with Claudio, he is treated to the sight of a woman doing far more than talking with a man at a window; he is also far from callous after hearing reports of Hero's death. As Celestino Deleyto has observed (99–100), Keanu Reeves's Don John has much of his malevolence tacitly motivated by conventional trappings of homosexuality (as seen in Welles's and Branagh's takes on Iago): if only he liked women, all might be well.

In Shakespeare's playtext, heterosexual males are not all that fond of women either. Claudio and Benedick continue to joke about cuckoldry until the play's end, just before their marriages to Hero and Beatrice. In Branagh's version, by contrast, expressions of male doubt about female constancy are regularly cut from early scenes and banished from the conclusion. Also largely banished are any suggestions that Dogberry's ineptitude as constable has an indolent amiability as one of its foundations. Branagh includes Verges's address to Dogberry, "You have been always called a merciful man, partner," and his superior's reply, "Truly, I would not hang a dog by my will, much more a man who hath any honesty in him" (3.3.61–64). But these lines are heard as ironic, as the "two comic psychopaths" (Branagh 1993, 51) are physically threatening to the watch and each other. Borachio and Conrade are roughed up, on-screen as well as off, by Dogberry's company, described by Branagh as "The Three Stooges meet Terminator II." Male aggression—a more pervasive, often threatening force in the play—is relegated to the middling sort, the citizenry of Messina rather than its aristocrats, and is contained by comic conventions. Most curious of all, it is credited with resolving the play's central dilemma: a scarred and beaten Borachio confesses to Don Pedro that "these shallow fools have brought to light" (5.1.233–34) the plot against Hero's honor. Not content with overhearing his account, they have apparently extracted a public statement by force.

The interplay between force and social order is a frequent theme in Shakespeare's history plays, but also in his visions of the pre-Christian West. Both *Julius Caesar*, which is as fascinated by the aftermath of the title character's assassination as by the act itself, and *King Lear*, set in a scrupulously pagan world, explore the validity of claims that power has received transcendent sanction. Both plays include skeptics toward such claims—Cassius in *Julius Caesar* and Edmund in *King Lear*—and would-be architects of belief in supernatural support of the social order—first Caesar himself and then Antony in ancient Rome, first Lear himself and then Edgar in ancient Britain. While self-serving, the arguments of the skeptics should not be readily discounted, since the party of belief is comprised of people acting out of self-interest or out of the dutiful conviction that others need belief. Cassius reinterprets celestial signs that blaze forth Caesar's right to rule; Caesar chooses whichever form of divination best agrees with his ambition or self-regard. Edmund suspects that the idea of a divinely-decreed correspondential order is merely a prop for the present social system, one that excludes illegitimate sons from being heirs; for his part, Edgar stages a miracle for his father's benefit, but does not believe in it himself. Ultimately, even Edgar must prosecute his right to inherit his father's title—and identity—by force of arms.

Film versions of the two plays have, at times, found unsettling resonances between these themes and the political events of the twentieth century. Joseph L. Mankiewicz's 1953 *Julius Caesar* not only looks back at the rise of fascism (Willson 2000, 143) but also considers the consequences of its defeat. In many ways, Mankiewicz seems anything but transgressive in his approach to filming Shakespeare. For this project, he adapted himself almost completely to the studio system: he relied on established and up-and-coming stars; he recycled sets from the 1951 remake of *Quo Vadis* that had been shipped back from their Italian locations. He did so, not surprisingly, for the sake of economy. The executives at MGM would agree to the film only if it could be made within a very modest budget. Within these constraints, however, he was able to make a literate and involving interpretation of Shakespeare's play. On one level, the MGM stars, two notable British imports, and a host of contract players deliver the kind of character studies one might expect. At the same time, Mankiewicz uses the play to comment on the chilling combination of demagoguery and conformism then shaping U. S. politics. In this, he proved himself not merely transgressive, but defiant.

Senator Joseph McCarthy's "Red Scare" campaign had hit political dissent hard, especially in Hollywood. Careers were sharply curtailed or simply ended by panic-stricken studio heads both eager to prove their patriotism in the burgeoning Cold War and fearful of the consequences should they not appear sufficiently anti-Communist. Projects deemed too critical of the capitalist system were stopped or, when too much prestige or clout was involved, made politically palatable. The film version of Arthur Miller's *Death of a Salesman* is perhaps the most notorious example of ideological bowdlerization. On stage, Willy Loman was (and remains) the tragic everyman who plays by all the economic rules and is still ground down by his pursuit of the American Dream. In the 1951 film, Loman (as played by Frederic March) is transformed into an eccentric, a neurotic—a poor soul incapable of living up to the common-sense codes of free enterprise. To further counteract Miller's critique, Columbia Pictures decided that the film should be released with a companion short, *The Life of a Salesman*, which presents its protagonist as normal, hardworking, successful, and destined for greater rewards. Seen in this cultural context, Mankiewicz's *Julius Caesar* pulls very few punches. It could do so, in part, because of the supposed historical distance; Shakespeare himself explores the foundations of political life most overtly in his histories. Elizabethan authorities simply would not tolerate the depiction of contemporary events (and leaders) on the stage. The MGM *Julius Caesar* also succeeded as political commentary because of the idea that Shakespeare, as high art, was inherently apolitical—a category that often includes, however, "right" political thinking, as in Olivier's *Henry V*.

John Houseman, the producer of *Julius Caesar*, had tested that idea in the 1930s when he collaborated with Orson Welles on the "fascist" staging of the play. Mankiewicz was the brother of another former partner with Welles, who contributed to the screenplay of *Citizen Kane*. Together, they had learned from Welles's insights and mistakes—they would work within the studio system—and from Olivier's successes in filming Shakespeare. Olivier's *Hamlet* and Welles's *Macbeth* and *Othello* all rely on narrative introductions at the outset; Olivier supplies a visual text along with his own voice-over. Houseman and Mankiewicz instead rely only on the visual induction (a Hollywood staple for historical films), but one that is accompanied by an ambiguous visual image: the imperial eagle. With its reminders both of Mussolini's coopting of the Roman past and of U. S. appropriations from classical republicanism, the eagle allows the opening quotation from Sir Thomas North's translation of Plutarch, which was Shakespeare's primary source, to have a wide range of political resonances (Crowl 149). When Julius Caesar was named "Dictator for Life," we are told, Cassius and Brutus decide to take desperate action. Caesar's dictatorial ways are established in the first scene, as republic-minded patricians are arrested for speaking publicly against Caesar's primacy and for removing adulatory garlands from his bust in a marketplace. The film, drawing from the play's own political analyses, is fascinated by the dynamics that transform a citizenry into a mob. The power of eloquence to initiate and to exploit that process had been documented in Germany and Italy alike; Houseman and Mankiewicz want to bring the lesson closer to home.

The totalitarian atmosphere continues in the aftermath of two simultaneous performances: Antony's three offers of a crown to Caesar, and Cassius's efforts to persuade Brutus that violent action is necessary to prevent Caesar from assuming any more power. Cassius and Brutus hear the roars of the crowd at each refusal of the crown, but do not yet know their significance. John Gielgud's Cassius signals to Edmund O' Brien's wonderfully plain-spoken Casca that they should speak; Caesar observes the silent exchange and immediately pronounces on the danger that Cassius might embody to anyone less than Caesar himself. Louis Calhern takes every opportunity to highlight the vanity and increasing infirmity of the still-charismatic title character. The production suggests that Caesar is drawn to the office of king precisely because he fears the waning of his personal strength and power. After Casca provides his sardonic account of the abortive coronation (complete with Caesar's fainting spells), he informs Brutus and Cassius that the impolitic patricians we saw earlier have been "put to silence." That fact registers all the more powerfully with James Mason's Brutus after Cassius's expert behind-the-scenes rhetoric. The republican cause requires a public spokesman, however, and Cassius is convinced that Brutus can fulfill that function. In the ensuing soliloquy, Cassius admits that the course he wants Brutus to adopt—the betrayal of his friend and patron, Caesar—is far from honorable or noble in itself. Nevertheless, the importance of the cause demands questionable means, including the manipulation of Brutus's sense of the popular will. He manufactures documents that praise Brutus and comment "obscurely [on] Caesar's ambition" (1.2.319–20). Despite this duplicity, we discover, Cassius is also motivated by a profound admiration for the friend he admits (to us) he is seducing. Unlike Iago, who similarly comments on his own unwillingness to trust himself, Gielgud's Cassius wants to be trustworthy and passionately desires that he be deserving of Brutus's friendship. Like Othello, Mason's Brutus takes such admiration as his due: it is a foregone conclusion that he will win the later argument between these allies.

As soon as Brutus agrees to lead the tyrannicides, Cassius constantly defers to him—usually with dire results. Brutus is incapable of perceiving Cassius's double nature and he is completely duped by Mark Antony, who outmaneuvers his political enemies at every turn. Marlon Brando's performance as Antony surprised many at the time; critics and audiences who believed him limited to sullen mumbling and passionate howls were not prepared for his presentation of sheer cunning. Brando's Antony is motivated by the desire for power and nothing else: his support of Caesar, his cagy negotiations with Caesar's assassins, and his public sorrow during the funeral oration all have political advantage as their ends. Shortly after beginning the oration, Shakespeare's Antony pauses to regain his composure and to allow his auditors to absorb and comment upon what he has already said. Brando's Antony turns away from the crowd at this point, apparently to hide his tears; Mankiewicz lets us see his averted face, which shows not grief but stern joy that his words and gestures have already had such an impact.

The same air of calculation is evident in Antony's coy mention of Caesar's bequest to the citizens of Rome:

> But here's a parchment with the seal of Caesar,
> I found it in his closet, 'tis his will.
> Let but the commons hear this testament—
> Which, pardon me, I do not mean to read—
> And they would go and kiss dead Caesar's wounds,
> And dip their napkins in his sacred blood . . . (3.2.128–33)

It is a statement designed to provoke interest in the contents of the document, to elicit complicity in their revelation. Senator McCarthy had employed a similar statement in launching his rise to national prominence.

In an address given in Wheeling, West Virginia, on February 9, 1950, he had announced that he could not at that time name all the communists and enemy spies employed by the U. S. State Department. Even so, he said, "I have here in my hand a list of 205." Soon much of the country joined in his efforts to make known the identities of Reds—real and imagined, past and present—regardless of the consequences. As a result, McCarthy wielded frightening influence within the Republican Party, in the Senate, and in American political life for over four years, a period which included the production and release of this film. At the end of the funeral oration, Brando's Antony is calmly approving of the riot he has provoked: "Now let it work. Mischief, thou art afoot, / Take what course thou wilt!" (3.2.260–61) is spoken by the actor not as an exclamation but as a calm assessment. In the turmoil, Antony can wrest power not only from his enemies but also from his allies, as Mankiewicz takes care to include the scene in which Antony blithely bargains for power with the lives of friends and family. The director's reading of the play's politics parallels his view of the political scene in his own time and place.

Released in 1971, *Peter Brook's Film of William Shakespeare's "King Lear"* (to give its full, forthright title) brings to cinematic life an Eastern European reading of the play and of Shakespeare. Brook was profoundly influenced by the writings of Czech scholar Jan Kott—who had himself been impressed by some of Brook's earlier productions, such as his 1955 *Titus Andronicus*. Kott's *Shakespeare Our Contemporary* explicitly connects *Lear* with the austere bleakness of Samuel Beckett's absurdist dramas (100–18); at the same time, Kott was reflecting the sense of everyday absurdity experienced by citizens of countries compelled to remain within the Soviet bloc. Indicators of these associations are evident in Brook's thoughts about the problems of adapting Shakespeare for film; they appear in a 1965 interview for *Sight and Sound*. A Shakespearean play is "a major achievement in writing," an artifact that allows for constant reinterpretation but also remains utterly itself:

> This object is there and it's like a sputnik, it runs round, and over the years different portions of it are nearer to you, different bits are further away. It's rushing past and you are peeling off these meanings. (qtd. in Manvell 134)

The term sputnik—Russian for co-traveller—refers to the first man-made satellite successfully launched into orbit around the earth, by Soviet scientists, in 1957. Some years after Brook's landmark Stratford 1962 staging of the play in response to Kott's reading, he continued to think about Shakespeare in terms of the great sociopolitical tensions of his time.

Brook worked on his film of *King Lear* beginning in 1968 and did not finish post-production work until 1970; shooting was done mostly on location in North Jutland, Denmark, during the winter of 1969. The landscape is pitilessly bleak, almost all sand and mud and snow, and the weather suitably harsh. The world of the play matches such a setting, especially after Brook had edited and realized the script to intensify its nearly overwhelming bitterness. On being chastened by Irene Worth's Goneril at her castle, this Lear incites his followers to riot, thereby ensuring that his knights will be taken from him; Robert Lloyd's Edgar shares in his illegitimate brother's resentment toward the older generation's rule (the student uprisings of 1968 continue to resonate here) and thereby makes himself more vulnerable to Edmund's machinations; in his disguise as Poor Tom, Edgar is beaten and abandoned; in his disguise as Caius, Kent (played by Tom Fleming) has his boots removed—in the dead of winter—when he is placed in the stocks.

Brook employs several distancing and disorienting techniques throughout the film, most notably during the scene on the heath, as Lear is consumed by both his madness and his increasing powers of empathy. In one take, the screen presents just one corner of Lear's skull as it is subjected to the storm's fierceness: the internal and external turmoil becomes one, but with no reassuring message of ultimate harmony or clarity. There is no place for *discordia concors*, a harmonious disharmony—the Renaissance notion of this jangling world's place amidst the music of the spheres—in Kott's or Brook's reading of the play, any more than there is in Samuel Beckett's dramatic cosmology.

What almost compels the audience to care, despite the stylistic irruptions and apparent moral void, is Paul Scofield's towering portrayal of Lear himself. The actor had appeared in Brook's Stratford stage production (before inhabiting a very different ethos in the stage and film productions of *A Man for All Seasons*) and brings the weight of that experience to bear here. His Lear becomes a heartrending ruin of deeply flawed greatness. His opening speeches betray the slightest hints of a stroke that may have prompted his decision to divide his kingdom. He tries desperately to maintain his dignity when Regan and Goneril combine against him: he delivers the line, "O fool, I shall go mad," with quiet calmness. When the mad king meets the blinded Gloucester, he plays the fool himself with canny relish: he directs the lines about adultery directly to the earl who has paid bitterly for his sexual indiscretions. Finally, though, Scofield's Lear comes to feel what wretches feel. He has shown compassion for the Fool; he has seen the disguised Edgar as an *ecce homo* figure (the suffering Christ as presented to the crowd by Pilate—a startling image in this assertively agnostic film of a play set in pre-Christian Britain); he has accepted Cordelia and asked her forgiveness and lost her forever. The shooting script indicates that Brook had intended to end the film, as the Folio version ends, with Edgar's dazed acceptance of responsibility. "The weight of these sad times we must obey" (5.3.324), says Edgar, marking the passage of one generation to the next. Brook considered having Edgar speak the concluding lines directly to the camera and then showing Edgar alone in this wasteland. The script finishes with "Then this picture also vanishes, until nothing has left a trace" (qtd. in Manvell, 152). But the actual film instead concludes with shots of Lear looking upward, falling slowly out of the frame, simultaneously leaving this life and searching an empty white sky for its meaning—perhaps a glimpse of Cordelia's spirit (as the script suggests earlier) or an acceptance of the void itself. Despite the film's own acceptance of a world filled with impersonal forces and inhuman political acts and inaction, Brook keeps one person—Scofield's Lear—in view until the very end. A kind of objectless hope animates Beckett's plays, and Kott was drawn to that spirit's potential for resistance as it could be enacted in Shakespeare and in the cultures of both the Western and Eastern blocs. Brook pays tribute to that spirit in the wake of the Soviet repression in 1968, of the Czech government's and people's hopes for reform, and in the context of the West's squandering of moral authority in Southeast Asia.

"A plague on both your houses" is Mercutio's dying curse, and Franco Zeffirelli's 1968 *Romeo and Juliet* presents the older generation's combatants in the feud between the Montagues and the Capulets as the most deserving recipients of that malediction. At a time of generational conflict, of radical questioning of the political landscape in the Cold War, Zeffirelli tailored his rendering of the play for an audience ready to assume "Give peace a chance" as its slogan. For it is the rivalry between the arriviste Lord Capulet—anxious to legitimize his clan's claim to status by marriage with the nobility—and the more patrician Montagues that leads to the destruction of their children. The differences between the families are evident in their garb: costume designer Danilo Donati gives bright, even garish colors to the *nouveaux riches* Capulets and somber, dignified shades of black and grey to the established Montagues. It is clear that the Capulets envy their rivals' status: Zeffirelli's Sampson and Gregory, servants to Capulet, are swaggering provocateurs, not bumbling clowns. The younger generation has taken the feud for granted, without fully realizing its dangers. The fatal conflict between Mercutio and Tybalt is all fun and games—so much so, that Mercutio's friends cannot believe the seriousness of his wound. Neither, at first, can Tybalt. In Michael York's memorable portrayal, the accomplished young swordsman is shocked at the sight of blood; it seems impossible to him that the horseplay has turned tragic.

John McEnery's Mercutio carries more than a hint of tragedy from the beginning. En route to the Capulets' ball, he wears a death's mask and in trying to assuage Romeo's misgivings simply cannot keep from proclaiming his own. The Queen Mab speech grows into a howl of unbridled misogyny—almost always evident in the character's wordplay—and, indeed, unrequited love for Romeo. Leonard Whiting's uncomprehending hero quiets his friend: "Peace, peace, Mercutio, peace! / Thou talkst of nothing" (1.4.95–96). The implicit pun on female anatomy built into *nothing* reinforces the sense that Mercutio is excluded from any dreams of fulfillment that Romeo might have. Instead, Romeo is transformed by a radiantly youthful Olivia Hussey—to the strains of Nino Rota's song, "What Is a Youth," a blend of Elizabethan sentiment and 1960s Europop. The very next day, when Mercutio is wounded as a result of Romeo's well-meaning intervention, he initially reveals his wound only to his friend—as sign both of intimacy and of bitter resentment. Even so, the judgment Mercutio renders goes beyond the bounds of Romeo's own involvement and absence. He pronounces a doom upon the elders, even if the children have to suffer most immediately for it.

Richard III, as adapted in 1995 by Ian McKellen and Richard Loncraine, also combines political concerns with issues of sexual orientation. For Zeffirelli, pathos linked the two spheres of individual and social experience; for McKellen and Loncraine, camp provides the medium for exploring both. Jonathan Dollimore has argued that a Shakespearean play-text such as *Antony and Cleopatra* is predicated upon what he calls "the profound truth of camp, the 'deep' truth of the superficial: if it's worth doing, it's worth overdoing." McKellen's and Loncraine's *Richard III* eagerly follows the Shakespearean injunction to overdo. Their film revels—as Dollimore reminds us about camp—"in a desire it simultaneously deconstructs, becoming a form of theatrical excess which both celebrates and undermines what it mimics" (147). Their film offers not only theatrical but also cinematic excess, as an array of movie conventions from the 1930s onward are gleefully and sometimes wickedly invoked. Among these conventions are some of the richest and most volatile materials associated with the camp sensibility: the Hollywood musical, the matinee idol, the ephemera of art deco styles and fashions, even the frequently alleged connection between homoeroticism and fascism.

The film directly connects with the theatrical history of *Richard III* via its origins in a celebrated Royal National Theatre production that opened in 1990 and continued, on tour, for over two years. Directed by Richard Eyre, this production realized an analogy that Ian McKellen had asserted for years in his one-man show *Acting Shakespeare*: that the Richard of the *Henry VI* plays and *Richard III* was a type for the totalitarian leaders of the twentieth century. From early on in the process of adapting the play—and the thirties-era production—for the screen, McKellen was thinking in terms of sexuality and in terms of jolting his audience with outrageous humor. Much of the sexualization and much of the drama is heightened to camp effect. This is not entirely McKellen's and Loncraine's doing; as Dollimore suggests, much of the extravagance is Shakespeare's own.

From the film's outset, McKellen portrays Richard as a sexual outsider: he is alienated from his family because of his incapacity to continue the York line in any form. Sexual frustration is a major component of McKellen's interpretation of the role. He had appeared as Iago shortly before tackling *Richard III* for the National Theatre production and—as is often the case with actors—saw a connection between the characters. McKellen, having "delved into the jealous psychology of a sexually frustrated husband . . . was prepared to explore Richard's humanity rather than reducing him to an emblem of wickedness" (McKellen 22–23). This Richard, in his way, was unmistakably sinned against as well as sinning (Eyre's production was initially staged in repertoire with Deborah Warner's staging of *King Lear*). He may sin against himself—as the desperate, conscience-stricken soliloquy after dreaming of his victims indicates—but he has considerable help, notably from his mother, the Duchess of York. McKellen is explicit on this point: Richard has suffered from his mother "verbal and emotional abuse which from infancy has formed her youngest son's character and behaviour" (McKellen 22). Little wonder, then, that in the screen adaptation several of Queen Margaret's bitterest lines are assigned to the Duchess herself (Buhler 2000, 45).

Richard's villainy inspires the filmmakers—as it inspires Shake-speare—to heights of extravagance. Sometimes the theatrical excess is registered by cinematic technique. Consider the scene between Richard and his newly arrested brother Clarence, set in this case by the banks of the Thames and introduced by Richard himself, who unexpectedly leans into the camera frame from the upper right. Even as he describes his plot "To set my brothers, Clarence and the King, / In deadly hate, the one against the other" (1. 1. 34–35), the jocular delivery and jaunty camerawork suggests that Richard has somehow stumbled into his own story. He becomes, briefly, a passerby who has wandered onto the set and into camera range; he also becomes, briefly, an intrusive journalist covering the story for our benefit, but even more for his own. The film version of Richard's conquest of Anne is, as many commentators have observed, considerably muted from the stage version. Some of the muting likely results from literalizing the locale: Bob Crowley's set for the National Theatre merely suggested a morgue or field hospital; Tony Burrough's setting for the film makes it clear this is a mortuary. The performance style contributes to a quieter, even more somber tone. One supremely theatrical effect from the stage production did survive and was intensified: Richard's offering Anne a ring as a kind of betrothal between them. The published screenplay describes how Richard "slowly lifts his right hand to his mouth and, with his teeth, pulls off his family signet-ring . . . [then] slides the ring, wet with saliva, onto her engagement finger" (McKellen 85). The erotic charge of the scene, which was considerable on stage, is heightened by the use of closeups here. Kristen Scott Thomas's Anne quietly gasps as the ring actually slides onto her middle finger. She can barely utter her next line, a last gesture toward resistence: "To take is not to give." The sexuality, however, is to a great extent autoerotic—as Richard initially performs a kind of fellatio on himself—and this feeds the bitter, self-regarding exuberance of Richard's own commentary on what has transpired between Anne and himself: "Upon my life she finds, although I cannot, / Myself to be a marvellous proper man" (1.2.256–57). His manner with assorted victims of the recent war waiting in the hospital's corridors is solipsistically merry. Richard then dances his way upstairs, as a tune that would befit a musical from the era blares on the soundtrack.

As McKellen tells it, Richard with Anne "inspires himself by playing the fantasy role of romantic lover" (80), as embodied by a panoply of "screen heroes": he mentions Clark Gable, Clifton Webb, David Niven, and Douglas Fairbanks by virtue, in part, of the stylized moustache they wear and that this Richard wears by McKellen's own choice. The role of romantic lover is not only fantastic for Richard, but for anyone—the role is part of a fantasy aggressively mounted, marketed, and naturalized in the 1930s. The arbitrariness of the marks of the screen hero, though, underscores the constructed quality of the role itself and invites the detached mirth of camp: the pencil-line mustache is now something of an emblem for director John Waters, perhaps today's shrewdest student and auteur of camp sensibility.

Richard later tries to replicate his success with Anne by trying to coerce Elizabeth, his brother's widow, to agree to a marriage between him and her daughter. Despite her apparent acceptance, Elizabeth simply buys time in order to counter not only Richard's schemes, but also his misogyny and dysfunction. This is trumpeted in the film through an audacious rearrangement of the playtext—and further revision of history—by having Richmond marry Princess Elizabeth before the battle of Bosworth Field. The marriage remains Queen Elizabeth's doing: in the role, Annette Bening registers relief and joy at the ceremony. She also enjoys this strategic triumph over Richard and his desperate (and humiliating) attempt to seduce her into consenting to an alliance. Not only does she telegraph her intentions to Richard's rival: the Queen has apparently marched young Elizabeth straight to Richmond's camp and expectant embrace.

Instead of being visited in the night by the same ghosts that so terrify his adversary, Dominic West's Richmond enjoys "fairest-boding dreams" that are here inspired by the lovely young woman with whom he has spent the night. It is Princess Elizabeth, and not an attendant lord, who asks him: "How have you slept, my Lord?" The scene self-consciously echoes Zeffirelli's cinematic rendering of Romeo and Juliet's aubade, their leave-taking after their only night together. The film's idealized presentation of easy, comfortable sexual love on the eve—and the morn—of a portentous battle nearly demands an ironic response. The film goes to extremes in marking Richard and Richmond as polar opposites and this continues in the final battle. While Richard abandons the wounded Ratcliffe and executes Tyrrell for even suggesting retreat, Richmond waves off his men to pursue Richard alone. Such clichés of the action-adventure movie are accompanied by auditory and visual overstatements. The music for this final "chase" is a melodramatic rewrite of Isaac Albeniz's virtuoso guitar composition, "Asturias." Looming over Richard as he tries to elude Richmond, we see an impressively phallic smokestack which has survived the barrage of artillery. Although meant to be part of "a massive abandoned factory," the location, it turns out, is the old Battersea Power Station. The contrast between Richard's presumption and Richmond's potency could not be clearer.

Nevertheless, the film concludes by calling their differences into question. When cornered by Richmond on the girders of the ruined factory, Richard reaches out and invites his enemy to join him. He uses words that in the playtext appear as the couplet prefacing Richard's oration to his troops: "Let's to it pell-mell, / If not to Heaven, then hand-in-hand to Hell!" (5. 3. 312–13). He falls backward, while Richmond fires his revolver superfluously after him. West's Richmond then looks directly at the camera—as no one else in the film has done, other than Richard—and smiles quietly, a bit smugly, as we hear Al Jolson's version of "Sittin' on Top of the World." What kind of exchange has occurred by which both pretenders to the throne feel, as McKellen says, "that they are sitting on top of the world" (286)? At this point, we see Richard's body plummet from the girders, with the massive tower again in the background. We then see Richard grinning as he falls into flames. The song's lyrics apply in several uncanny ways: there is an echo of James Cagney's character in *White Heat* bellowing "Top of the world!" to his mother with fiery explosions surrounding him (see Loehlin 75); there are also the verses that aver that "A bundle of money don't make me feel gay, / My sweet little honey is makin' me say: / I'm sittin' on top of the world." Kathy M. Howlett (148) has noted how the radical instability of the film's closing framework can demand "that the viewer's sense of what is going on" historically and morally "also be found vulnerable" and subject to reconsideration.

Both Richard's villainy and his humanity—in less moralized terms, his otherness and identity—are alternately communicated and ironized. Similar strategies with Elizabethan and Jacobean playtexts were employed by Derek Jarman, first with his *Tempest* and then with his "improvement" (his own term) of Marlowe's *Edward II*. In the published version of the screenplay for the latter film, Jarman notes how he insisted on letting the homosexual characters be unsympathetic; he records that Andrew Tiernan "is not playing Gaveston in a way that will endear me to 'Gay Times'" (Jarman 1991, 20). He also comments on McKellen's public avowal of being gay and his subsequent receiving of honors from the government of John Major:

McKellen's knighthood is . . . shocking: wining and dining in the erroneous belief that his honour improves our situation. There are many gay men with Tory hearts who believe in this honour. I don't.

It was brave of Ian to come out—but that is all he had to do. (Jarman 1991, 106)

McKellen's and Loncraine's camp *Richard III* is to some extent a response to Jarman's *Queer Edward II* (the title of the published screenplay) and to Jarman's critique of McKellen's public persona as "A Knight, Out." There are a few unmistakable echoes of Jarman in *Richard III*. For example, the same actor, Roger Hammond, largely represents the Church for both films. In *Edward II*, he is the Bishop of York, representing alarm at the king's sexual politics and coercing Edward into approval of his favorite's banishment; in *Richard III*, he is "the Archbishop" who is Richard's first principal defector and who later presides over Richmond's marriage to Princess Elizabeth. In addition, the use of "Sittin' on Top of the World" at the end is inspired, at least in part, by Jarman's integrating Cole Porter's "Everytime We Say Goodbye" (as sung, on camera, by the Eurythmics' Annie Lennox) into the farewell scene between Edward and Gaveston. The differences between the films, however, are profound. Jarman worked with dramatic characters whose sexuality is discussed directly in the play; McKellen and Loncraine work both with a text that is less direct and a stage tradition that interacts with that text. Just as Shakespeare's sexuality is less certain than Marlowe's, so sexuality in *Richard III* is more elusive than in *Edward II*.

A more insistently transgressive adaptation of Shakespeare—but one that generally avoids the political dimension—can be found in Derek Jarman's own 1980 *The Tempest*. Prospero's island, here, is Britain itself, with the interiors shot primarily at Stoneleigh Abbey (the ancestral home of the Leigh family, contributing to a romantic-era conception of Prospero as an anachronistic magus) and the exteriors, shot in deep blue filter, along the coast at Bamburgh. Jarman's critique of the self-contradictions of mainstream, heterosexist culture centers on the deposed Duke of Milan. As Prospero, Heathcote Williams is presented as a benign Alastair Crowley figure, both drawn to the vertiginous world of kabbalistic magic and unsettled by it. He experiences the physical storm of the play's title as a nightmare and his retreat from physicality finds expression in his polarized servants, Ariel and Caliban. Jarman draws upon the stage convention of a vaguely eroticized relationship between Prospero and Ariel, when that spirit is played by a woman. Karl Johnson's Ariel, unmistakably male, is a beautifully aloof presence in white, an object of desire abstracted into a pale wraith. In contrast, Caliban is portrayed as sheer appetite, an embodiment of Freud's idea of the "polymorphous perversity" of infantile sexuality. Blind performance artist Jack Birkett, who billed himself as The Incredible Orlando (with a sly allusion to Virginia Woolf's hero/ine), tackles the role with appropriate relish: he gestures raunchily at Miranda, even spewing raw egg at her; he passionately insists "I must eat my dinner" when Prospero faults him for shirking his duties; we even see him, as an adult, nursing at Sycorax's breast before Prospero's arrival. The last flashback, though, appears when Prospero confronts Ariel with his former condition as thrall to Caliban's mother; it connotes Prospero's distaste toward the body (especially the maternal body) and suggests he has projected that distastefulness upon Caliban.

Birkett would later play a cross-dressing Thersites in Jonathan Miller's production of *Troilus and Cressida* for the BBC Shakespeare series. More in keeping with the spirit of Jarman's *The Tempest*, he would also appear as Titania in a vivid *A Midsummer Night's Dream*, a 1984 collaboration between Celestino Coronado and Lindsay Kemp. Coronado had done a wildly experimental film essay on *Hamlet* in 1976, stressing the internal divisions and sexual conflicts within the title character and the language he employs: two actors, Anthony and David Meyer, play Hamlet. That version gave Jarman a precedent for exploring similar dynamics in Prospero, something the director acknowledges in casting David Meyer as Ferdinand in his *Tempest*. Prospero's trial of Ferdinand takes on both sadomasochistic and alchemical resonances (moving from Freud to Jung, perhaps) as Ferdinand must be "sublimated" before he and Miranda can be united. Miranda, too, has apparently been subjected to taming in the past, though with mixed results. In an inspired bit of casting, punk diva Toyah Willcox is a gloriously rebellious daughter, by turns sullenly resentful and gleefully impulsive. Even as she unwittingly follows her father's plan in proposing marriage to Ferdinand, she surreptitiously hands him the key to his shackles.

Similarly, Jarman genially subverts the sexual politics of the play's normalizing marriage by means of the festival he conjures up to celebrate it. First, Ariel is directed to fetch the mariners who have been kept asleep on the other side of the island. He is about to open the door in order to leave on this errand when he catches himself, grins as if to say "What was

I thinking?," and then vanishes. If he is to be relegated to spritely status, he may as well have fun with it. The campiness of the film's celebratory masque indicates the kind of fun he and Jarman have in mind. The mariners appear in gleaming white sailor suits and dance energetically to a hornpipe; the entire production seems equal parts Busby Berkeley and Gilbert and Sullivan. Ariel trades his workman's coveralls for a white tuxedo to serve as master of ceremonies, introducing jazz singer Elisabeth Welch for a rendition of Arlen and Kern's "Stormy Weather" (Welch reportedly gave the song its London debut back in the 1930s). The mariners now happily serve as chorus boys to the sunnily gowned vocal-ist, a literal diva—a goddess.

With the marriage secured, the families and kingdoms reconciled, and the homoerotic celebrated all at once, Jarman concludes the film with the suggestion that *The Tempest* and its consequences have somehow been confined to Prospero's own mind. We see Prospero asleep in the festival room, now darkened; he sits in the chair that Miranda had occupied as Ferdinand's consort. Ariel grins at his erstwhile master, then sits and intones the song that the play's character sings while he assists Prospero in adopting his ducal garb:

> Where the bee sucks, there suck I,
> In a cowslip's bell I lie;
> There I couch when owls do cry.
> On the bat's back I do fly
> After summer merrily.
> Merrily, merrily shall I live now,
> Under the blossom that hangs on the bough. (5.1.88–94)

He will not disturb Prospero with such language, however, which is brac-ingly sexualized in the new context. He walks quietly past the still-sleep-ing duke, takes one last look, and then runs away, laughing. We hear, in voice-over, Prospero's summary of the masque performed for the young couple, beginning with "Our revels now are ended," and concluding with "our little life / Is rounded with a sleep" (4.1.148–58). The screen fades to black and the first credits declare the film to be "Dedicated to the memory of Elizabeth Evelyn Jarman," the director's mother who had died in 1978. Jarman's first revision of the play, in 1975, had depicted Prospero as insane, "rightly imprisoned by his brother," and "playing all the parts" (Jarman 1984, 183). After reflecting on his mother's "eighteen years of illness, borne with such serenity" (184), the idea of a circumscribed life retaining and rediscovering vitality took precedence over the earlier conception. The director's own "messing with Will Shakespeare" (1984, 206), both neglected and reviled at the time of the film's release, was a conscious attempt to rediscover the vitality of the playtext.

Peter Greenaway's 1991 *Prospero's Books* and Trevor Nunn's 1996 *Twelfth Night* demonstrate how the very act of making a Shakespeare film can be consciously experienced as transgressive. Both these filmmakers—if for very different reasons—assume some measure of disapproval on the part of the authorial presence they invoke and present. Greenaway is first and foremost a visual artist, trained as a painter and art historian before moving to the cinema. He is also, though, fascinated by the possibilities of hypermedia, the depth of interplay between images and text made possible by the new digital technologies. His first experiment along these lines was *A TV Dante* (1989), which examined the first cantos of Dante's *Inferno* through a dizzying array of sights and sounds, of readings, representations, and commentaries. The voice-over provides the organizing principle for much of *Prospero's Books*, his adaptation of Shakespeare's *The Tempest*, since for the bulk of the film Greenaway borrows from the idea Jarman had rejected: this Prospero, played by John Gielgud (who had served as the voice of the Roman poet Virgil for *A TV Dante*), speaks for—or with—all the characters until very late in the play. There are two commentators, however. Along with Prospero's own voice and his impersonations, an unidentified narrator provides information about the specific volumes in the exiled duke's possession. Making use of Graphic Paintbox technology, Greenaway allows these fictional hybrids of actual Renaissance texts to come alive, to be ever-changing hypertexts. He adds these technological effects to the brilliant cinematography of long-time collaborator Sacha Vierny (whose work can also been seen in such classics as Alain Resnais's *Hiroshima, Mon Amour* and Luis Buñuel's *Belle de Jour*).

Curiously, though, the playtext itself is presented only in its most attenuated forms. Douglas Lanier (1996) has written insightfully of Greenaway's film as "Drowning the Book," alluding to how *Prospero's Books* actualizes Prospero's pledge to cast his book of magic into the sea "deeper than did ever plummet sound" (5.1.56). At the end of the film, we see the many aspects (or emanations) of Ariel assist Prospero in consigning his library to the waves; throughout the film, the playtext's language is realized and then overwhelmed by sheer visual representation. What makes the language easier to overwhelm, however, is Greenaway's insistence on disconnecting it from two sources of its power: verse itself and actorly performance. While Gielgud's voice pays tribute to the musicality of Shakespeare's language, Greenaway shows that language as prose, not poetry. Prospero here is a surrogate for Shakespeare, writing all the dialogue and rehearsing all the scenes himself. We see his quill scratching the words onto parchment, but as they take shape they form paragraphs, not verse lines. In the move from the vertically oriented page (▮) to the the horizontally-oriented screen (■)—such as the widescreen format of high-definition TV—Greenaway has prevented himself from conveying the visible sign of word as verse. At the same time, in the move from the interaction of different voices to the interplay of different media, Greenaway deliberately sacrifices both drama and emotional play. The director has drained the book before drowning it.

Even so, the film contextualizes Shakespeare's play within Renaissance art, cosmology, history, literary culture, psychology, and technology in provocative and instructive ways. Greenaway sets his Prospero to work in a recreation of Michelangelo's Laurentian Library (see Figure 8); he reconnects the denizens of the island with Early Modern attempts to depict the inhabitants of the New World in visual terms; he turns the most youthful aspect of Ariel into the putto of an Italian fountain, endlessly urinating (and also suggests that conjuring up a storm is little more than "making water"). He withholds the possibility of human interaction until Prospero himself is ready to feel compassion—and even then stages the play's denouement in an aggressively static manner. More provocatively, Greenaway makes the survival of the Shakespearean canon—Prospero's manuscript is placed at the front of the First Folio, where *The Tempest* first appeared in print—dependent on Caliban, who despite his resentment of language rescues the last of Prospero's books from the sea. Finally, the film shows the liberation of Ariel, who runs toward the camera as the on-screen cast applauds, blending into the groups of performers and then re-emerging more and more youthful. The youngest Ariel takes flight and in laborious slow motion rises out of view, having freed himself of the confines of the screen.

Greenaway feels that filmmaking in itself can be liberating; there can be no sharper contrast in attitude than that provided by Trevor Nunn in his assessment of what it was like to bring *Twelfth Night* to the screen. Despite his own wide experience in extravagant stagings, directing the original productions of Andrew Lloyd Webber's *Cats, Starlight Express,* and *Sunset Boulevard* (along with the first English-language production of

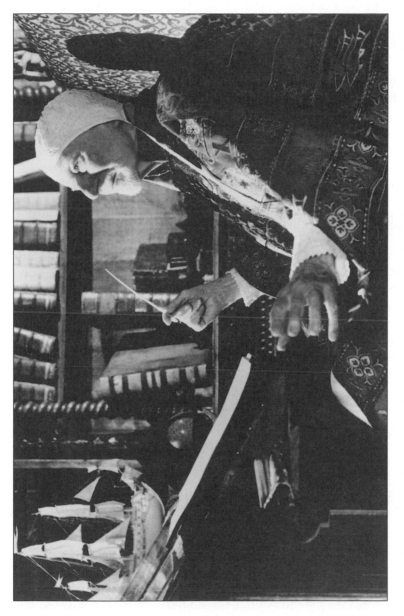

FIGURE 8. John Gielgud as Prospero in the library envisioned by director Peter Greenaway for *Prospero's Books* (1991). Photo courtesy of Jerry Ohlinger's Movie Material.

Les Misérables), Nunn was profoundly uncomfortable with the process of adapting what he terms "the text I most love" (iii) to what was hoped would be a mass-market audience. The introduction to the published screenplay repeatedly voices his frustration at the Hollywood executives and southern California audiences who conspired to force him to provide explanatory introductory materials establishing not only the story line but also Feste's role as narrator, observer, and (it is suggested) orchestrator of what follows. The powers given to an "allowed fool" here are expansive; Nunn feels, in reaction, particularly constrained. Film, Nunn argues, "is even more an amalgam of compromises than the theatre" (xiv), and at least the stage would allow him to do the play "without cutting or changing a word" (xvi).

The emphasis on language comes from Nunn's time with the Royal Shakespeare Company, including nearly twenty years as its artistic director. During that time, he (and most people involved with the RSC) was greatly influenced by John Barton, an academic-turned-director who combined close textual analysis with canny stage instincts. Most things an actor needs are on the page, advises Barton (see his *Playing Shakespeare*, esp. 25–32, 150–56). But what happens when vast amounts of text must be abandoned? Nunn's solution—one he addresses briefly in his introduction—is to rearrange the text so that thematic and dramatic parallels can serve to highlight one another. For Nunn, *Twelfth Night* is "one of those rare phenomena, the perfect work of art, like Mozart's *Figaro* or Billy Wilder's *Some Like It Hot*" (iv). Nunn's choice of masterworks is deliberate. Both involve cross-dressing and gender confusion: Mozart's Cherubino—usually played by a woman on the operatic stage—is persuaded to dress as a woman by the countess he adores; Wilder's film shows men attempting to hide from gangsters by disguising themselves as part of an "all-women" band. Surely, though, the perfection of such works must depend not only upon individual components—whether Cherubino's aria, "Voi che sapete," or Joe E. Brown's closing words of acceptance, "Nobody's perfect!"—or on their thematic parallels, but on the arrangement of those materials, the architecture of the whole. Even so, Nunn felt that he must change the sequence of events, the "*chronology* of the story" (xi, Nunn's emphasis) for the play to work on cineplex screens. So, "trembling and expecting an imminent thunderbolt" (Nunn, it appears, remains a communicant of the church of Shakespeare), he set out to divide and conjoin scenes and even speeches in mapping out the shooting script and, later, in the process of editing.

What results, interestingly enough, is a version of the play that high-lights the division and reunion of sister and brother. Nunn's visual pro-logue (with Feste's account heard in voice-over) shows Viola and Sebas-tian onboard ship before the storm that founders the vessel. At what might be a nineteenth-century version of a Twelfth Night (January 6th, the last day of Christmas) festival, the twins indulge in cross-dressing as they sing a Victorian-style setting of "O Mistress Mine" to a delighted audience. Branagh, too, in *Much Ado About Nothing*, uses as introductory material a song that is heard in the middle of the play. Sebastian's mascu-line baritone asserts itself in the line "That can sing both high and low," and while both are dressed in female "Oriental" garb, they also both sport mustaches beneath their veils. Sebastian removes Viola's mustache, but before she can attempt to remove his, the storm hits. There is time to gather some belongings (which will conveniently come ashore with Viola) but soon Viola is washed off-deck. Sebastian dives underwater to rescue her and we briefly see them, underwater, hand in hand. They reach the surface, are driven apart by the waves, and are left to be rescued, respec-tively, by Antonio and the Captain, whom we have seen at the party.

The film, then, opens on a somber note and sustains it remarkably. Nunn removes the lines that suggest Viola's hope that Sebastian has sur-vived: she is so grief-stricken that she seeks to join her brother in death. The group of survivors has to hide from some of Orsino's soldiers and, while taking refuge in nearby woods, stumble near a belated funeral pro-cession led by Olivia in honor of her recently deceased brother. Taking all of this in is Ben Kingsley's enigmatic and melancholy Feste, watching atop a seacliff. Imogen Stubbs's Viola assumes her male identity not only so she can join Orsino's service in safety, but also as a living memorial to the brother she believes has drowned. The Victorian setting lends a cul-tural authenticity to the signs of grief that Olivia hopes to maintain and that Viola expresses in her very disguise.

Much as Branagh had attempted to "improve" such characters in *Much Ado* as Claudio and Don Pedro, Nunn downplays the narcissism of Orsino. The duke, as played by Toby Stephens (son of Robert Stephens, Branagh's Ancient Pistol), still admires that Olivia can "pay this debt of love but to a brother" (1.1.33), which here allows the disguised Viola to recall her last view of Sebastian. But Nunn excises the lines in which he anticipates "How will she love when the rich golden shaft / Hath kill'd the flock of all affections else" and when "Her sweet perfections with one self king"—namely himself—are "fill'd" (34–38). His indulgence in matters of love to the neglect of other affairs of state is implicitly explained by a wounded arm. And, as with *Much Ado*, the emotional economy of the play demands that elements suppressed in one area must emerge in another. With a more earnest Viola, there is ample room for a more giddy Olivia, which Helena Bonham Carter eagerly supplies. With a less self-romanticizing Orsino, there is ample room for a yet more self-indulgent Malvolio. Nigel Hawthorne presents his stern regime as head of Olivia's household staff as the counterpart to his lingering desire to be lord of the manor in fact. Alone in his rooms, he reads French erotic romances (*L'Amour* is the title we see), sips brandy (its decanter discreetly hidden in a hollowed-out book), and assumes such gentlemanly garb as a sumptuous dressing gown and the yellow stockings that will contribute to his downfall. A hilarious and poignant take later on will reveal that Richard E. Grant's Sir Andrew also wears yellow, not knowing that "'tis a color she [Olivia] abhors." In public, Malvolio insists on wearing and constantly adjusting a toupee (which the cast members quickly dubbed "Colin"), reluctant to accept the encroachments of age.

The centerpiece of this autumnal view of the play is Feste's own version of "O Mistress Mine." Nunn intersperses scenes involving Viola/Cesario and Orsino with the playtext's original scene. After Feste has established a plaintive tone with his version of the song, accompanying himself on the concertina, Nunn cuts to Orsino's house where the same tune is heard on the piano. Back at Olivia's, the revellers, Sir Toby and Sir Andrew, are uncharacteristically reflective in response to the song. Returning to the duke's castle, we then see the growing intimacy between Cesario and "his" master, including some jealousy on Orsino's part (does he already suspect Olivia's motives in wanting to see the young messenger?) that his young attendant is in love. We hear Orsino's admission that male devotion is wavering and his advice to Cesario: "Then let thy love be younger than thyself, / For women are as roses whose fair flower, / Being once displayed, doth fall that very hour" (2.4.36–38). As Feste sings, "What's to come is still unsure," Imelda Staunton's Maria sees an opportunity to appeal directly to Mel Smith's Sir Toby. She provides harmony for the final verse of the song: "In delay there lies no plenty, / Then come kiss me, sweet and twenty. / Youth's a stuff will not endure." The last line is repeated with increasing urgency by Feste, as Maria aims a pleading gaze at her mistress' uncle. This Maria will only briefly hesitate to defy Malvolio and engineer his humiliation, all for the sake of attracting Toby—who is all that the day has left for her to seize.

The film is lovely to behold, as realized by Sophie Becker's production design and Clive Ticknor's photography; the Victorian setting allows for sumptuous Pre-Raphaelite visions to guide decisions in costuming, decor, and casting the extras. Both Olivia's veil of mourning and the shimmering blue dress that proclaims an end to grief are indebted to painters of the adopted period. Shaun Davey's music contributes greatly to the unfolding of the story, as motifs recur and combine; this is, after all, a play much dependent on song, one that opens with a line about music as "the food of love" and that closes with Feste's "The Wind and the Rain." All of the principals are gifted comic performers, provoking genuine laughter throughout. The overall mood, though, is bittersweet. Sir Andrew is finally disabused of his dreams of marrying Olivia and of his thought that Sir Toby was actually a friend. Sir Toby and Maria do indeed marry, but their departure from Olivia's estate seems a matter of settling down and settling for less. Sebastian's rescuer, Antonio (the ubiquitous Nicholas Farrell), is happy that his beloved's sister is alive, but palpably wounded that he is wed to Olivia. Even this giddy Olivia—whose double takes at seeing the twins together are deliciously overdone—feels sympathy for a much-abused Malvolio, who may agree not to "be reveng'd upon the whole pack" of Olivia's household but who still has to leave. Feste himself, the instigator of all, is none too pleased with the sum of Malvolio's travails and abruptly retreats.

What *is* happy about this ending is the reunion of brother and sister. All Sebastian has to do is once more remove his sister's false mustache and he can ignore Viola's request that he "not embrace" her until her "masculine usurped attire" (5.1.250–51) has been changed for feminine garb. In the screenplay, which reflects Nunn's shooting script, the expressions of their acceptance of each other's identity is limited to touching each other's hands, faces, and tears (123). In the actual film, by contrast, the performers find that the intensity of their joy can best be expressed by an exultant, tearful embrace. As Feste returns to the seacliff, singing to Davey's upbeat setting for the concluding song's wistful words, we see the outcasts from the celebration and we see the fortunate couples, Olivia with Sebastian, and Orsino with Viola. Because the credits begin to roll at this point, audiences might be tempted not to pay attention to Nunn's final twist on the story. The song nears its end, the couples embrace, and the twins reach beyond their new partners to join hands once again, as they had underwater.

Feste may get the last words—and Kingsley, speaking rather than singing, repeats the song's final "every day" twice—but Sebastian and

Viola enjoy the true resolution in Nunn's retelling. The marketing of the film stressed the transgressive nature of the materials, drawing parallels with other gender-bending films (not, however, Wilder's *Some Like It Hot*): "Before Priscilla crossed the desert, Wong Foo met Julie Newmar, and the Birdcage was unlocked, there was . . . *Twelfth Night*." Strangely, the most transgressive elements in the resulting film involve Nunn's own anxiety about rearranging Shakespeare's materials; only Welles has been more daring in restructuring the plays. His suggestion that sibling devotion can outweigh all other forms of love also savors of the transgressive. In making the suggestion, however, he may also have touched upon a connection between Shakespeare's life and art that has been little commented upon. Of the two Shakespearean plays that involve twins, *Comedy of Errors* and *Twelfth Night*, it is the latter that involves not two males but a male-female pair, the kind of twins to which Shakespeare himself was father. *Twelfth Night* was written after the death of Hamnet, the male twin, at the age of eleven; as Richard P. Wheeler notes (147–52), the play provides a series of fantasies on the theme of restoring the dead male twin to life. The playwright was grateful that daughter Judith had survived, and perhaps he gained a greater appreciation for her; without question, he knew all the more keenly that youth's a stuff will not endure. Some boundaries are not socially constructed, even if means of coping with them are.

CHAPTER EIGHT

— ◇ —

Gaining in Translation

KATHERINE: Your Majesty shall mock at me, I cannot speak
your England.

—Shakespeare, *Henry V*

When filmmakers adapt Shakespeare for cinematic performance in languages other than English, they often take the opportunity not only to translate the playtexts into film more "freely" but also to comment on the cultural differences marked by language itself. Such differences intrigued Shakespeare, as several plays hinge on the significances attributed to language and dialect. Near the end of *Henry V*, Princess Katherine, the "capital demand" (5.2.96) of the conquering invader of her country, is keenly aware of her vulnerability in political terms and in linguistic ones. She cannot speak the King's English, and therefore cannot negotiate anything like a separate identity for herself or her people before her enforced marriage to the English king. Lest the situation be presented too starkly, the playtext also focuses on Henry's professed inabilities in French and in courtship language more generally: we and the princess, in being moved "to laugh at" (5.2.187) his artfully awkward efforts, are disarmed.

But the play goes on to announce that the unified empire of England and France—and even the internal unity within England—will not last. The French powers will reassert themselves in the Hundred Years' War, while the Wars of the Roses will resolve only after a descendant of Katherine's second marriage claims legitimacy, in effect, by "right and title of the female." Henry, Earl of Richmond and grandson of Katherine and Owen Tudor, will defeat Richard III and marry Elizabeth, Richard's niece and the daughter of his predecessor Edward IV. Henry's granddaughter, Elizabeth I of England, was the flower and conclusion of the dynasty he founded.

Throughout Shakespeare's history plays, languages other than English are associated both with female power and with the often obscured sources of Tudor authority: France and Wales. Command of authoritative language in English is consistently associated with effective rule—and not only in the history plays. Comic figures ranging from Armado in *Love's Labors Lost* and Bottom in *A Midsummer Night's Dream* to Dogberry in *Much Ado About Nothing* "prove" how much they deserve their lack of status by virtue of their unwitting misuse of language. Elites, by contrast, can exploit the slipperiness of words, as another aspect of their power. Young Hal, before becoming Henry V, sneers at the linguistic ineptitude of Francis, a tavern boy; Sir John Falstaff is similarly dismissive toward Mistress Quickly's ill-chosen words. In the history of Shakespearean performance as well, command of the King's English has been valorized: some of the distaste aimed at the 1935 Warner Brothers *A Midsummer Night's Dream* stemmed not from textual liberties but from "non-Shakespearean" accents. Such valorization functions most strongly, however, within English-speaking communities. As a result, Shakespearean performances in languages other than English have not been as constrained by notions of linguistic propriety. The cinematic results of such freedom have regularly proved to be some of Shakespeare's most vigorous and compelling interpretations. The plays often gain in translation to the screen as a consequence of being translated from English; the films benefit, too, from their keen awareness of the cultural issues involved in linguistic as well as cinematic translation. What follows is a series of brief national "histories" of Shakespearean filmmaking, each placing special emphasis on the interrelation between language and political or cultural authority.

REPORT OF FASHIONS IN PROUD ITALY
(from *Richard II*)

As suggested in chapter four, filmmakers in Italy were drawn to Shakespeare's materials, if not always strictly to his plays, from the earliest days of the Film d'Arte movement. In many Italian adaptations, cultural priority is asserted for the film, rather than the text; stressing the play's source materials—or at least the locales that could be said to have "inspired" them—can effectively displace at least some of the playwright's authoritative status. In 1910, Gerolamo Lo Savio directed two of Italy's most famous performers, Ermete Novelli and Francesca Bertini, in sharply compressed versions of *King Lear* and *The Merchant of Venice*. Brilliantly hand-tinted (as were many early films) for their original release, *Re Lear* places special emphasis on the scenes featuring the principal actors: the reconciliation scene between Novelli as Lear and Bertini as Cordelia departs from the film's usual rushed pace. We see the old king slowly, tearfully regain his wits under the gentle ministrations of his devoted daughter. With Bertini as Jessica, *Il Mercante di Venezia* understandably focuses on the tensions that exist between her character and that of her father, Shylock, played by Novelli. His grief at losing her to the Christian Lorenzo goes far in justifying his campaign for revenge; he becomes, at key moments, more a tragic than a comic "villain." Lo Savio's 1911 *Giuletta e Romeo* (also featuring Bertini) takes similar liberties with Shakespeare's playtexts: hadn't the events taken place on the very streets that served for the film's location? The director follows the eighteenth-century stage practice of permitting the lovers one last scene together. Long before Juliet looked into the still-seeing eyes of Romeo in Baz Luhrmann's film version, Bertini had awakened in the Capulet tomb to find Gustavo Serena not yet dead, but suffering the dire effects of the apothecary's potion.

Enrico Guazzoni first tackled Shakespeare's variations on Roman history in his 1910 account of *Brutus*. He followed his 1912 triumph, *Quo Vadis*, with a grandly scaled biography, *Giulio Cesare*. Filmed over the course of four years, it was released in 1914 and featured the wonderfully named Amleto Novelli (Ermete's son) in the title role. The actor's name may be the most Shakespearean thing about the production, although title cards prepared for English-speaking audiences increasingly echo *Julius Caesar* as the film approaches the fateful assassination. A free rendering of *The Winter's Tale*, *Una Tragedia alla Corte di Sicilia* (1913) reclaims the story for its Italian locale: under Baldassare Negroni's direction, the ill-fated courtier Antigonus is not devoured, off-stage, by a bear (as the playtext memorably dictates) but tossed into Sicily's own Mount Etna. Despite the departures from Shakespeare in favor of source materials and local color, the energy and ingenuity of the camerawork and the performances in both these films presage what could happen when the playtexts themselves provided more of the basis for cinematic expression rather than constraints against it.

Strangely, later Italian filmmakers have not fulfilled that promise. Renato Castellani's version of *Giuletta e Romeo* (see chapter five) regularly resorts to a version of Shakespearean language that its film techniques find incompatible. In part, this is strategic: Castellani wants to champion the powers of his medium. But he has constructed too easy a foil in the round tones of Laurence Harvey, his Romeo, and John Gielgud, his Chorus. In Franco Zeffirelli's reworking of *The Taming of the Shrew* and in his *Romeo and Juliet*, we can sense an impatience with the cadences of Received Pronunciation mouthing Shakespeare's lines in English. In his *Hamlet*, however, Zeffirelli calls upon several products of the Royal Shakespeare Company and the Royal National Theatre to provide more reliable delivery of Shakespearean verse than his principal performers sometimes manage. Choosing to make Shakespearean films in English has often led these directors to concede too much to a presumedly authoritative approach to the language: only Zeffirelli's 1986 film of *Otello*, Giuseppe Verdi's operatic retelling, is completely free of such subservience.

HOW LIKE YOU THE YOUNG GERMAN?
(from *Merchant of Venice*)

Film adaptations of Shakespeare's plays in Germany show the profound influence of that country's greatest Shakespearean stage director, Max Reinhardt, whose productions nevertheless often allowed their spectacular elements to overwhelm the text, even in translation. Reinhardtian spectacle animated a now-lost 1913 *Macbeth*, which combined English actors Arthur Bourchie and Violet Vanbrugh in the two lead roles with a German cast and crew, led by director Ludwig Landmann. The siege of Dunsinane Castle was given full treatment, as was the scale of the Macbeths' retinue (Ball 185–86). That same year, more direct borrowings from Reinhardt's *Dream* appeared in an updated *Ein Sommernachtstraum* directed by Stellan Rye and featuring as Puck Grete Berger, who would appear as a worker in Fritz Lang's silent masterwork *Metropolis*. The screenplay, by Rye and Hanns Heinz Ewers, a specialist in fantastic eroticism, expanded on the disturbing qualities of the fairy realm rediscovered by Reinhardt and suggested in his own Hollywood version for Warner Brothers. A 1925 version went even further in the direction of the carnivalesque: Berlin censors deemed it unsuitable for children and an English reviewer, Oswald Blakeston, candidly pronounced it "Rabelaisan" (Ball 297–98). Scattered descriptions suggest an exercise in Weimar decadence, à la *Cabaret*, complete with jazz band, a Puck played by Valeska Gert (who had already worked with Bertold Brecht), and disruptive commentary on the title cards provided by Expressionist poet and provocateur Klabund (born Alfred Henschke). Audiences were presented with all this and Werner Krauss, the Iago of Buchowetzki's *Othello* and the Shylock figure in Felner's *The Jew of Mestri*, as Nick Bottom.

The rise of the Nazi regime precipitated a mass exodus of artists and intellectuals from Germany. Reinhardt himself would leave in 1933, followed by legions of actors and directors, including many who had trained or worked with him. A few individuals remained, notably Krauss and Ewers, a writer for the 1913 *Dream*, who would write a fictionalized biography of blackshirt "martyr" Horst Wessel (who reportedly appears in Rye's other 1913 film, *The Student of Prague*). Only a 1935 *Merry Wives of Windsor* (Guntner 100) attempted to bring Shakespeare to the screen during the ascendancy of Joseph Goebbels's Ministry for Popular Entertainment and Propaganda, despite its interest in film and despite National Socialist claims that Germans and Anglo-Saxons were natural allies. Fully political appropriations of Shakespeare in service of the Reich would apparently have to wait until England's subjugation. After the Second World War, German filmmakers would be drawn to the story of Hamlet, whose alleged uncertainty about what course of action to take and whose insistence on uncovering the truth both resonated with the postwar generation. Helmut Käutner's 1959 *Der Rest Ist Schweigen* (*The Rest Is Silence*) offers an updated version of the play, complete with concerns over family involvement in wartime profiteering. The title—Hamlet's last words— reflects not only German reluctance to speak openly about the recent past but also a more wide-ranging suspicion toward language, which had been abused in so many official announcements and euphemisms. (Arthur Miller's drama *All My Sons*, an American tragedy that explores conflicts between success and responsibility, offers an intriguing intertext. The plot centers on the role of defective parts in the deaths of servicemen in the Second World War and how families come to terms with who is truly responsible.) In 1960, Franz Peter Wirth produced a very effective *Hamlet: Prinz von Danemark* for West German television, featuring Maximilian Schell in the title role as a charismatic figure, one who should have been trusted to assume his father's throne. Wirth's production explicates the political dimensions of the tragedy in ways that have yet to be matched (Rothwell 172), although Branagh's hints about the nature of Hamlet Senior's regime appear indebted to this version.

LIKE MUSCOVITES OR RUSSIANS, AS I GUESS
(from *Love's Labors Lost*)

We have already explored Russian-language Shakespeare in connection with Sergei Yutkevich's grandiose *Othello* (see chapter two) and considered some of the political allegorizing at work in the film's depiction of Desdemona's hero-worship and even in the use of color in the final scenes. There is no mistaking the political spin placed on another 1955 Soviet production, Yan Fried's larkish *Dvenadtsataya noch*, or *Twelfth Night*: taking advantage of the all-too-brief cultural thaw after Stalin's death, Fried and company present a gleeful fairy-tale version of the play. The melancholy strain in the text which would be so fully explored in Trevor Nunn's version has been laughingly excised. Only Malvolio is somber here and is associated with all the dour repressiveness of the cultural apparatchiks—party functionaries—who had held sway under Stalinism. The playtext's status as Other—marked as English and as Renaissance—enhances, rather than undermines, its cultural authority and therefore its capacity for witty dissent.

The film hastens to establish that both Viola and Sebastian have survived the shipwreck that separated them. This helps to lighten the mood immediately—showing that Viola's hopes that her brother indeed lives are well-grounded—and helps audiences accept actress Klara Luchko in both roles. So convinced is Viola that she and Sebastian will eventually be reunited that when they set eyes upon each other at the film's conclusion, she simply calls out his name and rushes to embrace him; none of the playtext's moving lines of uncertainty (can this be true?) survive in Fried's adaptation. Her cheerfulness from the start leaves her susceptible to the appeals of romance: she determines to assume male disguise primarily to gain access to a very attractive Orsino, played by Vadim Medvedev as something like Prince Charming. Viola's own charms as Cesario prove irresistible to Alla Larionova's Olivia, whose sumptuous estate proclaims the wealth that undeniably attracts both Sir Andrew and Malvolio. Which is not to say that this Olivia is personally unattractive: Larionova joins the rest of the cast and the vibrant settings in contributing to a film of storybook beauty throughout. Cinematographer E. Shapiro captures the energy in vibrant Sovcolor; Fried cannot resist moving from scene to scene via old-fashioned wipes, instead of dissolves; A. Zhivotov contributes glorious music. It is unfortunate that this film is most widely available in a badly dubbed, black-and-white video version; the colors are lost and the capable actors' own voices are heard only during the songs. The energy of the production comes through nevertheless.

Mikhail Yanshin's Sir Toby Belch displays Falstaffian proportions in girth and appetite. His friend and victim Sir Andrew is played by Georgi Vitsin as a thin, dim, sweet-natured Stan Laurel to Yanshin's stout and scheming Oliver Hardy. We see the sweetness in a moving, but funny take on Sir Andrew's unsuccessful campaign for Olivia's affection, leading a full consort of musicians to serenade her, his arms holding a vast number of roses. He is foolish, but he is also abjectly fond. For this reason, perhaps, he is not summarily dismissed by Toby at the end. Vasili Merkuriev's Malvolio is grandly stern, with a rococo extravagance to his hair and beard (imitated by designer Dante Ferreti and director Terry Gilliam in imagining the lead character for their 1988 film, *The Adventures of Baron Munchausen*) that proclaims his self-love, the vanity that will be his downfall. There is no pity at his humiliation: when Olivia informs him that the letter which seemed to fulfill his dreams was written by "Maria's hand," she and her entire household cannot contain their laughter.

The last words remain Feste's, but the Russian-language "The Wind and the Rain" is sung in an upbeat manner. Bruno Freindlich, as Feste, serves a celebratory purpose from beginning to end: he introduces the film, singing while seated on a window sill—an image that returns at the conclusion. He makes Olivia laugh outright when he chooses to "catechize" her about her brother's death and insists on riotous foolery (even animal sounds) when Malvolio attempts to curb Sir Toby and Sir Andrew. At the end of the film, after Malvolio storms off vowing revenge, Feste races up a flight of stairs and releases two birds in a magic act expressive of newfound freedom. Smiles and laughter abound, such as when Viola laughs at the thought of Olivia's desire for "Cesario" and when Antonio simply beams at Viola's and Sebastian's meeting. The festivity is infectious, the delight in shaking off restraint is palpable from the screen. The thought that real-life Malvolios could vengefully assert themselves on "the whole pack" (5.1.378) of revelers has been banished, with the ambitious steward, if only for a time. (For analyses of the political context of this film, in connection with the 1955 *Othello*, see Osborne.)

Grigori Kozintsev's 1964 version of *Hamlet* and 1970 version of *King Lear* show the passing of that time. While his *Gamlet* (the Russian title) includes enough of a political charge to be interpreted as an anti-Stalinist fable by some (Kliman 1988, 112–113), the world in which Kozintsev sets the tragedy suggests little hope for renewal. As the Prince of Denmark, Innokenti Smoktunovsky finds himself blocked in every direction. His return to Elsinore feels like an imprisonment, as the camera focuses on the massive drawbridge rising and the gate closing once he has entered. When Claudius tries to engage his attention, Hamlet is already trying to escape, leaving his chair in the council chamber empty and quickly moving downstairs. His first soliloquy is given in voice-over as an internal monologue, heard as he first walks against the flow of Claudius's retinue and then as he attempts to "mingle" with those celebrating the marriage Hamlet finds so troubling.

If this Hamlet is frustrated by his family, then Anastasia Vertinskaya as Ophelia is simply ground down by hers. We see her first dancing to stylized harpsichord music (evocative of the Elizabethan virginal, another keyboard instrument), not so much enjoying the dance as dutifully cultivating the attributes of a courtly young woman. After Polonius's death, she is caged in a metal corset and suppressed under the heavy, dark fabric of a mourning dress. Her death is marked by a hint of release, as Kozintsev's cinematographer Jonas Gritsyus has the camera follow the flight of a seabird over the expansive ocean. This image, perhaps recalling Feste's release of two birds at the end of Fried's *Twelfth Night*, signals only a brief respite. When the film returns to Ophelia, for her funeral, we are confronted by another sign of her imprisonment. After Hamlet has confronted Laertes, after he has gazed at her face as she lies in her coffin, after all the mourners have left, we see the lid placed firmly over her. The Gravedigger pounds heavy nails into the lid, keeping her in place once more.

By contrast, Hamlet seems to experience some deliverance in his own death. Knowing the poison will soon take its course, he walks out of the chamber where the duel had taken place and heads toward the sight of the open sea. Vladimir Erenberg's Horatio offers to assist him, but Hamlet refuses; he sits down, delivers his last line—"The rest is silence"— and turns his head away. When Fortinbras's men carry the prince's body in funeral procession, they march through the courtyard and across the drawbridge, out of the castle. The gate is lifted; Hamlet is free from that prison at least, if not the "king of infinite space" (2.2.255) he might once have wished himself. Kozintsev leaves us, however, with shots of the impassive gaze of peasantry, the implacable surge of the waves, and one of the stone walls of the fortress that is Elsinore. Dimitri Shostakovich's closing music scrupulously avoids any suggestion of transcendence, in keeping with the director's conviction that humanity and mortality implicate one another. When Hamlet had conversed with the gravedigger, the screen showed us a broken headstone in the shape of a cross looming behind the men, both of whom appear ready to be swallowed up by the earth itself.

Kozintsev then turned to Shakespeare's most unflinching look at human mortality and vulnerability, *King Lear*. His *Korol Lir*, shot during 1967 to 1969, and released in 1970, begins where *Gamlet* had ended, with a bleak landscape inhabited by the poorest of the poor. While Brook, almost simultaneously, was exploring the play's depiction of cruelty in his film, Kozintsev instead emphasizes the larger social context of the action—the "poor, naked wretches" of whom Lear has "ta'en too little care" (3.4.32–33) until he is reduced to their condition. We see peasants and beggars labor up a hill in sight of the castle where Lear will divide his kingdom. Thinking themselves secure in their place above such fellow creatures, Gloucester, Kent, and Edmund begin their discussion of who, they believe, really matters: the king himself, his daughters' present husbands and one future spouse. "I thought the king had more affected the Duke of Albany," opines Kent in the play's first words, and the film's framing of the line adds to its power. The king does not "affect"—care for—any of his subjects; he merely wants their obedience to his demands. When Cordelia and Kent dare to deny his royal pleasure, he expels them not only from his regard but from the body politic. Yuri Yarvet, as Lear, declaims his sentences against daughter and adviser before the assembled citizenry.

In casting Yarvet in the role, Kozintsev was underscoring his conviction that there was indeed no difference between ruler and the ruled: Estonian-born, not a native speaker of Russian, the actor had originally been considered for the role of the Fool. His gaunt, aged face, his slight frame, and his sometimes manic intensity would have lent themselves well to such traditional casting. But the director knew where his Lear was headed, toward the common state of humankind, and wanted the king to shows its marks already. Kozintsev himself describes the banishment scene in *"King Lear": The Space of Tragedy*, his diary of the film's production: "The people without rights, the crowds in their thousands, await their fate outside. . . . The old man, who is no different from them, seems to them like a god" (36). Yarvet is a deliberately unimposing figure at the outset; any grandeur connected with him comes from his capacity for tragic suffering, for painfully learned empathy with his fellow creatures. The actor communicates such insight with gestures, more than words, much as Kozintsev communicates meaning as much by filling the screen whenever possible with "the thick of life" (Kozintsev 82), as by Boris Pasternak's admired Russian translation (itself a foreign presence for Yarvet).

In Kozintsev's view, Lear comes to choose common humanity, without fully realizing what it entails. He cannot accept the version of rule his daughters seek to impose upon him, even as others calmly accept—why would they not?—the "new" order of things. As the director describes it:

> When the King thought that he was the one chosen among many, he was living not in a real world (which he did not know), but in a fictitious world (which he imagined to be reality). Leaving the boundary of the estate where Goneril and Regan now reigned, he was beyond the bounds of the fictitious (what he thought was true); and now he was walking in the world. . . . Lear was alone among men, sat apart from the rest. Then he became the same as everyone else, indistinguishable from the rest; grief has but one face (191, 195).

This is why Cordelia's troops have difficulty in finding him; he cannot now be distinguished from the mass of refugees in this time of civil war. As Lear himself bitterly observes to Gloucester and the still-disguised Edgar: "they told me I was everything. 'Tis a lie, I am not ague-proof" (4.6.104–105).

Even so, at the end, this Lear demands attention of the crowd—now assembled soldiers from the recent wars—not because he is king but because of his suffering. Yarvet astonishingly negotiates between utter grief and unflinching acceptance of the worst that could be: the sight of Cordelia hanging from the battlements. His commands to "Howl" reverberate through the castle's ruins, but then Lear quietly meditates on Cordelia's murder and his dispatch of those responsible. Only the finality of her death provokes new outrage: Yarvet's delivery of "Never, never, never, never, never" (which Kozintsev allows to echo beyond even Shakespeare's daring five times) is harrowing. His illusory hope for Cordelia's survival—"Look there, look there"—is delivered in quiet wonder, an everyday miracle. At that very point, however, he collapses. The calm conviction registers even beyond death. After Lear gives up the ghost, his face and Cordelia's remain composed. Their bodies are carried on a single bier, and the procession pushes aside a small, weeping figure, the tragedy's most anguished mourner. It is Oleg Dal's young Fool, "the last man to stay by" Lear (Kozintsev 238), whose wistful pipe playing—presented as a clarinet solo in Shostakovich's score—opens and ends the film. His music suits a vision of the world that accepts death—we see, in the final shot, peasants attempting to salvage and rebuild their village—even as it confronts the enormities that often inflict it. This Fool is privileged (at least by Lear) as a truth-teller not only in language but in sheer sound; he must go beyond language to fulfill his function. He becomes, in this version, a figure for the artist: Shakespeare himself, Kozintsev and Shostakovich and Yarvet, whom the director described as having "spiritual grace" (234) enough to embody Lear's journey toward such acceptance, defiance, and vulnerability.

I'LL PUT A GIRDLE ROUND ABOUT THE EARTH / IN FORTY MINUTES
(from *A Midsummer Night's Dream*)

Akira Kurosawa first engaged with Shakespeare in his 1957 *Kumonosu-djo* (*The Castle of the Spider's Web*), an adaptation of *Macbeth* (released in the United States in 1961 as *Throne of Blood*). He said farewell to Shakespearean materials nearly thirty years later, with *Ran* (*Chaos*), his 1985 adaptation of *King Lear*. *Kumonosu-djo* is rightly considered a masterwork: if not the greatest adaptation of Shakespeare on film, it is certainly one of the most impressive films ever inspired by Shakespearean materials. Much has been said about Kurosawa's ability to find in Japanese history cultural analogues—or sometimes replacements—for the settings and social structures operative in the playtexts. The director's most impressive act of translation goes beyond differences in language and culture, beyond differences in medium. In apposition to the rich cultural intertexts at work in Shakespeare's plays, Kurosawa puts into play Japan's own complex history; in opposition to the physical limitations of the stage, Kurosawa sets film's power to suggest the limitless. These translations, however, underscore the director's sense of the tragic. While other filmmakers, such as Olivier, celebrate film's relative freedom through confident adaptation and appropriation, Kurosawa powerfully explores how a sense of limitless possibilities can be dizzying, disorienting, haunting. Kozintsev learned from Kurosawa in approaching filmic tragedy as a matter of the spatial, not only the verbal, or individual, or even societal. The Soviet director could write about "The Space of Tragedy" in *Lear* in part because the Japanese director had established it as central to his vision of *Macbeth*.

Toshiro Mifune, the actor most frequently used by Kurosawa in his films, plays Washizu, the Macbeth figure of *Kumonosu-djo* (see Figure 9). The arc of his tragic career is marked by shifting conceptions of space and by the character's increasingly desperate attempts to impose certainty, to achieve closure in the face of a featureless void. The film establishes the void in the scene that follows his fateful meeting with a single ghost-like figure (instead of three "weird sisters"). After being lost in the woods, after hearing the strange predictions of the spirit, he and Miki, the Banquo character (played by Minoru Chiaki) find their way onto open fields. But the landscape is shrouded in mist and they cannot find their bearings. The two warriors, mounted on horseback, impulsively choose one direction after another, riding across the screen this way and that, quickly losing heart and trying a different way. There are no words, only the sound of the horses' hooves. Kurosawa, with photographer Asakazu Nakai, sustains the scene for so long that the audience is invited to participate in the desire for closure. Surely some direction, any direction, is preferable to this impulsive crisscrossing in a void. The film then provides such resolution both for the viewers and for the characters, as the warriors finally gain sight of the castle where Washizu will attempt to embrace and control his fate.

Kurosawa, then, offers a distinctive interpretation of the playtext. Despite an unseen Chorus's judgment (heard both at the beginning and end of the film) about the perils of ambition, Washizu is brought down less by his ambition than by his desire to find certainty. As he contemplates the murder of his king, Macbeth wishes "that but this blow / Might be the be-all and the end-all, here, / But here upon this bank and shoal of time" (1.7.4–6). Washizu will do anything to grasp at that surety: the impassive quiet of Asaji, his wife, sitting motionless in large, empty rooms, does as much to provoke his action as her challenges to his bravery and manhood. After she must finish the job of killing Kuniharu, the warlord, Washizu accepts his new status, but then attempts to guarantee the rest of the oracle by naming Yoshiteru, Miki's son, as heir. When Asaji

FIGURE 9. Toshiro Mifune struggles toward an illusory certainty as Washizu, the Macbeth figure in Akira Kurosawa's 1957 film *Kumonosu-djo* (*Castle of the Spider's Web*). Photo courtesy of Jerry Ohlinger's Movie Material.

declares that she is expecting a child, the new situation prompts a series of decisive actions. Washizu orders Miki's death, then kills one of the assassins himself at the news of Yoshiteru's escape. He strikes at the apparition of Miki's spirit with his own sword, growing more determined the more the hollowness of the prophecy becomes clear.

Finally, the very landscape grows fluid with the movement of the wood toward the castle and Washizu's troops grow restless. He accuses them of seeking security by surrender, yet demands that they follow him into certain destruction. With his wife dead and their child stillborn, he longs for death. His wish is granted in a frightening manner, as his warriors aim their arrows at him. His passing is anything but peaceful, as he staggers in pain—now resisting, rather than inviting, final stasis. He could have stayed on the wooden balcony from which he addressed his troops, fixed in place by dozens of their arrows now lodged in his body. Pinned in corner after corner, he struggles free each time. In what could have been the coup de grace, an arrow pierces his throat; a brief but complete silence overwhelms the soundtrack. He cannot speak, cannot cry out. Instead of surrendering at that moment, he somehow makes his way downstairs, ready to struggle for a new, indeterminate future. As Washizu, Mifune stares at the troops, just past the camera; as in the sequence on the plain, Kurosawa holds the shot long past what we might expect. The openness is too much for Washizu, who in the act of reaching for his sword (perhaps to kill himself?) suddenly collapses and dies. Rather than show any resolution to the warfare, however, Kurosawa simply returns to the fog, the shifting forest, the sound of the wind. Such openness is Kurosawa's point: he withholds any victory speech, such as that found in Shakespeare's playtext (however problematic it might be); he frustrates any hope on the audience's part that a new order can or should be established. The film offers a glimpse of the warriors outside the castle, apparently determined to attack regardless, and then a return to the opening chant. The screen shows a monument—possibly Washizu's—but the words proclaim that his spirit still cannot find rest. As E. Pearlman has observed, Kurosawa "has frustrated our natural desire for closure" (256); the director has done so, in part, because that desire is in itself what has doomed Washizu.

Shortly after his success with *Kumonosu-djo*, Kurosawa attempted another filmic translation of Shakespeare, a version of *Hamlet* set in post-war Japan, 1960's *The Bad Sleep Well*. Here, too, he seeks for visual analogues to the imagistic power of Shakespeare's language, as well as cultural analogues for the playtext's situations. *The Bad Sleep Well* complicates the problems of translation by setting the action of *Hamlet* in modern-day, and therefore Westernized, Japan. The opening sequence shows a wedding reception that awkwardly blends European music and custom with the trappings of old Japan and new business; pivotal scenes take place in a bombed-out factory. The dynamics of royal succession and the intrigues it can inspire have been replaced by the struggles of the salaryman to gain and consolidate power in a corrupt corporate world; feudal notions of honor and loyalty are ruthlessly exploited by those in economic power. What has happened to the play is also, Kurosawa suggests, what is happening to Japan in the aftermath of the Second World War. Within such transformations, traces of the original persist. In this version, the Hamlet figure is Nishi (played, much against type, by Mifune) who seeks to find out the truth about his father's suicide. He assumes a friend's identity, joins his father's firm (even marrying the daughter of the executive he suspects), and learns that his father was forced out of a window in order to keep the company's corruption from exposure. An ancient custom—choosing death rather than shame—can persist but has here been coopted by those who, without conscience, can deflect both shame and death onto others.

The film is a tour de force exercise in shifting perspectives (as in Kurosawa's *Rashomon* of 1950) and identities. Everyone closely observes each other—paralleling the obsessive spying in Elsinore—but no one is quite certain who the objects of their scrutiny really are. Reporters seek to uncover the latest scandal, unaware of how their gaze has been manipulated; Nishi confirms all of his suspicions, only to discover that he cannot translate his knowledge into vengeful action; his scheming father-in-law Iwabuchi believes another staged death will solve his problems, but (like Washizu/Macbeth) cannot guarantee its consequences. The mist that stands for uncertainty in *Kumonosu-djo* is replaced here by cigarette smoke, which accompanies every official obfuscation. Kurosawa may also be paying tribute to Olivier's *Hamlet*, which veiled its Elsinore in fog; Kurosawa therefore may have inspired Branagh's visual joke in *A Midwinter's Tale*. He is assuredly returning to the indeterminacy explored in his earlier adaptation of Shakespeare: there is a moral void in the social world depicted here, a radical destabilization of truth, value, and identity that provokes Nishi's outrage and might well inspire Washizu's brutal attempts at certainty.

The Bad Sleep Well has inspired a version of *Hamlet* set in the corridors of corporate power in present-day New York City: Michael

Almereyda's film, released in 2000, presents Ethan Hawke—as a deeply ambivalent heir—in the title role. Traces of Kurosawa also appear in the Finnish *film noir* satire, appropriately shot in black-and-white, *Hamlet Goes Business* (*Hamlet liikemaailmassa*), irreverently directed by Aki Kaurismäki in 1987. In this version. Elsinore is a failing business, thanks to the Claudius-figure's campaign to corner the world market in bath toys; the Ghost is more interested in saving the company than in revenge. Throughout his 2000 *Hamlet*, Almereyda pays tribute to his eclectic sources: when his Ophelia (played by Julia Stiles) returns gifts and other "remembrances" to Hamlet, she includes a rubber duck. The greatest debt, however, is owed to Kurosawa's film, with its use of social contexts and cinematic intertexts (such as the post-war detective films that influenced Olivier's *Hamlet*) to explore Shakespeare's sense of tragedy.

Ran (*Chaos*), Kurosawa's 1985 revisioning of *King Lear*, replaces the evocative black and white of the two earlier films with vivid, strangely beautiful color. The strangeness of the beauty, as shot by longtime collaborator Nakai, rests in the savagery and desolation of the events depicted: how can sights so horrifying or heartrending be beautiful? Aristotle had wondered about the aesthetic impact of the events described in the poetic drama of ancient Greece; again, Kurosawa attempts to redefine tragedy into predominantly visual, rather than verbal, terms. The Lear figure, Hidetora (played by Tatsuya Nakadai), is first seen hunting, an activity merely described in the playtext (as when the king and his retinue return to Goneril's castle) or which provides materials for metaphoric reflections on what is, in actuality, Nature. Kurosawa visually associates the practice with the condition at the heart of the film, chaos, for he superimposes the title over the image of Hidetora preparing to shoot. Arrows will be used by Hidetora to explain the division of the kingdom to his three sons (not only a rewrite of Shakespeare's daughters but a revision of a Japanese legend about faithful sons) and to demonstrate the importance that they stay allied. The old man asserts that three arrows bundled together cannot be broken, while a single arrow can. It is Saburo (played by Daisuke Ryu), the male Cordelia figure, who protests against the division of the kingdom and who angrily breaks such a bundle apart. His protests, unheeded, and his later attempts at negotiating a peace, contribute to the coming dissolution.

The seeds of chaos were sown long before, however. Hidetora has been a merciless warrior and daughters of his past enemies have now entered into political marriages with two of his sons. When one, the Lady

Kaede (played by Mieko Harada), seeks to disempower and humiliate Hidetora it unleashes waves of brutality. As the skirmishes escalate, Kurosawa fills the screen with one horrific vision after another. "Is this the promised end?" asks Kent in the playtext at the sight of Lear carrying the strangled Cordelia; "Or image of that horror?" replies—with yet another question—the stunned Edgar (5.3.238–39). The depiction of warfare in *Ran* deliberately invokes the apocalyptic feeling of these lines. During the crucial battle, we hear sounds of chanting both detached from the carnage and in outrage against it. Only at the moment when Taro, the eldest of Hidetora's sons, is killed at the order of Jiro, the middle brother, does the soundtrack provide the actual sounds and screams of war. (Welles's *Chimes at Midnight* has had an impact here.) Kurosawa has linked the West's most influential story of the final conflagration with its most enduring account of the Primal Murder, Cain's assault on Abel. History begins, yet again.

Frustrated in his attempt to choose death over the shame of defeat, Hidetora goes mad and like Lear upon the heath is left nearly alone in the open fields. Only Tango, the Kent figure, and Kyoami the fool, played by the Japanese tranvestite performer Peter (sometimes spelled Peater), remain in attendance. Madness, however, is no refuge from the grief of loss: Saburo dies in his father's arms. As in *Komonosu-djo*, Kurosawa both removes any gesture toward closure and chillingly explores the consequences of seeking it. In his quest to remove any possible challenge to his power, Hidetora had ordered that Tsurumaru, the son of one enemy (and brother of Jiro's first wife), be blinded. He is cast adrift when his sister, Sue, is seen as an obstacle by Kaede and they must flee. At one point, she leaves him in order to retrieve his beloved Noh flute (recalling both the soundtrack of *Kumonosu-djo* and the fool in Kozintsev's *Lear*) and promises to return. Kurosawa deftly combines such elements of Shakespeare's playtext as the blinding of Gloucester, the fidelity of Cordelia, the fierceness of Goneril and Regan, and the persistent (but doomed) hopefulness of Edgar (and his cure for Gloucester's despair) into a single, poignant subplot. Sue, it turns out, is killed on her sister-in-law's command. We see her fallen body, the flute still clutched in her hand. Tsurumaru is left alone. He steps, tentatively and dangerously, toward the cliff. The void, which so terrified Washizu, now overwhelms us with its emptiness, its silences, and, in Kurosawa's vision, sheer beauty. The space of tragedy is infinite, both everything and nothing.

HOW SAY YOU BY THE FRENCH LORD?
(from *Merchant of Venice*)

We conclude this survey of Shakespearean films in languages other than English where we started this chapter, in France, the land that King Henry V so desired. The weight of cultural and political history has affected in profound ways the adaptation and appropriation of works by England's national poet into French. Since the time of Voltaire's indictment of the playwright's alleged "savagery" (Voltaire singled out *Hamlet* for particular scorn), Shakespeare has served as a site of contestation through centuries of imperial rivalry between England and France, through alliances almost as bitter as their conflicts, and through ongoing French concern with the preservation of its language and culture. The linguistic obstacles were more easily circumvented during the silent era, so the adaptations (such as Bernhardt's staging of the duel scene in *Hamlet* and Méliès's filmed Shakespeares) were generally less adversarial than what followed. The arrival of sound in film, however, made questions of language unavoidable—except by avoiding Shakespeare altogether. For nearly two decades, no version or adaptation of a Shakespeare playtext was made in France. Maurice Tourneur's inspired 1939 *Volpone*, based on the satiric comedy by Shakespeare's friend and rival Ben Jonson, makes the linguistic avoidance even clearer. Though Jonson's sharp social criticisms in themselves might appeal more readily than Shakespeare to the Gallic sensibility, this version hedges its bets by multiplying the processes of translation: the screenplay is based on a French stage adaptation of a German stage adaptation of Jonson's original.

Even before the onset of sound, however, there were versions that foreshadowed an adversarial relationship, including the irreverent 1910 *Romeo Turns Bandit* (Ball 115), which sets the love story very much in the early twentieth century. *Shylock*, adapted from *The Merchant of Venice* in 1913, also takes several liberties (beginning with the title), despite quickly establishing a suitably "Renaissance" setting. The film starts with its star, Harry Baur, dressed first as a modern financier; he then transforms into Shylock, whom the title cards proclaim "a living symbol of cunning and greed." (Baur would later play the avaricious and cynical Volpone in Tourneur's version.) Anxieties about international finance combine with unabashed anti-Semitism to bring the moneylender to life for contemporary audiences. Baur, as Shylock, laughs directly at the camera, raising his cloak as if to surround the audience with it. When Antonio and Bassanio visit him to borrow money on Bassanio's behalf, they interrupt one of his miserly revels, as he showers himself with gold coins. A large and boisterous audience attends the proceedings at which Shylock attempts to collect the bond; not surprisingly, they cheer with enthusiasm when the disguised Portia traps him with the letter of the law. The playtext's humiliation of Shylock is not enough, here. Shylock appears at Portia's house in Belmont, throwing himself prostrate and begging for a more lenient penalty. He's there in part to serve as additional documentation for Portia's revelation that she was, indeed, the young jurist who outwitted him. He is also there as a further opportunity for laughter and revulsion. His protests are haunting enough in act 4 of Shakespeare's playtext, which avoids bringing him directly to Belmont; they become even more poignant here, separated from the direct threat against Antonio. In this version, the happy ending enjoyed by the Christians is made utterly dependent on Shylock's defeat—and made secondary to it, however unintentionally. Baur's own death at the hands of the Gestapo during the Nazi occupation of France adds yet another unsettling note to post-Holocaust viewing of this film.

Les amants de Verone, André Cayatte's 1949 look at *Romeo and Juliet* as cinematic material, broke the long silence ironically inspired by bringing sound to film. The cinematic medium becomes very assertively the grounds for the encounter, as Cayatte and co-screenwriter Jacques Prévert propose a film project, a modern-day version of *Romeo and Juliet*, as the backdrop for his story involving a young Venetian glassblower, who wins a place as an extra and stand-in for the actor playing Romeo, and the daughter of a corrupt and powerful family. The dizzying denouement involves the "real-life" characters, drawn into the realm of representation, dying on the Venetian film set depicting a Veronese tomb.

In 1962, Claude Chabrol also used a filmic enterprise as the centerpiece for *Ophélia*, his 1962 seriocomic dissection of adaptation and translation based—and very much dependent—on *Hamlet*. The film presents the story of Yvan, the son of a deceased factory owner, whose mother has married his father's brother. The parallels with *Hamlet* are clear enough, but the provincial Yvan doesn't make the connection until Olivier's version reaches the village *ciné*. After Yvan hears (in dubbed French) the lines about "'Tis not alone my inky cloak" (1.2.77) that embodies the prince's grief, he begins to see his own situation in terms of the play. The name of the village, Erneles, becomes an anagram for Elsener—a Gallic version of Elsinore. His childhood friend Lucy, daughter of the factory's manager, becomes an Ophelia who must choose between him and her father, now cast in the role of Polonius. When Yvan, assuming his own "antic disposition," addresses the manager (played by Robert Burnier) as Polonius, the response is gruffly dismissive: "Never heard of him!"

Convinced that his uncle must have been responsible for the death of his father and encouraged by the community's unfamiliarity with the play (or resistance to applying it to their own lives), Yvan sets out to prove his uncle's guilt in the same way Hamlet did, by means of performance. Instead of a play-within-a-play, however, screenwriter Martial Matthieu provides us with a cinematic "dumb show": a silent film that Yvan produces and then screens before the family and all the village's leading citizens (anticipating the video "Mousetrap" that appears in Almereyda's recent film adaptation). He collects actors from the village, including the local gravedigger, and instructs them, Hamlet-style, not to outdo the modesty of nature in their roles. Not only "the rest" is silence, but the action is as well. Amidst the film's amusing and affectionate parodies of silent melodramas, the message that Claude Cerval poisoned his brother and married his brother's widow Claudia (the names provide additional inspiration for Yvan) is unmistakable. When a profoundly shaken Claude first resolves to kill Yvan and then takes his own life instead, it appears as though he has been moved by guilt over the crime of murder. Chabrol and Matthieu provide an additional twist, however, that reveals how ingeniously wrong—and profoundly Oedipal—Yvan's translation and adaptation have been: Claude turns out to have been Yvan's real, biological father.

Jean-Luc Godard's deconstructed *King Lear* nervously meditates on the relation between text, stage, and film, and on the nature of artistic authority and autonomy. Released in 1987, the film comments on its own making, announcing its status as the aftermath of a project gone awry with the Cannon Group (best known, especially at the time, for such action-adventure series as the *Death Wish* and *American Ninja* films). "Shot in the Back" is a repeated title card, suggesting both betrayal by film executives and tenacity on the part of Godard himself, who continues to make his *King Lear* even after the opportunity for a big-budget enterprise is gone. The deliberately fragmented "story" first presents the project's initial, Hollywood-style Big Concept: translate the story of *Lear* from ancient Britain to present-day Las Vegas, from monarchy to the Mafia. Norman Mailer and his daughter will serve as not only a Lear and Cordelia, but also as Writer and, apparently, Muse. When that fails, after a single day's shooting, Burgess Meredith and Molly Ringwald take the place of the Mailers. Meredith and his Lear study the sources of their character, Don Learo, by reading Albert Fried's *The Rise and Fall of the Jewish Gangster in America*, a book that focuses on Bugsy Siegel's ambitions in Las Vegas (and which influenced the Warren Beatty feature *Bugsy*). Godard's film itself considers the transformations first visited on U. S. culture by the Las Vegas entertainment model and then on transnational culture by the Americanization of both commerce and art.

American culture—and the English language it transforms and promulgates—have a lot to answer for. Enter American-born director and *enfant terrible* Peter Sellars as William Shakespeare, Jr., the Fifth, who has been commissioned by the Cannon Cultural Division and Her Majesty's Royal Library (there's Anglo-American culture for you, suggests Godard) to recover and reassemble the works of his namesake. He overhears Meredith/Learo and Ringwald/Cordelia speaking in a hotel restaurant, immediately recognizes the Lear-like qualities of their words, and both interrupts and transcribes the conversation. Although text-obsessed, Shakespeare, Jr., is also haunted by filmic ancestors. We see him meditate on the images (with no identifying titles or spoken names) of filmmakers who attempted to refine or resist the strictly narrative cinema (Metz 188–208): French directors like Jean Renoir and François Truffaut, Italian directors like Luchino Visconti and Pier Paolo Pasolini, expatriates like Fritz Lang and (at least professionally) Orson Welles. Welles's name had figured in the first discussions with Cannon Films, though his death in 1985 decided a casting issue that finances would doubtless have complicated. Welles the Hollywood outcast, a non-canonical (or Cannonical) interpreter of Shakespeare, the director who rearranged multiple texts into a single film like *Chimes at Midnight* and who insisted on a tension between word and image, is one of Godard's inspirations here.

As cinematic devotee, Godard appears more or less as himself in the film and as "The Professor" (of belief in film), Dr. Pluggy, who wears a wig made of sound cords and jacks. Pluggy speaks in a deliberately slurred voice, which not only "accords with his distrust of words" (Donaldson 1990, 207) but also recalls the faint hints of incapacitating stroke in Paul Scofield's Lear for director Peter Brook. The history of *Lear* on film is further invoked when a "Professor Kozintsev" joins in Pluggy's experiments, bringing in a clip from "his" version, adding Yuri Yarvet's Estonian-inflected Russian translation of the English word "nothing" to a dizzying montage that includes the French icon of Liberté and an antic, self-devouring wolf from a Tex Avery cartoon.

The film concludes with wild juxtapositioning between the tragic and the comic, the living and the dead, the patriarchal text and the feminist rejoinder to it, the European and American. We are shown how Sellars/Shakespeare, Jr., discovers that Lear and Cordelia may share a (bloodstained) bed, followed by the sight of Godard/Pluggy testing Ringwald's/Cordelia's virtue and identity by means of a fireworks sparkler; we see Cordelia lying on a rocky shore, while Meredith/Learo gazes out at the ocean, holding the rifle that may have shot her in the back; we hear fragments of *Lear* and Shakespeare's sonnets mingle with the final words of Virginia Woolf's *The Waves* and their defiance against death. Godard suggests that there is potential in refigured language not to "redeem" tragedy but to face it more directly. Finally, the screen reveals Sellars in an editing room hoping to piece together this very film with Mr. Alien, who enacts the filmic theory of *suture* by using needle and thread (Bennett 67, Silverman 205–206). The editor is played by Woody Allen, devoted filmmaker and perhaps unwitting and insidious agent, for all his self-deprecation and sly cultural critiques, of what Anglo-American culture is doing to the rest of the world and specifically to the world of filmic art.

In the face of what seems a consuming "love," so intense that not even the village of Erneles could be spared in Chabrol's film, Godard offers to Shakespeare both acknowledgment and strategies of evasion. He *will* not (rather than cannot) "speak your England" unless it is in terms of his own complex, resolutely visual and disruptive approach to cinema. The stress on the visual goes beyond the mechanics of the medium and situates film technologies in the shifting geography of transnational culture.

CHAPTER NINE

◇

Conclusion:
The Next Century of Shakespeare

HECTOR: The end crowns all;
And that old common arbitrator, Time,
Will one day end it.

—Shakespeare, *Troilus and Cressida*

The end of the first century of Shakespearean film may signal a new age
in the negotiations between the media and the body of literary and theatrical work associated with William Shakespeare. In 1998, a witty romp
through the playwright's early career, *Shakespeare in Love*, offered both a
version of the man behind the plays and a series of fanciful—and highly
unlikely—explanations for the inspiration for his works. The film was a
critical success and something of a surprise hit at the box office; the film
garnered numerous industry awards, including the Oscar for Best Picture.
Shortly after the 1999 Academy Awards, a new film version of *A Midsummer Night's Dream* was released, which was intended to be a more
faithful adaptation of an actual playtext. The response from audiences
and reviewers alike was decidedly more mixed. It is tempting to explain
the different responses by judging one as "Shakespeare Lite"—less intel-
lectually filling and therefore easier for a general audience to consume—
and the other as "Shakespeare in Earnest"—with both the benefits and

179

disadvantages that attend such an approach. While those broad characterizations have some validity, much more is going on in the films and, I would argue, in the reactions to them. What the next century holds may be heralded by the first serious film adaptation ever attempted of *Titus Andronicus*, long thought to be one of Shakespeare's most problematic plays.

The screenplay for *Shakespeare in Love* was written by Marc Norman, a veteran of offbeat Hollywood productions such as *Zandy's Bride*, and Tom Stoppard, whose first staged script was the *Hamlet* send-up *Rosencrantz and Guildenstern Are Dead* and whose directorial debut on screen was the film version of that play. While most likely not participants in a conventional collaboration, the two writers still produced an intriguing synthesis of backstage romance and lighthearted existentialism. The backstage romance proposes that William Shakespeare's muse must have been, at all times, a flesh-and-blood woman. Lady Viola turns out to have inspired at least one of the earliest of his sonnets, "Shall I compare thee to a summer's day?"; most traces of that sonnet's homoerotic context (since most of the sequence addresses itself to a fair, young man) and its deliberate complication of Petrarchan love-poetry conventions are erased here. Even *Romeo and Juliet* took its ultimate shape, according to the film, thanks to that attractive noblewoman, devoted to plays, working both behind the scenes and in front of them. The existential comedy arises from the interaction between the "real life" of the film's characters—both historical and imagined—and the emotional life of the characters in the play Shakespeare creates. The combination of the two strategies allows for greater playfulness than either one of them might have produced alone.

The backstage romance approach is familiar enough: it provided the rationale for the MGM short *Master Will Shakespeare*, in which the playwright ardently identifies with Romeo. It has also led to such successful Shakespearean spinoffs as *Kiss Me Kate*, based on *The Taming of the Shrew*, *A Double Life*, a 1947 Ronald Colman vehicle (directed by George Cukor and written by Ruth Gordon and Garson Kanin) about an actor consumed by his performance as Othello; and Kenneth Branagh's *A Midwinter's Tale*. In *Master Will Shakespeare*, prospective audiences for the Leslie Howard/Norma Shearer *Romeo and Juliet* were assured that the playwright was not only as stage-struck as the best of them but was deeply, personally involved in the presentation of love in that particular play. *Shakespeare in Love* makes a similar case, explaining that *Romeo and Juliet* was inspired by his own direct experience with a "star-cross'd" romance. There is no acknowledgment here of Shakespeare's widely known and widely read sources for the play, most notably Arthur Brooke's 1562 poem, *The Tragicall Historye of Romeus and Juliet*: it all must have been sketched from life.

The second approach, the existential comedy, is also familiar enough—if only from Stoppard's own work. *Rosencrantz and Guildenstern Are Dead* takes a delightful look not "backstage" but at the imagined semi-lives of minor characters who are, well, just that: minor, stage-bound characters. Stoppard's non-Shakespearean play *Travesties* interrogates the distinctions drawn between reality and all forms of memorial reconstruction, including memoirs and history. Even *A Double Life*, with its borrowings not only from *Othello* but also from *Hamlet* (a version of "The Mousetrap" affirms the lead character's guilt), played with the sometimes indistinct boundaries between reality and its representations. In *Shakespeare in Love*, we are presented with the case of lovers who not only inspire but enact the roles that Shakespeare creates: when Will (played by Joseph Fiennes) and the Lady Viola (Gwyneth Paltrow) play Romeo and Juliet on the stage of the Curtain, they are merely consummating in aesthetic terms what they had long been doing in her chamber. Because of this, the normative heterosexuality at work in the backstage romance plot is very happily compromised. Will-as-Romeo loves Viola-as-Juliet because their own love is fated to end: the actual male-female romance parallels the imagined one. At the same time, however, Viola-as-Master Thomas Kent-as-Romeo also loves Master Will Shakespeare, who writes the lines for her/him and Juliet alike. While a more accurate depiction of the sonnets' genesis would probably center on a figure much like Lord Wessex, Viola's vain and arrogant suitor, the interplay among stage, page, and bed effectively invokes the transgressive spirit of Shakespeare's questioning of gender roles.

Along with the Shakespearean spirit, the film provides the Shakespearean letter in abundance. Borrowing from George Bernard Shaw's biographical flight of fancy, *The Dark Lady of the Sonnets* (in which Shakespeare jots down any interesting turn of phrase for later use), *Shakespeare in Love* collects familiar lines from a wide variety of Shakespeare's plays but also puts them in the mouths of his contemporaries. The game is announced early on in the fulminations of Makepeace, a puritan preacher, against the two theaters, the Rose and the Curtain:

> Under the name of the Curtain, the players breed lewdness in your
> wives, rebellion in your servants, idleness in your apprentices and

wickedness in your children! And the Rose smells thusly rank by any name! I say a plague on both their houses! (Norman and Stoppard 8)

Shakespeare himself is contributing to the storehouse of language during his pre-Freudian session with Dr. Moth, a character loosely based on Elizabethan astrologer Simon Forman. The first thing out of his mouth is "Words, words, words," long before Hamlet tells Polonius that is what he's reading. Half-remembered, half-formed lines recur: "All ends well"; "You will never age for me"; "Oh, my lord, you will not shake me off." The invented dialogue falls comfortably into iambic meter, most appropriately when Viola and Will discuss the death of Christopher Marlowe, who showed what blank verse could do for drama: "You never spoke so well of him"; "He was not dead before." Even though these are not complete blank verse lines, they still draw power from its basic rhythm.

While Shakespeare's words appear in the general conversation, so do later turns of phrase, such as being nervous about the first time one has "played the Palace." Perhaps the most egregious variation on a cliche is heard in this exchange between the playwright and Philip Henslowe, owner of the Rose Theatre (played by Geoffrey Rush):

> WILL
> What do we do now?
> HENSLOWE
> The show must . . . [*searching for the next idea*] you know . . . [*he's not sure*]
> WILL
> [*Impatiently*] Go on!

The formulation of the prime theatrical directive is done off-the-cuff, without great fanfare, and as a collaborative enterprise. For all the myth-making in *Shakespeare in Love* about individual genius, the film also places the playwright in a lively and inventive cultural context. Passersby contribute language, colleagues and rivals offer ideas (some very bad, some very good), and the next generation of playwrights (represented by a young, bloody-minded, and mean-spirited John Webster) provokes a crisis that leads to Shakespeare's first triumph.

The filmmakers treat earlier versions of Shakespeare as collaborators, too. The Rose and Curtain here owe a considerable debt to Olivier's vision of the Globe in *Henry V*, as does director John Madden's presentation of a solitary actor facing the all-encompassing audience in such a setting. Another delightful quote from the Olivier film transforms an expository device into a crucial element of the plot. Olivier's *Henry V* opens with a playbill, first fluttering in the breeze and then filling the screen with information about the play's performance that very day at the Globe. In *Shakespeare in Love*, one of dozens of self-congratulatory playbills printed by moneylender-turned-theater-angel-and-actor Hugh Fennyman (played by Tom Wilkinson) slaps Lord Wessex in the face and is retrieved by Viola. With this information, she is determined to attend the debut of *Romeo and Juliet*. The film's concluding sequences show Shakespeare's imaginative creation of scenes for *Twelfth Night*, which somehow (telepathically?) parallel Viola's experiences in the New World. This conclusion more than glances at Trevor Nunn's filmic prologue, with its depiction of Viola underwater before surfacing into a new identity in an unknown land. (It ignores, however, the alternative autobiography with which Nunn's film resonates, Shakespeare's grief at the death of a son rather than a separation from a lover.)

While such references to the early and recent history of Shakespeare on film add to the comedic impact of *Shakespeare in Love*, similar gestures in Michael Hoffman's 1999 *A Midsummer Night's Dream* often get in the way of the fun. Enjoyment is what Hoffman did intend and what affected many of his decisions about location, lighting, and structure in the play. Shakespeare's mythic Athens becomes Monte Athena, a village set in Tuscany. Branagh's idyllic *Much Ado About Nothing* had set a standard for amiable fun and for downplaying the darkness at work—if only in the background—in most Shakespearean comedies. This world is changing, thanks to technological marvels such as the bicycle and the phonograph record, and women's roles may change as well, but Hoffman's Monte Athena comes across as benign as Branagh's reconfigured Messina does. If the city with its rigid rules is its own kind of idyl (and Oliver Stapleton's cinematography presents it as such), then the release offered by the forest must be of a non-idyllic sort. Hoffman moves the forest inside, to a claustrophobic sound stage on the Cinecittà lot, where Federico Fellini had done much of his innovative work. The fairy world is reminiscent of Fellini's *Satyricon*, in its way, and presents the classical gods, with their sensuality, as the Italian equivalent of English pre-Christian folklore. Below Monte Athena is the *mons veneris*, the anatomical and metaphorical mount of Venus, since Hoffman seems to want his audience to associate the lovers' adventures with an encounter with their sexual subconsciousness. Such a reading, however, is hard to reconcile with Hoffman's stated intention of avoiding a "dark" version, either visually or psychologically. Believing that "psychological darkness works against comedy, especially if it's sustained for a long period of time" (LoMonico 12), he wanted a sound stage's control over lighting and a farcical mechanism, supplied literally by that newfangled bicycle, to lighten the tone. Victorian-style fairies, inspired by artists such as John William Waterhouse and George Frederic Watts (just as Reinhardt's and Dieterle's *Dream* reached back to Fuseli), also seem out of place amidst the Ovidian satyrs and nymphs already populating Hoffman's forest-world.

Interestingly, the film version of *Dream* that most closely predates Hoffman's adaptation invokes the same time period, the 1890s, but is far less constrained by it. Adrian Noble's little-seen 1996 film of *A Midsummer Night's Dream*, made for Britain's Channel Four and based on his Royal Shakespeare Company production of the previous year, alludes to High Victorian English decadence, but also includes later technology— such as the radio and the motorcycle—along with the more turn-of-the-century bicycle. The range of cultural references is justified by Noble's shrewd framing device: we are seeing a boy's dreams, which are inspired by a reading of the play as illustrated by Arthur Rackham, best known for his edition of Grimm's *Fairy Tales* and other works aimed at children (Burnett 97–99). The boy, played by Osheen Jones, tries to come to terms with his parents' sexuality and previous coming-of-age. By situating the play both in a young male's subconscious and in reflections on a cultural moment marked by an interest in fantasy and aesthetic "indulgence," Noble is free to explore the play's syntheses of innocence and eroticism, and of darkness and light. He does so far more fully than Hoffman does in his film, despite the clear influence of Noble's version.

Once nineteenth-century Tuscany was decided as the setting for Hoffman's version, other filmic intertexts presented themselves,. especially the Merchant-Ivory adaptation of E. M. Forster's *A Room With a View*, with its use of bel canto. Italian opera—and the new technology of the phonograph—figure not only on the soundtrack but in the storyline: Nick Bottom's ability to make a purloined gramophone work greatly impresses the fairies that attend on Titania. This Bottom must be impressive, because Hoffman is also employing star-system strategies in his Shakespearean adaptation. Kevin Kline is the most clearly bankable actor and Michelle Pfieffer the most bankable actress in the production; the story, then, emphasizes the importance of their encounter as Bottom and as Titania over all other story elements. (This emphasis had been anticipated in the seventeenth century by the unknown librettist for Henry Purcell's opera *The Fairy Queen*, also based on Shakespeare's *Dream*.) Bottom is supplied with an unhappy marriage, embodied in a wife whom we hear speak only Italian. In fact, a similar character was at one time under consideration for the Warner Brothers' *A Midsummer Night's Dream*, perhaps expanding Bottom's role in deference to James Cagney's status as a featured player (Jackson 40). In Hoffman's *Dream*, Bottom's passion for the theater serves as both a cause of conflict and an escape from it. His sojourn in the forest strangely confirms his manhood, if not his marriage, as a final added scene with him returning home after *Pyramus and Thisbe* suggests.

Despite Hoffman's devotion to Shakespeare—his labors of love include the founding and sustaining of the Idaho Shakespeare Festival—his *Dream* is often ill at ease with the playtext's strategically decentered plot. Expanding on Bottom's story is needed to "unify the action for the audience" (LoMonico 10), as well as to strengthen Kline's role. The film is also regularly resistant to the playtext's language. Stanley Tucci's Puck is supposed to know which lover should be given the love spell "by the Athenian garments he has on," but by the time he stumbles upon Dominic West's Lysander—an unintended target—the ardent young man has shed his clothes altogether (see Figure 10). The sequence recalls West's appearance as a newlywed Earl of Richmond in the Loncraine/ McKellen *Richard III*. The film's discomfort with the text is established as a motif in an early scene. When Theseus must tell Hermia that her father is right (if not just), that she must accept his choice for her husband, or die, or enter the convent, he consults a book of Monte Athenian law and marks the place with a red ribbon. The book looks alarmingly like a folio volume; Theseus never consults it again. As Theseus, David Straithairn seems tentative and uncertain, symptomatic of the film's frequent incapacity either to synthesize materials or to throw them into sharper juxtaposition. None of the promising and able cast makes a very strong impression, although Rupert Everett (who appears as Christopher Marlowe in *Shakespeare in Love*) presents an intriguingly languid Oberon and although the mechanicals, led by Roger Rees as Peter Quince, find most of the laughs for most of *Pyramus and Thisbe*.

Even that scene's comedy, however, is undercut by directorial choice. At the conclusion of the play-within-a-play, Francis Flute (played by Sam Rockwell) succeeds in genuinely moving the audience by giving Thisbe's

FIGURE 10. Lysander (Dominic West) surprises Helena (Calista Flockhart) with his sudden passion in Michael Hoffman's *A Midsummer Night's Dream* (1999). Photo courtesy of Jerry Ohlinger's Movie Material.

last lines a quiet, heartfelt delivery. The aristocratic audience—who hardly heckles at all in this version—is deeply impressed, even though most of the lines Shakespeare wrote for the role are patent nonsense:

> These lily lips,
> This cherry nose,
> These yellow cowslip cheeks,
> Are gone, are gone!
> Lovers, make moan;
> His eyes were green as leeks. (5.1.330–335)

Hoffman implies, somewhat surprisingly, that it doesn't matter what the words mean at all. That notion may be behind the visual excess (why must Puck appear on the back of a tortoise, even if the sight is reminiscent of a famous fountain at Florence's Pitti Palace?) and the combative film-codes of the production. The void left by language—in an English-speaking production—may have prompted such energetic efforts to fill it.

One hundred years after scenes from Herbert Beerbohm Tree's theatrical production of *King John* were recorded on film and presented to audiences, scenes from a forthcoming cinematic release of a Shakespearean adaptation were screened in one of the most public venues imaginable, Times Square. Innovative director and stage designer Julie Taymor took her work in progress to the streets of New York City—after excerpts had also been shown at the 1999 Cannes Film Festival—and showed excerpts from *Titus*, her radical revisioning of Shakespeare's *Titus Andronicus*. Fox Searchlight, the distributor of the film, purchased time on the Panasonic Astrovision screen situated at the intersection of Broadway and 7th Avenue. Taymor's vision of the play lends itself to such a venue. Her eye for spectacle was sharpened by her experience in adapting Disney's *The Lion King* (with its own borrowings from *Hamlet* and assorted other Shakespearean materials) for the Broadway stage. She has set Shakespeare's bloodiest tragedy in a setting that recalls the spectacular aesthetic of 1930s fascist and futurist Italy and incorporates elements from the present day. Elliot Goldenthal's music just as effectively ranges across times and genres. While the overall design gestures back toward the Orson Welles and John Houseman stage version of *Julius Caesar* and to the stage and film versions of *Richard III* featuring Ian McKellen, it also connects with this play's earliest stage history: Elizabethans loved to mix time periods. A pen-and-ink drawing from the 1590s or 1600s, for example, depicts elements from the play and reveals a heady combination of historically "Roman" garb with contemporary dress and armament (Shakespeare, plate 9). Taymor adopts an even more eclectic approach to historical period, building upon her own stage experience. The director was responsible for an ambitious, deeply disturbing stage production of *Titus Andronicus* for New York's Theatre for a New Audience in 1994: many elements of design and interpretation survive and are intensified onscreen. For the film version, Taymor has also tapped into the power of "star-delivery" Shakespeare. Casting Anthony Hopkins (Claudius in Tony Richardson's film and stage *Hamlet*) as the vengeful Titus is both obvious and inspired. Since Titus exacts his revenge, in part, by serving one of his enemies her own children in a macabre feast, who better to play the role than the actor who so vividly brought to life the screen's most memorable cannibal, Hannibal Lecter from *The Silence of the Lambs* and, later, *Hannibal*? As Tamora, Jessica Lange continues a career of literary adaptation seen in *O Pioneers!* and in *A Thousand Acres*, the film version of Jane Smiley's novelistic rewrite of *King Lear*, she ably exploits her own star quality in embodying a character that Taymor describes as someone who "could have come out of Visconti's 1930s [setting] film *The Damned*" (Blumenthal and Taymor 198).

Taymor also returns to the playtext itself. Although she has slyly claimed to have pitched the project to possible backers by calling the play Shakespeare's *Pulp Fiction* (it is, more accurately, his *Reservoir Dogs*), her sense of the play's importance connects the violence of the play with our own age's problematic relationship with violence and its representations. In arguing that now is the proper time to revive what "had been condemned as one of Shakespeare's worst plays," she points obliquely to the work of Quentin Tarentino and Oliver Stone and the genres such directors revisit:

> Our entertainment industry thrives on the graphic details of murders, rapes, and villainy, yet it is rare to find a film or play that not only reflects the dark events but also turns them inside out, probing and challenging our fundamental beliefs on morality and justice. For *Titus* is not a neat or safe play, where goodness triumphs over evil, but one in which, through relentless horror, the undeniable poetry of human tragedy emerges in full force, demanding that we examine the very root of violence and judge its various acts. (Blumenthal and Taymor 183)

The film frames this examination by focusing on a representative of a new generation of the Andronici, young Lucius. It opens with the child, played by Osheen Jones, enacting war games on a kitchen table, energetically destroying an ample meal, pouring out ketchup for the blood, and tossing his toy soldiers about. Taymor has cast the same young actor who supplied the frame-story for Adrian Noble's 1996 *Dream*, but her 1994 stage production had already focused on Lucius. His pastime comes to a sudden end as his father (we later learn) seizes him and brings him to an arena, where he is held aloft before unseen crowds as a budding participant—and possible sacrifice or high priest—in Roman warrior culture. His grandfather, Titus, returns in victory and mourning after battle with the Goths; the Roman troops enter the arena with the exaggerated movements of mechanical men. One of the roots of violence, Taymor argues, is the transformation of bloodshed first into play and then into piety.

The connection between violence and the sacred is made explicit in the play itself, as Shakespeare shows the surviving Andronici choosing to reject Tamora's pleas for mercy and instead to slaughter her eldest son in a ritual of vengeance. The elder Lucius, here played by Angus MacFadyen, addresses Titus:

> See, lord and father, how we have perform'd
> Our Roman rites. Alarbus' limbs are lopp'd,
> And entrails feed the sacrificing fire,
> Whose smoke like incense doth perfume the sky.
> (1.1.142–45)

Taymor and cinematographer Luciano Tovoli show the entrails being deposited in a brazier, sharpening our sense of shared outrage with Tamora even as she plots yet more exquisite revenge. The utter complicity of Roman culture in all the outrages that follow is deftly represented in Taymor's version. Aaron the Moor, Tamora's lover, is both a rousing comic villain in Harry J. Lennix's performance (Lennix played Aaron in Taymor's stage version) and a compelling mirror image of "the dark side of the Roman character" (de Sousa 111) which has already judged him for his black skin and his status as cultural outsider. Even the relatively virtuous characters of Lavinia, Titus's daughter (played by Laura Frasier), and Bassianus, brother to the new emperor, cannot escape this cruel logic. They sneer at Tamora for desiring Aaron, who Bassianus claims has remade her honor in the image of "his body's hue, / Spotted, detested, and abominable" (2.3.73–74). Already doomed to be victims of Aaron's scheming, they also share in provoking the crimes (and what follows is presented as such) about to befall them.

Patriarchy itself is under critique in Shakespeare's playtext—which may in itself be a reason for its later neglect—as is absolute rule. Titus dutifully forgoes any claim to the throne, preferring that the late emperor's eldest son, Saturninus, succeed his father in proper patrilineal fashion. When the senate and people of Rome concur (as broadcast over SPQR radio news), Alan Cumming's extravagant Saturninus begins to exercise arbitrary power, claiming Lavinia, betrothed to his brother, for his own. (Taymor communicates the new ruler's decadence through alert allusions to Fellini's *La Strada* and *Satyricon*.) Lavinia's brothers and Bassianus understandably object, despite Titus's acceptance that the emperor's desires—as well as his word—must be law. As they try to defy the imperial and paternal will, Titus grows more and more wrathful, killing his son Mutius for daring to oppose him. Later in the film, after Lavinia has been raped and mutilated and left alive to increase her own anguish and her father's, Taymor provides a horrific vision of Mutius as a sacrificial lamb, foreshadowing Lavinia's own eventual fate at the hands of her father and calling to mind the biblical story of Abraham and Isaac. All the "nightmare" sequences—including Alarbus's limbs aflame, Lavinia as a Marilyn Monroe figure, the masque of Revenge as Tamora hopes Titus perceives it—also recall Greenaway's Graphic Paintbox visuals depicting the contents of Prospero's library.

Taymor unflinchingly engages with a variety of texts, both visual and literary, that are implicated in the playtext and in our culture's under-standing of Shakespeare generally. The plot of *Titus Andronicus* hinges upon a cruel re-enactment of the story of Philomel in Ovid's *Metamor-phoses* and upon Lavinia's ability to use that text in order to explain what has been done to her. Taymor's film also presents Lavinia's plight as a vicious parody of the myth of Daphne, also retold by Ovid. Where Daphne, seeking to avoid being ravished by Apollo, was tranformed into a laurel tree, Taylor shows Lavinia abandoned on one of countless tree trunks, with branches set in place of the hands her attackers have cut off. In both cases, the written text, again represented by a folio volume, is taken seriously. So too is the language, spoken in a variety of accents and delivered with a sure sense of metrical power and range; some of the guid-ance here was provided by longtime Royal Shakespeare Company voice specialist Cicely Berry.

Taymor also confronts ideological revisions of Shakespeare, especially rebutting Branagh's sometimes sanitized looks at violence in his *Henry V* and *Much Ado About Nothing.* Titus and his soldiers return from the war against the Goths covered in mud, but find no justification in hardship as Branagh's Henry does. They grimly wash off the mud under huge conduits, a visual echo not only of Roman "civilization" (the aqueducts) but also of the exuberant bathing—by both sexes—that marks the return of men from battle at the start of Branagh's *Much Ado.* Another reminder is provided by Geraldine McEwan, who played a lady-in-waiting for that director's *Henry V,* and who appears here as the Nurse who helps Tamora deliver the child she had conceived with Aaron. Alice appears pleased by Henry's conquest of Katherine and of France at the end of Branagh's film; the Nurse in *Titus* is disgusted by the child's blackness and will pay for that disgust with her life.

As Aaron asks, "is black so base a hue?" (4.2.71). Romans think so, projecting onto the color their own savagery. Taymor reassigns crucial lines in order to underscore the process of enculturation in such attitudes. In the playtext, Titus's brother Marcus kills a fly. The grieving Titus, who has lost nearly all his children, feels such empathy with the creature— "how if that fly had a father and a mother?" (3.2.60)—that he rebukes Marcus for the deed. Taymor makes young Lucius responsible for the fly's death and gives him the line explaining that he killed the fly because it was "black [and] ill-favor'd," because it was "Like to the Empress' Moor," Aaron (3.2.66–67). Titus, although he has perceived that Rome itself is but "a wilderness of tigers" (3.1.54), can extend his powers of sympathy across species, but not across race. The deed is now acceptable, so long as the fly "comes in likeness of a coal-black Moor" (3.2.78). He applauds the boy's initiative and joins in, stabbing at the dead insect with a knife. Hopkins, as Titus, expertly negotiates the shifts from quiet compassion to jocular cruelty. Despite this approval, young Lucius will break free of the cycle of violence at the end of the film. After the grisly feast, which all the guests taste and enjoy, one retributive murder quickly follows another. Titus stabs Tamora (through the throat, recalling the end of Kurosawa's *Kumonosu-djo*); he is slain by Saturninus, who is in turn killed by the elder Lucius, Titus's only surviving child. He is offered the crown his father refused; he, however, accepts it. The new emperor pledges that he will "heal Rome's harms and wipe away her woe" (5.3.148), but only after he fulfills his filial obligations: mourning his father and exacting stern revenge upon his enemies, alive or dead. Aaron, valiantly unrepentant, is sentenced to be buried "breast-deep" (which Taymor shows) and starved to death; Tamora's body will be cast outside the city. Since they were pitiless, Lucius argues, no pity may be shown to them—on pain of death.

In all this, Aaron's infant child is left to face an uncertain fate. Shakespeare's playtext brings him on-stage, apparently in the arms of one of Lucius's followers, but no words are spoken concerning what will happen to him. For the Theatre for a New Audience production, Taymor had him brought on-stage in a tiny coffin (Blumenthal and Taymor 37); despite the older Lucius's assurances to Aaron that the child would be spared, the economy of retribution demanded payment. The film, instead, shows the beautiful child brought into the arena in a cage, which is handed to young Lucius. The son of Aaron and Tamora is entrusted to the youngest Andronicus. On the soundtrack, the infant's cries blend with the calls of innumerable birds (also heard at the conclusion of the stage version). As the film ends, the boy walks away from the viewer, carefully carrying the baby. They pass through an archway, leaving the arena where cruelty, racial difference, piety, and entertainment had merged. Overlooking a grassy plain and the sea beyond, they face the dawn. Just as the sun rises above clouds on the horizon, the frame freezes. The film's idea of the future, though still uncertain, allows for some hope.

Taymor's *Titus* suggests new ways for film and Shakespeare both to emerge the stronger as a result of the Shakespeare Test. In part because of the play's status as "unworthy" of Shakespeare, Taymor has been able to bypass the sometimes deadening authority established around the playwright and thereby to unleash more of the critical and emotional energies that truly animate the text. Her approaches do not entirely rely, however, on the unfamiliarity or alleged unsuitability of the playtext. W. B. Worthen has suggested (190–91) that conscious efforts at estranging familiar patterns of Shakespeare performance could result in richer productions and in more insightful readings of those productions; similarly, re-examining Shakespeare and film from different perspectives can lead to richer realizations of both. This book is an attempt to contribute to the processes of re-examination. It would indeed be a hopeful sign for the next century of Shakespeare on-screen—cinematic or digital or from yet another technology—if filmmakers see in Shakespearean playtexts (whether neglected or not) new insights into their media and new potentials for them. Many of the strengths in Taymor's *Titus* derive from her personal negotiations between stage and film; most of the successful adaptations of Shakespeare for the screen have served as interventions in cinema's ongoing relationship with the literary, the dramatic, and the other visual arts. Audiences for film and for Shakespeare can better make their own interventions through informed, shared responses to these always unlikely and always inevitable partners. As arbitrator, time will decide, but with our direction.

WORKS CITED

Addenbrooke, David. *The Royal Shakespeare Company: The Peter Hall Years.* London: Kimber, 1974.

Anderegg, Michael. *Orson Welles, Shakespeare, and Popular Culture.* New York: Columbia University Press, 1999.

Andrew, Dudley. *Film in the Aura of Art.* Princeton: Princeton University Press, 1984.

Ball, Robert Hamilton. *Shakespeare on Silent Film.* New York: Theatre Arts Books, 1968.

Barton, John. *Playing Shakespeare.* London: Methuen, 1984.

Bennett, Susan. *Performing Nostalgia.* London: Routledge, 1996.

Berger, Harry, Jr. *Second World and Green World.* Berkeley and Los Angeles: University of California Press, 1988.

Blumenthal, Eileen, and Julie Taymor. *Julie Taymor: Playing With Fire.* New York: Harry N. Abrams, 1995.

Boose, Lynda E., and Richard Burt, editors. *Shakespeare the Movie.* London: Routledge, 1997.

Bourdieu, Pierre. *The Field of Cultural Production.* Ed. Randal Johnson. New York: Columbia University Press, 1993.

Branagh, Kenneth. *"Hamlet" by William Shakespeare.* New York: W. W. Norton, 1996(b).

———. *"Henry V" by William Shakespeare.* London: Chatto and Windus, 1989.

———. *A Midwinter's Tale.* New York: Newmarket Press, 1995.

———. *"Much Ado About Nothing" by William Shakespeare*. New York: W. W. Norton, 1993.

———. "Notes for the Film Program" for the premiere of *William Shakespeare's "Hamlet."* Castle Rock Entertainment, 1996(a).

Bulman, James C., editor. *Shakespeare, Theory, and Performance*. New York: Routledge, 1996.

Buhler, Stephen M. "'By the Mass, Our Hearts Are in the Trim': Catholicism and British Identity in Olivier's *Henry V*," *Cahiers Elisabéthains* 47 (April 1995): 55–70.

———. "Camp *Richard III* and the Burdens of (Stage/Film) History," in Burnett and Wray.

———. "Double Takes: Branagh Gets To *Hamlet*," *Post Script: Essays in Film and the Humanities* 17.1 (Fall 1997): 43–52.

———. "Ocular Proofs: *Othello* Films on Video," *Shakespeare* Magazine 3.3 (Fall 1999): 17–19.

Burnett, Mark Thornton. "Impressions of Fantasy: Adrian Noble's *A Midsummer Night's Dream*." In Burnett and Wray.

Burnett, Mark Thornton, and Ramona Wray, editors. *Shakespeare, Film, Fin de Siècle*. London: Macmillan, 2000.

Cohen, Louis Harris. *The Cultural-Political Traditions and Developments of the Soviet Cinema 1917–1972*. New York: Arno Press, 1974.

Collick, John. *Shakespeare, Cinema, and Society*. Manchester: Manchester University Press, 1989.

Coursen, Herbert R. *Teaching Shakespeare with Film and Television*. Westport, CT: Greenwood Press, 1997.

Crowl, Samuel. "The Roman Plays on Film and Television." In Davies and Wells.

Danson, Laurence. "Gazing at Hamlet, or the Danish Cabaret." *Shakespeare Survey* 45 (1992): 37–51.

Davies, Anthony, and Stanley Wells, editors. *Shakespeare and the Moving Image*. Cambridge: Cambridge University Press, 1994.

Deleyto, Celestino. "Men in Leather: Kenneth Branagh's *Much Ado About Nothing* and Romantic Comedy." *Cinema Journal* 36.3 (Spring 1997): 91–105.

de Sousa, Geraldo U. *Shakespeare's Cross-Cultural Encounters*. New York: St. Martin's Press, 1999.

Détienne, Marcel. *Dionysos Slain.* Trans. Mireille Muellner and Leonard Muellner. Baltimore: Johns Hopkins Press, 1979.

Dixon, Wheeler Winston. *It Looks at You.* Albany: State University of New York Press, 1995.

Dollimore, Jonathan. "Shakespeare Understudies: The Sodomite, the Prostitute, the Transvestite and Their Critics." In *Political Shakespeare.* Ed. Jonathan Dollimore and Alan Sinfield. Second edition. Ithaca, NY: Cornell University Press, 1994.

Donaldson, Peter. *Shakespearean Films/Shakespearean Directors.* Boston: Unwin Hyman, 1990.

———. "Taking on Shakespeare: Kenneth Branagh's *Henry V.*" *Shakespeare Quarterly* 42.1 (Spring 1991): 60–71.

Edwards, Anne. *Vivien Leigh.* New York: Simon and Schuster, 1977.

Ellis, John. *Visible Fictions: Cinema, Television, Video.* London: Routledge and Kegan Paul, 1982.

France, Richard, editor. *Orson Welles on Shakespeare.* New York: Greenwood Press, 1990.

Garrick, David. *Catharine and Petruchio.* London, 1756; rpt. London, Cornmarket Press, 1969.

Guntner, J. Lawrence. "Expressionist Shakespeare: The Gade/Nielsen *Hamlet* (1920) and the History of Shakespeare on Film." *Post Script* 17.2 (Winter/Spring 1998): 90–102.

Guntner, Lawrence, and Peter Drexler. "Recycled Film Codes and the Study of Shakespeare on Film." In *Deutsche Shakespeare-Gesellschaft Jahrbuch 1993:* 31–40.

Guynn, William. *A Cinema of Nonfiction.* Rutherford, NJ: Fairleigh Dickinson University Press, 1990.

Hedrick, Donald. "War is Mud." In Boose and Burt.

Henderson, Diana E. "A Shrew for the Times." In Boose and Burt.

Hill, Errol. *Shakespeare in Sable: A History of Black Shakespearean Actors.* Amherst: University of Massachusetts Press, 1984.

Hirsch, Foster. *Laurence Olivier on Screen.* New York: Da Capo Press, 1984.

Hodgdon, Barbara. "Kiss Me Deadly; or The Des/Demonized Spectacle." In *"Othello": New Perspectives.* Ed. Virginia Mason Vaughan and Kent Cartwright. Rutherford, NJ: Fairleigh Dickinson University Press, 1991.

Holderness, Graham. "Shakespeare Rewound." *Shakespeare Survey* 45 (1992): 63–74.

Howard, Tony. "When Peter Met Orson: The 1953 CBS *King Lear*." In Boose and Burt.

Howlett, Kathy M. *Framing Shakespeare on Film*. Athens: Ohio University Press, 2000.

Hurwitz, Gregg Andrew. "Transforming Text: Iago's Infection in Welles' *Othello*." *Word and Image* 13.4 (October-December 1997): 333–39.

Jackson, Russell. "A Shooting Script for the Reinhardt-Dieterle *Dream*." *Shakespeare Bulletin* 16.4 (Fall 1998): 39–41.

Jackson, Russell, and Robert Smallwood, editors. *Players of Shakespeare 2*. Cambridge: Cambridge University Press, 1988.

Jarman, Derek. *Dancing Ledge*. Ed. Shaun Allen. London: Quarter Books, 1984.

———. *Queer Edward II*. London: BFI Publishing, 1991.

Jennings, Talbot. *"Romeo and Juliet" by William Shakespeare*. New York: Random House, 1936.

Jorgens, Jack J. *Shakespeare on Film*. Bloomington: Indiana University Press, 1977.

Jorgensen, Paul A. "Castellani's: *Romeo and Juliet*: Intention and Response." *Film Quarterly* 10.1 (Fall 1955); rpt. in *Focus on Shakesperean Films*. Ed. Charles W. Eckert. Englewood Cliffs, NJ: Prentice-Hall, 1972.

Kachur, B. A. "The First Shakespeare Film: A Reconsideration and Reconstruction of Tree's *King John*." *Theatre Survey* 32 (May 1991): 43–63.

Kliman, Bernice W. "Branagh's *Henry V*: Allusion and Illusion." *Shakespeare on Film Newsletter* 14.1 (December 1989): 1, 9–10.

———. "Gleanings: The Residue of Difference in Scripts: The Case of Polanski's *Macbeth*." In *Shakespearean Illuminations*. Ed. Jay L. Halio and Hugh Richmond. Newark: University of Delaware Press, 1998.

———. *"Hamlet": Film, Television, and Audio Performance*. Rutherford, NJ: Fairleigh Dickinson University Press, 1988.

Kott, Jan. *Shakespeare Our Contemporary*. Trans. Boneslaw Taborski. Garden City, NY: Doubleday, 1964.

Kozintsev, Grigori. *"King Lear": The Space of Tragedy*. Trans. Mary Mackintosh. Berkeley and Los Angeles: University of California Press, 1977.

Lanier, Douglas. "Drowning the Book: *Prospero's Books* and the Textual Shakespeare." In Bulman.

———. "Now: The Presence of History in *Looking for Richard.*" *Post Script* 17.2 (Winter/Spring 1998): 39–55.

"Laurence Fishburne Stars in Movie of Shakespeare's *Othello.*" *Jet*, Jan. 15, 1996: 32–35.

Levine, Lawrence W. "William Shakespeare and the American People: A Study in Cultural Transformation." *American Historical Review* 89.1 (February 1984); rpt. in *Rethinking Popular Culture: Contemporary Perspectives in Cultural Studies.* Ed. Chandra Mukerji and Michael Schudson. Berkeley and Los Angeles: University of California Press, 1991.

Loehlin, James N. "'Top of the World, Ma': *Richard III* and Cinematic Convention." In Boose and Burt.

LoMonico, Michael. "'Is All Our Company Here?': An Interview with Michael Hoffman." *Shakespeare* 3.2 (Summer 1999): 9–13.

Lyons, Bridget Gellert, editor. *Chimes at Midnight.* New Brunswick, NJ: Rutgers University Press, 1988.

MacCabe, Colin. *Tracking the Signifier. Theoretical Essays: Film, Linguistics, Literature.* Minneapolis: University of Minnesota Press, 1985.

Mallin, Eric S. "'You Kilt My Foddah': or Arnold, Prince of Denmark." *Shakespeare Quarterly* 50.2 (Summer 1999): 127–51.

Manvell, Roger. *Shakespeare and the Film.* New York: Praeger, 1971.

Marcus, Leah S. *Unediting the Renaissance: Shakespeare, Marlowe, Milton.* London: Routledge, 1996.

Marriette, Amelia. "Urban Dystopias: Reapproaching Christine Edzard's *As You Like It.*" In Burnett and Wray.

Maus, Katharine Eisaman. "Horns of Dilemma: Jealousy, Gender, and Spectatorship in English Renaissance Drama." *ELH* 54 (1987): 561–83.

McDonald, Russ. *The Bedford Companion to Shakespeare.* Boston: Bedford Books, 1996.

McKellen, Ian. *William Shakespeare's "Richard III."* Woodstock, NY: Overlook Press, 1996.

McKernan, Luke. "The Real Thing at Last." In *Walking Shadows: Shakespeare in the National Film and Television Archive.* Ed. L. McKernan and Olwen Terris. London: BFI, 1994.

McPherson, James A. "Three Great Ones of the City and One Perfect Soul: Well Met at Cyprus." In *"Othello": New Essays by Black Writers*. Ed. Mythili Kaul. Washington DC: Howard University Press, 1997.

Metz, Christian. *Film Language: A Semiotics of the Cinema*. Trans. Michael Taylor. Chicago: University of Chicago Press, 1991.

Mullaney, Steven. *The Place of the Stage*. Chicago: University of Chicago Press, 1988.

Mulvey, Laura. *Visual and Other Pleasures*. London: Macmillan, 1989.

Newman, Karen. "'And Wash the Ethiop White': Femininity and the Monstrous in *Othello*." In *Shakespeare Reproduced*. Ed. Jean E. Howard and Marion F. O'Connor. New York: Methuen, 1987.

Norman, Marc, and Tom Stoppard. *Shakespeare in Love: A Screenplay*. New York: Hyperion, 1998.

Nugent, Frank S. "Review of MGM *Romeo and Juliet*." *New York Times*, Aug. 21, 1936. 12:2.

Nunn, Trevor. *William Shakespeare's "Twelfth Night."* London: Methuen, 1996.

Occhiogrosso, Frank. "Cinematic Oxymoron in Peter Hall's *A Midsummer Night's Dream*." *Literature/Film Quarterly* 11.3 (1983): 174–78.

Olivier, Laurence. *"Henry V" by William Shakespeare*. London: Lorrimer, 1984.

———. *On Acting*. London: Weidenfeld and Nicolson, 1986.

Osborne, Laurie E. "Filming Shakespeare in a Cultural Thaw: Soviet Appropriations of Shakespearean Treacheries in 1955–6." *Textual Practice* 9.2 (Summer 1995): 325–47.

Pearce, Craig, and Baz Luhrmann. *William Shakespeare's "Romeo + Juliet."* New York: Bantam Doubleday Dell, 1996.

Pearlman, E. "*Macbeth* on Film: Politics." In Davies and Wells.

Plantinga, Carl R. *Rhetoric and Representation in Nonfiction Film*. Cambridge: Cambridge University Press, 1997.

Rothwell, Kenneth S. *A History of Shakespeare on Screen*. Cambridge: Cambridge University Press, 1999.

Rothwell, Kenneth S., and Annabelle Henkin Melzer. *Shakespeare on Screen: An International Filmography and Videography*. New York: Neal-Schuman, 1990.

Schoenbaum, S. *William Shakespeare: A Documentary Life*. New York: Oxford University Press, 1975.

Shakespeare, William. *The Riverside Shakespeare*. Second edition. Ed. G. Blakemore Evans. Boston: Houghton Mifflin, 1997.

Shaw, Bernard. *Our Theatres in the Nineties*. 3 volumes. London: Constable, 1932.

Silverman, Kaja. *The Subject of Semiotics*. New York: Oxford University Press, 1983.

Sinfield, Alan. "Royal Shakespeare: Theatre and the Making of Ideology." In *Political Shakespeare*. Ed. Jonathan Dollimore and Alan Sinfield. Second edition. Ithaca, NY: Cornell University Press, 1994.

Sinyard, Neil. *Filming Literature*. London: Croom Helm, 1986.

Skura, Meredith Anne. *Shakespeare the Actor and the Purposes of Playing*. Chicago: University of Chicago Press, 1993.

Spoto, Donald. *Laurence Olivier*. New York: HarperCollins, 1992.

Starks, Lisa S. "The Veiled (Hot) Bed of Race and Desire: Parker's *Othello* and the Stereotype as Screen Fetish." *Post Script* 17.1 (Fall 1997): 64–78.

Taranow, Gerda. *The Bernhardt Hamlet: Culture and Context*. New York: Lang, 1996.

Taylor, Neil. "The Films of *Hamlet*." In Davies and Wells.

Thompson, Ann. "Asta Nielsen and the Mystery of *Hamlet*." In Boose and Burt.

Thomson, David. *Rosebud: The Story of Orson Welles*. New York: Alfred A. Knopf, 1996.

Uricchio, William, and Roberta E. Pearson. *Reframing Culture: The Case of the Vitagraph Quality Films*. Princeton: Princeton University Press, 1993.

Vardac, A. Nicholas. *Stage to Screen: Theatrical Method from Garrick to Griffith*. Cambridge, MA: Harvard University Press, 1949.

Vaughan, Virginia Mason. *"Othello": A Contextual History*. Cambridge: Cambridge University Press, 1994.

Weinbrot, Howard D. "'An Ambition to Excell': The Aesthetics of Emulation in the Seventeenth and Eighteenth Centuries." *Huntington Library Quarterly* 48.2 (Spring 1985): 121–39.

Wheeler, Richard P. "Deaths in the Family: The Loss of a Son and the Rise of Shakespearean Comedy." *Shakespeare Quarterly* 51.2 (Summer 2000): 127–53.

Williams, Simon. *Shakespeare on the German Stage. Volume I: 1586–1914.* Cambridge: Cambridge University Press, 1990.

Willson, Robert F., Jr. "Kenneth Branagh's *Hamlet,* or The Revenge of Fortinbras." *Shakespeare Newsletter* 47.1 (Spring 1997): 7, 9.

———. *Shakespeare in Hollywood: 1929–1956.* Madison, NJ: Fairleigh Dickinson University Press, 2000.

Worthen, W. B. *Shakespeare and the Authority of Performance.* Cambridge: Cambridge University Press, 1997.

Zavarzadeh, Mas'ud. *Seeing Films Politically.* Albany: State University of New York Press, 1991.

Zeffirelli, Franco. *Zeffirelli: The Autobiography of Franco Zeffirelli.* New York: Weidenfeld and Nicolson, 1986.

INDEX OF
SHAKESPEAREAN
PLAYS AND FILMS

$$\diamond$$

(Photographs are indicated by **bold** numerals; productions are listed in chronological order.)

GENERAL INDEX

———— ◇ ————

(Photographs are indicated by **bold** numerals.)

207